DELIVERANCE

THE DIARY OF MICHAEL MAIK

**In Memory of the
Destroyed Jewish Community
of Sokoly, Poland**

Translated from the Hebrew by
Laia Ben-Dov

Edited by
Avigdor Ben-Dov

Published by JewishGen

**An Affiliate of the Museum of Jewish Heritage—A Living Memorial to the Holocaust
New York**

Deliverance - The Diary Of Michael Maik
In Memory of the Destroyed Jewish Community of Sokoly, Poland

Copyright © 2020 by Avigdor and Laia Ben-Dov
All rights reserved.
Second English Printing, revised and with an index: January 2020, Shevat 5780

Translated from the Hebrew by Laia Ben-Dov
Edited by Avigdor Ben-Dov

Published by JewishGen, Inc.
An Affiliate of the Museum of Jewish Heritage
A Living Memorial to the Holocaust
36 Battery Place, New York, NY 10280

JewishGen, Inc. is not responsible for inaccuracies or omissions in the
original work and makes no representations regarding the accuracy of
this translation. Digital images of the original book's contents can be
seen online at the New York Public Library website. The mission of the
JewishGen organization is to produce a translation of the original work,
and we cannot verify the accuracy of statements or alter facts cited.

Printed in the United States of America by Lightning Source, Inc.

Library of Congress Control Number (LCCN): 2020931770
ISBN: 978-1-939561-87-9 (hard cover: 276 pages, alk. paper).

Cover photograph: Lopochowo Forest (near Sokoly), with kind permis-
sion from *Yad LeZehava* Holocaust Museum, Kedumim, Israel.
Back Cover photo and all others: with kind permission from Moshe
Maik, of Blessed Memory, and the Sokoly Emigre Society in Israel, Tel-
Aviv.

Publication History:

Original publication (Yiddish): *Sefer Zikaron L'Kedoshim Sokoly: Yizkorbuch Sokoly,* Moshe Grossman, reviewer; Avraham Yitzhak Lev and Moshe Maik, co-editors; published by Orli Printers, Tel Aviv, 1962.

Hebrew translation from the Yiddish: *Sokoly B'Maavak L'Chaim,* Shmuel Kalisher, translator, Sokoly Emigre Society in Israel, Tel-Aviv, 1975.

First English edition (taken from the translation of the diary portion in the Hebrew Yizkor book): *Deliverance: The Diary of Michael Maik*; Laia Ben-Dov, translator; Avigdor Ben-Dov, editor; published by Keter Press, Jerusalem, Israel, 2004.

Second English edition of the softcover book *Deliverance: The Diary of Michael Maik* , now in hard cover, revised and provided with an annotated index, map and photographs. Publisher, JewishGen, an Affiliate of the Museum of Jewish Heritage – A Living Memorial to the Holocaust, New York, 2020.

ACKNOWLEDGEMENTS

With deep appreciation to **Moshe Maik,** of blessed memory, for permission to translate and publish the events recorded in the Diary of his father, Michael Maik of blessed memory, during the War years 1942-1945, "…so that future generations would remember and not forget," …and to **Rachel Loebel** for lending us her expert proofreading and editorial assistance on short notice.

Also, in grateful appreciation to those private individuals who assisted financially, but who prefer to remain anonymous, and to the following institutional sponsors:

Yad LeZehava **Holocaust Research Institute**, Kedumim, Israel for providing financial assistance, assisting in the preparation of the manuscript of this *Diary* for publication and providing a cover photo.

יד ושם רשות הזיכרון לשואה ולגבורה, הקרן לתמיכה בספרי זיכרונות של יצולי שואה

Yad VaShem **Remembrance Authority for the Holocaust and Heroism**, Jerusalem, Israel: The Support Fund for the Publication of Books of Memoirs by Holocaust Survivors — for providing financial assistance.

The Azrieli Shopping Centers, Azrieli Center and IC of the Azrieli Group — for providing financial assistance.(Note that the content, editing and data are the sole responsibility of the editor).

רשת קניוני עזריאלי, מרכז עזריאלי, ו-IC מקבוצת עזריאלי התכנים, העריכה והנתונים הם על אחריותו של המחבר

JewishGen Yizkorbooks in Print Project — for their assistance in publishing through their organization the second edition of the English. translation of the *The Diary of Michael Maik* (English with index).

Notes to the Reader:

In order to obtain a list of all Shoah victims from Sokoly, the reader should access the Yad Vashem web site listed below; one can also search for specific family names using family name option. These lists are continually updated by Yad Vashem, so it is worthwhile to periodically search these lists.

There is much valuable information available on this web site, including the Pages of Testimony, etc.

http://yvng.yadvashem.org

A list of this book and all books available in the Yizkor-Book-In-Print Project along with prices is available at:

http://www.jewishgen.org/Yizkor/ybip.html

For additional reading from complete English translation of the Hebrew Yizkor book go to:

https://www.jewishgen.org/Yizkor/sokoly/sokoly.html

DISCLAIMER

The contents, information, and editing of this book are the sole responsibility of the editor, and the appearance of the names of sponsors mentioned above are not intended to imply any endorsement or approval of the work.

JewishGen and the Yizkor Books in Print Project

This book has been published by the **Yizkor Books in Print Project**, as part of the **Yizkor Book Project** of JewishGen, Inc.

JewishGen, Inc. is a non-profit organization founded in 1987 as a resource for Jewish genealogy. Its website [www.jewishgen.org] serves as an international clearinghouse and resource center to assist individuals who are researching the history of their Jewish families and the places where they lived. JewishGen provides databases, facilitates discussion groups, and coordinates projects relating to Jewish genealogy and the history of the Jewish people. In 2003, JewishGen became an affiliate of the **Museum of Jewish Heritage—A Living Memorial to the Holocaust** in New York.

The **JewishGen Yizkor Book Project** was organized to make more widely known the existence of Yizkor (Memorial) Books written by survivors and former residents of various Jewish communities throughout the world. Later, volunteers connected to the different destroyed communities began cooperating to have these books translated from the original language—usually Hebrew or Yiddish—into English, thus enabling a wider audience to have access to the valuable information contained within them. As each chapter of these books was translated, it was posted on the JewishGen website and made available to the general public.

The **Yizkor Books in Print Project** began in 2011 as an initiative to print and publish Yizkor Books that had been fully translated, so that hard copies would be available for purchase by the descendants of these communities and also by scholars, universities, synagogues, libraries, and museums.

These Yizkor books have been produced almost entirely through the volunteer effort of researchers from around the world, assisted by donations from private individuals. The books are printed and sold at near cost, so as to make them as affordable as possible. Our goal is to make this important genre of Jewish literature and history available in English in book form, so that people can have the personal histories of their ancestral towns on their bookshelves for themselves and for their children and grandchildren.

Binny Lewis, Yizkor Book Project Manager
Joel Alpert, Yizkor-Book-in-Print Project Coordinator

JewishGen
Yizkor Book Project

This book is presented by the
Yizkor Books in Print Project
Project Coordinator: Joel Alpert

Part of the
Yizkor Books Project of JewishGen, Inc.
Project Manager: Lance Ackerfeld

These books have been produced solely through volunteer effort
of individuals from around the world. The books are printed and
sold at near cost, so as to make them as affordable as possible.

Our goal is to make this history and important genre of Jewish
literature available in English in book form so that people can have
the near-personal histories of their ancestral towns on their bookshelves for themselves and for their children and grandchildren.

Any donations to the Yizkor Books Project are appreciated.

Please send donations to:
Yizkor Book Project
JewishGen
36 Battery Place
New York, NY 10280

JewishGen, Inc. is an affiliate of the
Museum of Jewish Heritage
A Living Memorial to the Holocaust

PREFACE

The *Diary* was originally handwritten in Yiddish and hidden during the War years, later to be reclaimed and incorporated as a part of the Yiddish book, *Sefer Zicharon L'Kodshai Sokoly: Sokeler Yizkor-buch* (*Memorial Book for the Sokoly Martyrs: Sokoly Yizkor-book*), Tel Aviv 1962, edited by Moshe Grossman and guided by two members of the Sokoly Émigré Society in Israel: Avraham Yitzhak Lev, of blessed memory, and Moshe Maik, of blessed memory, the only son of the author. The original Yiddish manuscript now forms a part of the documentation of modern Jewish history in a Jewish Holocaust museum collection, a fact that reflects its importance to the Jewish people.

In 1975, Shmuel Kalisher prepared a Hebrew translation of the Sokoly *Yizkor-buch* entitled *Sokoly B'maavak L'chaim* (*Sokoly, in a Struggle for Life*). It quickly became apparent to me that the *Diary* was particularly worthy of separate treatment and I therefore took it upon myself to publish it for the English-speaking world so that those with either limited or non-existent reading knowledge of Yiddish and Hebrew could read Michael Maik's story even without access to the yizkor books.

The Hebrew version of the *Diary*, like its Yiddish original, has its own character and style, which the editor and translator have attempted, insofar as possible, to retain. The author's mode of writing reflects his uncertainty and anxious state of mind in a period of great peril. Nevertheless, the *Diary* manages to provide the reader with a natural, but dramatic, narrative. The story itself has the vitality of real events happening to real people. It conveys the impact of these events, reported by an educated observer. The reader will no doubt recognize that the *Diary* possesses unique merits as revealed very soon after perusing its opening pages.

But Michael Maik's account of his ordeal under the German and Soviet regimes in Sokoly is more than just a dry retelling of facts that are now widely known. Even though it is factual history, the *Diary* is also a personal, true-life story that, it is hoped, will both enlighten and inform.

It was also Michael Maik's earnest wish that Jews would read his *Diary* and take to heart his plea that they should remember what "Amalek" did to the Jewish people, not in the distant past, but in his own generation. The

Diary is for everyone to read, not only for Jews. Naturally enough, Michael Maik appealed directly to his Jewish brethren to assume the greater responsibility for publishing his words:

> *Now, writing my memories, I doubt whether we will be privileged to see the light of the world after the Holocaust and whether my writings will reach the hands of Jews who will be able to publish them. At the moment, the end is not in sight. We lie, day and night, like living dead, buried under the ground in a dark bunker. …Will my writings be privileged to reach the hands of Jews? I doubt it! I wanted them to study these works well.* (p. 168)

Michael Maik did live to see the light of the world. His personal deliverance was in the life he and his family, and many thousands more like him, built in the re-established Homeland of the Jewish People, the State of Israel, to which he immigrated in 1949.

The *Diary* illuminates the dark side of human nature, but it also reveals the heroism and self-sacrifice of both Jews and Christians in the face of unparalleled fears and threats of death and destruction. Michael Maik's *Diary* gives us insight into how a few righteous men and women overcame their fears in order to provide the basic needs of life to complete strangers. These deeds – though far too few – should not go unrecognized. In the English language retelling of Michael Maik's story, I hope I have accomplished at least this much.

> Readers should be aware that, for technical reasons, Polish names and terms generally are presented in an Anglicized format, although the spelling of well-known places and names has been retained. Any errors or omissions that may appear in the text are solely the responsibility of the editor. Readers' comments and corrections are welcome.

Avigdor Ben-Dov
avigdorbd@gmail.com
Jerusalem, Israel
January, 2020

TRANSLATOR'S FOREWORD

Michael Maik wrote his *Diary* during the years 1942-1945, while he was hidden in an underground bunker. In the first part of the *Diary*, Michael recalls in detail the gradual degradation of the Jewish community of Sokoly, from the entry of the Germans until the expulsion of the Jews in November of 1942, from the point of view of one who was actually there at the time. What happened afterwards was written as the events occurred; the suspense and tension portrayed are very real.

Most of us have read at least some books regarding the Holocaust. We who were fortunate enough to have been born outside the Europe of those days cannot help regarding its horrors with a certain degree of detachment, regardless of the empathy we feel toward its victims. In translating the *Diary*, however, I found myself becoming more and more attached to the people and events described. When the work was completed, I felt as if I had, in a small way, experienced their trials and tribulations.

I am left with a profound sense of respect and admiration for the initiative of these ordinary people who, when required to do so, revealed in themselves an extraordinary amount of courage. It was a privilege to become acquainted with them.

Laia Ben-Dov

Geopolitical Information:
Sokoły, Poland: 52°59' N, 22°42' E
9 miles NE of Wysokie Mazowieckie, 21 miles SW of Białystok, 29 miles ESE of Łomża.

Alternate names for the town of Sokoly: [Pol]; Sokoli [Yid]; Sokoly [Rus]; Sekole

Jewish Population: 1,723 (in 1897), 1,558 (in 1921)

	Town	District	Province	Country
Before WWI (c. 1900)	Sokoly	Mazowieckie	Lomza	Russian Empire
Between the wars (c. 1930)	Sokoly	Wysokie Mazowieckie	Białystok	Poland
After WWII (c. 1950)	Sokoly			Poland
Today (c. 2000)	Sokoly			Poland

Nearby Jewish Communities:	Miles and Direction
Bialystok	19NNE
Brańsk	17SSE
Bruszewo	2W
Choroszcz	16NE
Ciechanowiec	17S
Czyzewo	19SE
Idzki	1N
Jabłonka	7WNW
Jamiolki	1N
Jedwabne	27NW
Jezewo	10N
Kobylin	29N
Kolno	40NNW
Kosewo	26W
Kruczewo Wypycho	1E
Lachy	3N
Łapy	6E
Łomża	27NNW
Lopuchowo	11N
Mazury	5WSW
Ostrów Mazowiecka	27WSW
Rutki	14NW
Śniadowo	23W
Suraż	11ESE
Tykocin	15NNE
Wizna	20NW
Wysokie Mazowieckie	9SSW
Zabludow	18E
Zambrów	16W
Zaręby Kościelne	20SSW
Zawady/Zawada	17NNW

BALTIC SEA

LITHUANIA

Vilnius ●

RUSSIA

POLAND

Lomza   Bialystok
  ●   ●
       ●
    SOKOLY

BELARUS

GERMANY

● Poznan   Warsaw ●
     ● Lodz

● Prague

CZECH REPUBLIC

● Krakow

UKRAINE

SLOVAKIA

250 miles
0

0   250 Km   500 Km

POLAND - Current Borders

Map showing Sokoly in Poland

Photographs of Sokoly

Market Day in Sokoly, 1916

Michael Maik

Chaim Yehoshua Olsha

Moshe Lipa Shulmeister

Yehudit Rachelsky
in forest with Issur
Wondolowicz

Issur Wondolowicz

Rav Yosef Rosenblum

Tsipora Tabak
as a young girl

Tsipora Tabak after the war,
in Israeli Army (IDF)

Avraham Goldberg as
a Polish Army Soldier

Shlomo Olsha with wife
Sarah Miriam Rabinowicz

Moshe Maik with Avraham
Yaakov Lev, co-editors of *Diary*

Beileh Ryfka, wife of
Avraham Yaakov Olsha
(parents of Shlomo)

Chaim and Avraham Goldberg,
Michael Maik, Tsipora Tabak,
Moshe Maik

Rashka, wife of Chaim Boruch
Goldwasser, son Moshe and
Daughter (unknown)

Monik Roseman, Moshe Maik,
Chaim Goldberg

On September 1, 1939, the German army invaded Poland, and the world Holocaust began. Prior to that, no one believed that the danger was so near and that it would reach such proportions of horror.

Ten days after the War started, bloodthirsty German soldiers burst into our town, Sokoly, and immediately began a mad rampage. Guided by young Poles, they passed through the homes of the Jews and abducted the leaders of the community, in particular, the Rabbi and the *shochtim* (kosher ritual slaughterers). Thus, it was decreed that our Rabbi, *HaRav* Yosef Rosenblum, was also among those who were tortured. They stripped him of his clothing and, when he was barefoot and almost naked, they forced him to jump and dance under a flood of well-aimed strikes of a rubber whip on his exposed back. They also pulled out their beards along with the skin, and forced them to sing and dance. At the end, they forced their captives to wash their vehicles. This hell lasted for two hours.

The Germans then pushed a frightened crowd of Jews into the old synagogue and, screaming and shouting, threatened to burn it down with them inside. Thus, they kept their captives terrified to death for many long hours.

The Germans burnt the nearby district city, Wysokie Mazowieckie, on the day they entered it, and not a single Jew was left alive there who didn't immediately flee. Although some of the people who were burnt out of Wysokie came to Sokoly to seek shelter, the day after their arrival, the Germans also burnt down two main streets of Jewish homes in Sokoly: 'Tiktin' Street and Gonasoweki Street. While the flames reached towards the heavens, the soldiers rushed around in the streets of the town like hunting dogs and abducted Jews along with the possessions that they had rescued from their burning homes. Again, they gathered hundreds of Jews, and filled the Christian church with them, as well as a house that was under construction near the Bialystok road. Among the crowd there also were a few Christians, and even a young priest. The Germans threatened to take revenge on the prisoners for the killing of three of their soldier companions by Poles in the village of Lachy (three kilometers from Sokoly). Because of this, they burned down the village of Lachy and murdered a few farmers, but without the addition of Jewish victims, they did not regard their revenge as complete.

Thus, about 500 imprisoned Jews lay in fear of death all that night. Whenever a door opened, the people trembled and their hearts beat faster, lest their end had arrived. Cries and painful wails were heard, that they would never again see their children, their wives and their dear ones, and take leave of them before they were sacrificed.

At seven o'clock in the morning, the door was opened and a few Germans entered. They ordered the prisoners to get up and form lines according to age: lines from age 30 and upward, after them from age 20 and upward, and at the end, youngsters up to the age of 20. At the beginning, all of them thought that they would be shot according to the order of the lines. With broken hearts, parents separated from their children; brothers from brothers. Unexpectedly, to their surprise, all the lines were released. The purpose of the Germans was to cause terror and fear among the people. With indescribable joy, all of them ran to their relatives to spread the news that, praise G-d, they were rescued from death.

Alter Slodky

When they had gone only a few steps away, the joy ended. Alter Slodky was lying in the middle of the street, next to the two-story house, in a puddle of his own blood.

Regarding Alter Slodky: he was a vigilant man, attached to, and active in the community. His intelligence was outstanding, and he always had a parable, joke, or slogan appropriate to the conversation. His black beard, encircling his face, was always neat and combed. Alter was a talented merchant; he supplied flour, salt, sugar, and oil to shop owners and bakers – at wholesale. He also had a general store, where he sold housewares, decorative items, and all kinds of candles. In his yard were a horse and a wagon, which he used for his business. His three sons were employed in bringing merchandise from Bialystok, and they traveled around to the landowners' courts and the flour mills in the villages.

On the High Holy Days, it was Alter's custom to serve, without any compensation, as the *chazzan* (cantor) for the *musaf* prayer in the large *beit midrash*. His voice was agreeable and his singing of the prayers gave much pleasure to the congregants.

Now, Alter Slodky is no more. His body lies in the street, split and blood-soaked.

Pelchok, the Fisherman

At a distance of a few steps away from Alter Slodky lies the old bachelor, Chaim Pelchok the fisherman, seriously wounded in his stomach. This is Pelchok, who supplied the Jewish residents of Sokoly with live fish for *Shabbatot* and holidays. We dedicate a few lines to his image:

On Shabbat and holiday eves, in the early hours of the morning, Pelchok would bring a wagon full of fish to the market in our town, and would loudly call out: "Women – Live, Flopping Fish!" Dozens of women, with bowls in their hands, would hurry out from all directions and push to buy the live, flopping fish. There were women who sat and waited from midnight in the fish market, worried that they would be late, Heaven forbid, and would not be able to get live fish in honor of the holy Shabbat. The noise and tumult among the women was immeasurable. They surrounded Pelchok's wagon like bees. But Chaim knew how to stand up to all of them. With one look he encompassed the entire crowd of women. He knew his customers well; he knew their weaknesses and their tastes. He knew who paid in cash and who took credit.

He hurried to weigh the fish and record sales in his book, while telling jokes with his clever tongue. He calmed discontented women, exchanging one fish for another, to the satisfaction of all of them.

Now, Chaim Pelchok lies on the main road, curled up in agony, seriously wounded, and struggling with the Angel of Death. His sister stands at his side, tearfully begging the Jews who are approaching to take him into the house. There is no stretcher. Eight Jews carried Chaim Pelchok in their arms. The victim bitterly cried out: "Jews, have mercy on me, let me die quickly, I cannot bear the suffering." They laid him in bed. It was shocking to hear him crying from his horrible suffering.

Alter Novak

A few minutes later, it became known that there were additional sacrifices that night. Alter Novak was a 60-year-old learned Jew, a former Telshe Yeshiva student, who was always happy and of high spirits. In the *beit midrash*, he would learn Torah with the yeshiva boys and *kollel* students. During prayers, he did not allow the congregation to talk. He used to check whether the *tsitsiot* of the children's "small *tallitot*" were kosher. He watched over the boys of bar-mitzva age and took care to see that they put on *tefillin* according to the requirements of the *Shulchan Aruch*. It was his custom to severely criticize rabbis and famous authorities, and to disqualify their opinions.

Alter frequently went around in the villages in order to buy "bargains," and it was his custom to joke around with the farmers. He took his only cow, which had a single horn, to pasture in abandoned places, because he wasn't able to give it to a shepherd. While he watched the cow, he would study a book or read a newspaper that he got from his neighbors. The evenings he would spend in the *beit midrash*. Now, it is all over. Alter is no more!

The New Rabbi, *Rav* Kalman 'Yankel'

The scorched body of the new rabbi of the *Mishnayot* group, *Rav* Kalman 'Yankel', lay at some distance. He was a quiet and honest Jew. He lived in an apartment with his youngest married daughter, his son-in-law, and his grandson. The family numbered five souls, who lived from the permanent support of their sons in America.

Being free from the worries of income, and being a person who was satisfied with very little, *Rav* Kalman's favorite occupation was to prepare a chapter of *Mishnayot* for his students and for the *minyan* of worshippers.

In the evenings, *Rav* Kalman would read chapters of *Mishnayot* to his students and the *minyan*, and would explain complications in a simple way that was understood by everyone. He loved to tell his students about fascinating deeds of the holy men and miracle workers. The community would "lick their fingers" from their Rabbi's stories. His group of students grew and grew. Jews who were known previously as simple Jews who had until then not dared to look into a book of *Mishnayot*, joined them. The Rabbi added to their fortitude and faith, and they became enthusiastic students who were able to learn and study the chapters by themselves.

Alas and alack! Of *Rav* Kalman 'Yankel', only his scorched bones and a pile of dust remained.

Rav Avraham 'Yossel'

The next sacrifice was *Rav* Avraham 'Yossel' [Shapira] (the son-in-law of Moshe 'Yossel'), who lay seriously wounded on the stones of the street. He was a *kollel* student with a patriarchal beard, a completely righteous, Heaven-fearing man, one of the 36 righteous ones [*Lamed Vovnikim*], who never stopped studying day and night.

From dawn until late at night, he would sit in the new *beit midrash*, in his father-in-law's seat at the corner of the wall on the eastern side, and learn *Gemara*. In his pleasant voice, he would explain to himself all the difficult passages, paragraphs in *Yoreh Deah, Choshen HaMishpat*, and the *Rambam*, as if he were teaching others. He stopped learning only to pray in the *minyan*. He refrained from ordinary conversation with anyone, because this was wasting time from Torah. He did not get involved, and was not interested, in conversations that took place near him on the subjects of war, politics, or turbulent events and daily matters. For him, there existed only the world of learning Torah and serving G-d.

He taught in order to support himself and his wife, but only a limited number of students, for a few hours a day. He and his wife, who was modest like he was, were satisfied with little, with bread and water, and they did not bear any jealousy towards anyone. On market days, *Rav* Avraham 'Yossel' would stop learning for a little while and go out shopping for such things as a quarter of a sack of potatoes, which would suffice for the Shabbat and the rest of the week, and ten bundles of wood for heating the house on cold days and for cooking.

A completely righteous man, he accepted with love the agony of his death; after all, he was no better than the ten martyrs, from Rabbi Akiva to Chananya ben Tradyon.

Rav Avraham 'Yossel' hovered between life and death for a long time, until G-d answered his pleas and death released him from his suffering.

Chaicha Allenberg; Avraham Yitzhak; and Mendel Lev

Another sacrifice to the Germans' brutality was a young, 20-year-old woman, 'Chaicha' [Chaya], the daughter of Baruch [Allenberg], the sexton [*shamas*] of the new *beit midrash*. She was an innocent and proper daughter of Israel.

Among the wounded that night were many Jews, who suffered for many long months afterwards until their wounds were healed. Among those seriously wounded were Avraham Yitzhak Lev and his [older] brother Mendel, the sons of Shmuel [Lev], the *Shob*.

The Double Hell

After the horrible night of hell mentioned above, more Jewish refugees from burnt-down Wysokie Mazowieckie flowed into Sokoly in order to find shelter and a roof over their heads. Many houses in Sokoly also went up in flames during those days. The lack of housing grew, and in spite of this all the refugees were absorbed among us, including even those who continued to flow in from the towns on the German border: Grabow, Kolno, Stawiski, Jedwabne, Myszyniec, and more. Those who came settled mainly in the portion of Sokoly that had not been burnt. We were forced to live in crowded conditions, three or four families in one small apartment. One bed was used for several people, and many slept on the floor.

At the beginning, somehow there was peace in the houses, but little by little, the occupants began to quarrel and argue among themselves, even brothers and sisters and relatives. It was especially difficult for them to compromise with regard to sharing the kitchen. One family was required to wait patiently until the family before them finished cooking. Fuel and food were acquired with a great deal of effort, bordering on danger to life. There is no doubt that the true woman of the house felt herself entitled to be more aggressive and to drive her neighbors and good friends, or relatives who were dear to her, out of her house. This was a double hell, inside the house and outside... .

Searches

The day after the night of horrors, a series of searches began. German gangs commandeered Jewish houses and went from house to house, searching for gold, jewelry, leather, manufactured merchandise, bed linen, and other expensive possessions, which, for the most part, were hidden.

With the help of Polish informers, former friends of the faithful "*Moshkim*," [from the word "Moses", *i.e.*, Jews] who knew the hiding places of their Jewish "friends," the Germans uncovered hidden cellars, false walls, double attics, in whose spaces goods and jewelry were hidden.

Among other things, at the home of 'Itzele' [Yitzhak Roseman], the son of Yisrael Chaim [Roseman], the belt-maker, they found a not-insignificant inventory of leather, shoes, and merchandise. Even in the houses of the poorest Jews, the Germans found something to steal and rob.

In the evening, the Polish *goyim* brought the Germans to Jewish girls. A few of them were raped. A great and bitter panic arose. The girls hid in barns, in attics and in cellars. A few of them succeeded in escaping to the villages, to the homes of farmers they knew. That night the Jews did not lie down to sleep; they sat on their packed possessions, which they had not yet had a chance to unpack after the night of the fire. All of them lived in constant fear that the Nazis would come and burn down the houses that remained after the first fire. Young men hid themselves and looked out through the cracks [in the walls] to see if they could see a German in the distance. The Germans kidnapped young Jews for manual labor and sadistic brutality.

In the streets of the town center and the marketplace, in the places where Germans were always around, not a single Jew was to be found. Even in the quiet lanes, the Jews would crawl on all fours, hugging against the walls and looking in all directions to make sure that the angels of terror were not in the vicinity.

During the nights, the din and whistling of the German military vehicles spread panic and the fear of death. It appeared that all seven gates leading down to hell had been opened and that the angels of terror went out in demonic bands, surrounding the wretched Jews, whose G-d had forgotten them. The tense situation continued thus for 12 days, from before *Rosh Hashana* until the *Neila* prayer on *Yom Kippur*.

On *Yom Kippur*, the Jews gathered in secret *minyanim*, and in choked, heart-rending voices, like the *conversos* in Spain, they conducted the prayers while looking out of the windows towards the street, to see whether the murderers had appeared.

The Good News after '*Unetana Tokef*'

At the hour of the *"Unetana Tokef"* prayer, the women in the women's section of the synagogue sobbed out loud and the men were forced to stop the prayer in order to quiet them.

Suddenly, two youths came running into the large *minyan*, with the news: "The Germans have left Sokoly! They have already taken down their field telephone…we expect the Soviets to enter Sokoly…"

The entire congregation looked in wonder at the young men who brought the news, and it was hard for them to believe what they were hearing; these things are miraculous….

The youths told everyone that they heard about an agreement between the Germans and the Soviets, according to which part of the conquered territory in Poland would be evacuated and handed over to the Russians. The knowledge that the Germans had retreated, revived the spirit of life. All those present raised their heads. Heaven and earth rejoiced. In one moment, the entire world changed from darkness to light and from sadness to joy.

In the congregation, the conversation turned to the relationship between the Soviets and the Jews. The *Neila* prayer in the Rabbi's *minyan* was conducted properly as it had been in prior years, while sensing the miracles and wonders that G-d had done for us. *Yom Kippur* ended in joy and with a wonderful feeling that cannot be expressed in words. The devout Jews believed that they had benefited from the merit of the righteous, elderly, brilliant scholar, *HaRav* Rabbi Avraham Epstein, who was still living, and that G-d had heard his prayers and supplications.

HaRav Epstein suffered paralysis when he reached the age of 70, and he was not able to walk. A wheelchair was arranged for him so that he would be able to move from place to place. While sitting in his chair, Rabbi Epstein received visitors for two hours every day. The elderly Rabbi passed away in 1940.

The Red Rescuers Have Arrived

The next day, soldiers of the Red Army entered the town. The people of Sokoly, from the biggest to the smallest, from the youngest to the oldest, men, women and children, all went out to the streets to greet the liberating soldiers. The Jews received the "Reds" with shouts of joy and enthusiasm. In comparison, the Poles stood disappointed. There were Jews among the soldiers. They talked with the citizens of the town and told them about life in the Soviet Union. Near the houses stood groups of Jews, among them shop owners, craftsmen and merchants, who asked about the chances for our people under Soviet rule.

Pessimists argued that for adults who observed tradition, it would be difficult to become adapted to the new regime. Private trade in Russia was thought to be speculation, subject to punishment. A profession and trade are hard to learn in old age. The elderly are not suited at all to hard labor. It is a rule with the Soviets that whoever doesn't work, doesn't eat...

In comparison, the optimists argued: Don't worry. The demon isn't as terrible as they are describing him...a Jew will become accustomed, will adapt himself and will accommodate himself to any condition in the world. We won't, G-d forbid, die of hunger, and we have nothing to lose. It is so good that we are rid of the accursed Germans, and far be it from us to pine for the lifestyle we had before the War, under the Polish regime.

The life of the Jews in Sokoly in recent years, before World War II, was bitter. Danger threatened the Jew when he walked in the street, and how much more so in the villages, or outside the town. The Polish *goyim* threw stones at the Jews. Next to the Jewish shops stood gangs of young Polish ruffians or "*Pikatniks*," clubs and cudgels in their hands, and they did not allow Christians to enter Jewish stores to shop, or to order work from a Jewish craftsman.

Occasionally, during market and fair days, the mob would break windows in Jewish houses. They destroyed Jewish kiosks, destroyed or stole the merchandise, and took the kerosene. And so, after morning prayers, they attacked *Rav* Alter 'the Preacher' from the old *beit midrash*. A straight and honest Jew who never argued with anyone, he earned a living through his own labor and a bit of support from his relatives in America. He would spend hours every day in the *beit midrash* in prayer, reciting psalms, and learning. One fine day *Rav* Alter was going home from the *beit midrash* and [on the way] they murdered him.

The hooligans disappeared. There was no justice and no judge. Peddlers and rag sellers, who would go around in the villages and supply the farmers with household needs, were endangering their lives every day. More than once, Jews returned from the villages beaten and injured by malicious brutality.

Twenty Months under the Soviet Regime in Sokoly

After the Red Army established itself in our town, the political bosses and organizers arrived: various commissars, the new civil administration, and organizers of town and village councils. They accepted [both] Jews and Poles as functionaries in all the institutions, without discrimination. For the most part, young Jewish women were hired as secretaries.

After some time, storekeepers and craftsmen were required to obtain business permits, at the price of a small payment. They were instructed to open their places of business and to sell everything at the prices that had existed before the War broke out. The value of the Polish zloty was set to equal the Russian ruble.

The storekeepers did not like these instructions, and they avoided them, managing their businesses to their own advantage. Trade with the farmers increased. The craftsmen were exchanging their products for food.

The wholesalers, Alter Rachekovsky and Yaakov Ginzberg, were unable to hide all the merchandise in their possession in the shop and storerooms, because buyers did not come to them. They sold damaged and old goods wholesale in the exchange trade, since this was an opportunity to get rid of them.

A short time later, government shops were opened and it was possible to purchase cheap goods, but these were rationed in amounts for personal use, and it was forbidden to make purchases for others. Long lines formed along the length of the street, and, to the extent that the sold products were the more important ones, such as clothing and food, many people joined the lines. The lines began to form at dawn and even at midnight, not being deterred by strong winds, storms, and bitter cold. Quarrels and arguments frequently burst out in the lines, even leading to blows, because of an insolent fellow who had pushed his way into a more forward position. In such instances, the police had to intervene to restore order.

For the most part, large families succeeded in profiting from the lines, because they brought a number of people to stand in line simultaneously, and even sent their children to Bialystok to stand in line there, so as to obtain various kinds of products. At that time, there was no danger in smuggling goods from Bialystok to Sokoly, and it was easy to bribe the police who were guards at the Kruczewo Train Station and at the crossroads. After a few months, the prospects for smuggling lessened, along with the prospects for trading by exchange.

Very slowly, life entered orderly channels. Merchandise began to be sold in exchange for Polish and Russian money, and almost all the people of Sokoly were employed.

Bread – By Rationing

There were two flour mills in Sokoly, operated by steam. One mill, on 'Tiktin' Street, belonged to 'Shabtil' [Shabtai] Esterovitz, and the other, on Gonosowekie Street, next to the new cemetery, belonged to the Pole, Krinski. Krinski bought the lot from 'Lazerke' Rosenovitz and there he built a flour mill and an electric power station. The Soviets nationalized both mills and temporarily left their owners as managers of the plants, after adding assistants, secretaries, cashiers, and workers. The Soviets also brought in new functionaries to manage the Kruczewo Train Station, the post office, and the telephone company, leaving one or two of the prior officials as foremen.

In rationing bread, one-half kilo per person was allocated in exchange for tickets, at the official price of 85 kopeks per kilo. At that time, there were five bakers working in Sokoly: Alter Radzilowsky ('Moisheke'), Dina Burstein, Hershel Olsha, Yechiel Somovitz, and Yisrael Hirshman the *Melamed*. The five of them worked cooperatively. Flour, wood, and yeast were supplied to them at government prices.

The Nationalization of Houses

The Soviets began to solve the housing problem according to their own methods. First, they nationalized the large houses belonging to both Jews and Christians, leaving their owners one or at most two rooms, according to the number of people in their families. Later, they nationalized the houses of the *Endekes* [members of the *N.D.K.* the Polish National Democratic Party, who supported the Germans and antisemitic acts] and whose owners had fled from the Soviets, along with public buildings such as the municipality, the village council, the fire station, the hall belonging to the Christian church, the courthouse, the school, the bathhouse, etc.

They quickly conducted inspections of these buildings, according to engineering plans. They requisitioned one *beit midrash* and synagogue building from the Jewish Religious Council. At the request of Rabbi Yosef Rosenblum, the Soviets allowed the Jews to keep the large *beit midrash*. The pious Jews showed satisfaction with this arrangement, because prior to this, they had thought and also had heard that the Soviets would persecute the Jews with regard to religious matters. Now, they found out that it was possible to compromise on the subject and somehow bear the situation.

In the middle-sized houses, the residents paid rent to a government official; the amount of rent paid was dependent on the resident's position and status. Self-employed merchants and workers paid more than laborers and clerks. The estimation of the assessments was done on the basis of permits from the municipality and the place of employment.

After repairs and improvements were made to the public buildings, new shops were opened and a sick fund and pharmacies were put into operation. Following these, a theatre, cinema, libraries, reading halls, schools and clubs were opened. The medical staff received a government salary and served the public without payment. The pharmacies sold drugs at low prices.

Warehouses were opened for gathering crops from the farmers and from the residents of the settlements, who were obligated to sell a portion of their produce to the government at a low price. The village councils each kept a card index, including details regarding the dimensions of the fields and orchards, the number of cattle, sheep and poultry. More warehouses were opened for storing animal skins, milk, butter, cheese, eggs and even wool and linen.

Kosher - Politically

The municipal functionaries were mostly Jews. Their salaries ranged between 150 and 600 rubles per month. In order to be accepted for a government position, one had to be politically kosher in the eyes of the local political bosses. The Lapchinsky family had special rights. The members of this family set their sights on important positions; they were glorified because of the distinction of their brother Chaim, who had rotted in prison for four years because of his Communist activities when he was a student at the Teachers Seminary in Bialystok.

However, when there was a lack of, and need for, officials, a bourgeois or former capitalist would also be appointed.

Income without Shops

During the second year of the Soviet occupation, all the private shops in Sokoly were closed, as were those in the entire surrounding area. This was not caused by an economic crisis, but rather by the Treasury's imposition of heavy taxes. The shop owners were required to return their permits to the Treasury Office and to officially testify that they were liquidating their businesses. It is surprising that, though it appeared otherwise, the economic situation of the middle-class and small merchants during the Soviet occupation was better than it had been during the Polish regime before the War. It is true that officially, the Soviets proclaimed war on speculators, but they actually did not intervene in the citizens' business; they did not conduct searches and they did not harm the merchants.

The Soviet soldiers craved all kinds of merchandise, and they were very thankful when the merchants sold to them. Thus, unofficial trading flourished and there was plenty of income.

Shadow of the Era

In spite of everything mentioned above, a shadow hovered above the heads of the populace. Arrests and imprisonments began; following denouncements, single persons and entire families were driven out and exiled to far-away places in Russia. Any suspicion, or a single denouncement, was sufficient for a person to be imprisoned. This happened, for example, to the former head of the community, Palek Goldstein. He was accused, as it were, of imposing heavy taxes on workers and extorting large sums from the public through a government loan that he imposed on the citizens during the last year before the War, with the help of the police and through pressure tactics. Palek was put in prison in Bialystok and from there sent to Russia.

In this manner, they also imprisoned and exiled Yona Zilberstein, the former head of the *Beitar* [Revisionist Youth] movement in Sokoly, *Beitar* being, in their eyes, a fascist party. Following this imprisonment, four members of the family of Label Zilberstein, a successful merchant before the War, were sent to Russia. He used to send boxcars full of chickens and eggs to Warsaw and other cities. He also had a business fattening geese.

To the list of those sent to Russia were added: the teacher Avraham Wasserman and Gedalia Slodky's family, which numbered five souls. Gedalia Slodky was the owner of a metal shop in Sokoly. His entire guilt was that one of his sons, Michael, had fled abroad through Lithuania.

Mendel Fleer, a cattle dealer and wholesale meat supplier, was in line to be exiled. He would sort out cattle for ritual slaughter and send them to be transported in boxcars. Once they found an animal in his possession without a veterinarian's stamp. He was immediately arrested and exiled to Russia.

The imprisonments and exiles had a bitter influence on the local Jews. Later, under the evil Nazi regime, all the Jews envied those who had been imprisoned and exiled to the Soviet Union.

And Even So, the Situation Was Better

The rabbis and *shochtim* worried that they would not have any income, because they did not have permission to legally manage the religious institutions, and the butchers had returned their permits and closed the butcher shops because of the heavy taxes imposed upon them by the regime. In spite of everything, the results were the opposite. The rabbis, the *shochtim* and the butchers made larger profits during the Soviet occupation than they had before the War.

The rabbis and *shochtim* supported themselves by slaughtering chickens, which was a free occupation, as well as from the slaughter of large and small animals, which was partially legal. In the slaughter of animals, the rabbis and *shochtim* were equal partners, and the butchers, who did not have business permits, cooperated with the farmers, who had the right to slaughter their cattle and sell the meat to customers without a business permit. They needed a veterinarian's stamp on the meat, as well as a permit from the village council stating that the animal had not been stolen. Only then, was the farmer entitled to slaughter the animal as he wished and sell the meat to the Jews.

The butchers took advantage of the opportunity and bought animals from the farmers, which they then slaughtered in the *kosher* slaughterhouse, and they sold the meat in the presence of the farmers; some of it was sold in Sokoly and the rest was taken to Bialystok for sale in the meat market, or to a Jewish butcher. Such trade was legal, the farmer taking the Jewish expert as his assistant.

During the Polish regime before the War, Jewish shop owners and craftsmen were persecuted, subject to trials and punishments for transgressions under the trading laws. In comparison to the trade that existed during the time of the *Endekes* [N.D.K.], the Jewish merchants felt freer under the Soviet occupation, even though they were legally subject to heavy punishment.

They Learned with Perseverance and Prayed with Devotion

When the Jews entered the large *beit midrash* in Sokoly in the mornings and evenings, they did not feel as if they were under the Soviet regime, of which they had been so afraid. The *beit midrash* was always full of groups praying together, *minyan* after *minyan*, as it had been in the past. In the evenings, all the tables were occupied by those learning *Gemara*. The Rabbi sat next to one of the tables, and gave lessons in the *Daf Yomi* to the *Gemara* Society. Next to another table, a *Rav* taught a chapter of *Mishna* to his students in the *Mishnayot* Society. In front of a third table, a famous teacher from Wysokie Mazowieckie taught a page of *Gemara* to his students from another *Gemara* Society. Behind the stoves and between the benches sat simple, innocent Jews, who talked to each other about various issues of the day; sometimes they told stories about the past.

But young men were almost never seen in the *beit midrash*, except for those who were retarded. Youths who wasted time, who were empty-headed and irresponsible like they were before World War

17

II, were almost non-existent now. Whoever was talented was easily able to find work in an office, the shops, a factory, or other institutions, or else they were occupied in privately smuggling merchandise.

The permanent yeshiva students in Sokoly, those who, in the years before the War, had filled the *batei midrash* and were busy day and night with Torah and service, were now seen in the *beit midrash* only infrequently, mostly on the Shabbat, because they sat at home all week, seriously studying Russian grammar and various Russian textbooks. Similarly, with the assistance of teachers, they also learned accounting and bookkeeping, so that they would be able to find employment in these professions and would be able to take their day of rest on the Shabbat instead of on Sundays. The holiness of the Shabbat was still felt everywhere, as it had been in the past. Thus, this era continued until June 22, 1941.

The Last Day

On Saturday night, June 21, 1941, the youths of Sokoly, of both sexes, were entertained at a dance in the hall at the fire station. The Russian army commanders and officers enjoyed themselves there until late into the night. After midnight, the youths went to sleep, not knowing that this was their last entertainment.

Sunday morning, the neighbors woke each other in order to pass along the news that during the night, the Germans had bombed the Malkin Bridge and made a lot of noise shooting rounds of ammunition on the Bialystok Road. A lot of people were injured, some of them Jews.

For a few minutes, great confusion arose. Hearts began to beat faster; had a war begun between Russia and Germany?! We thought that we already were rid of the Germans forever!

Many residents came to [Moshe] Maik to hear the news. At the time [of the beginning of the War], there had been only two radios among the Jewish population of Sokoly, one belonging to Mendel

Fleer and one to Alter Ginzberg; but the Germans had confiscated them at the time they first entered Sokoly.

Moshe Maik turned on the radio, and Hitler's speech to the German Army and Molotov's speech to the Russian nation were heard. By means of the radio, the Jews were informed that the Germans had already conquered a large area of the Polish-Russian territory and the Russian Army had dispersed and was conquered; thousands had been taken prisoner by the Germans. Molotov's last words, that Hitler would inherit the downfall of Napoleon in Russia, were of small comfort to the listeners. Now the destruction would begin.

Chaim Somovitz (the son of Yechiel Somovitz, the baker) said, "We are already lost, and we can no longer depend on miracles, like the first time…"

Then, we had no idea of the cruelty and barbarity of the Germans. The experiences we had at the time the barbaric soldiers entered the first time, when they stayed only 12 days, were enough to impose panic, confusion and fear of death upon us.

The optimists still comforted themselves with the hope that danger was still far away. They said, if a small country like Poland could hold out for two weeks before it was conquered by the Germans, then even more so, how would it be possible for them to conquer White Russia and the Ukraine any faster?!

But immediately many others came and told us that the Germans had bombed the Russian airport in Wysokie Mazowieckie and burned up all the airplanes that were there. Many injured Russian pilots were brought to Sokoly, and about two thousand Russian soldiers that were in Sokoly fled. Only a few soldiers remained in order to burn and destroy all the warehouses.

We were also told about horrible, heart-rending sights: about the last parting of the senior Russian officers from their families; about the crying and wailing of the wives and children of the Russian officers, who wanted to take some possessions with them, things that they would never be able to get in Russia, and now they did not have any room to take their precious treasures with them. There wasn't even room in the vehicles for their children who were squeezed and crowded in like sardines in a can. They argued and quarreled with each other over a more comfortable place in the vehicle.

The Commissar of the town, the managers and senior officials of all the institutions in Sokoly, were ensured of comfortable means of travel. In spite of this, they rented additional wagons to transport their possessions, at least to Bialystok.

"Good-hearted" Poles broke into shops and warehouses no less than the hoodlums, and they stole entire stocks of merchandise and all the possessions that they came across. They loaded wagons with sacks of sugar, manufactured goods, shoes and expensive possessions. There also were Jews who carried leftovers from the officers' empty houses. Towards evening of that same day, the Jews began to pack their possessions and hide some of them in pits, under the floors, and in secret locations. During the night, rumors spread that the Germans had already reached Wysokie Mazowieckie, and it was estimated that they would reach Sokoly at any time.

The Germans Re-enter Our Town

The next day at dawn, German tanks invaded Sokoly. A wagon, loaded with the possessions of Nissel Lapchinsky, who had been the chief manager of the cooperatives and stores under the Russian regime, stood on Bathhouse Street. From fear of the Germans, Nissel fled with his family to Bialystok.

At noon, a senior Soviet officer by the name of Kaposta was still seen in the streets of the town. This man later became famous as General Kaposta, the leader of the partisans in the Baranowicz Forests. That day, Kaposta arrived in a vehicle in order to transport the soldiers whom he had left there until the last minute. He even wanted to take his possessions from his apartment in

20

Shlomo Leibel Itzkovsky's house, but he had come too late, because the place had already been broken into and robbed. Tsippa Sarnivitz, the daughter of the locksmith Alter Sarnivitz, escaped with him from Sokoly.

With the re-invasion of Sokoly by the Germans, panic and confusion arose. During the first week, there still was no civilian rule. Many military vehicles, tanks, and artillery filled the streets and rushed through without a pause. They had been in the town for only a few hours, but this was sufficient for them to reveal their characters and satanic souls through cruelty and sadism towards the Jews.

Before the German "*Amstkommissar*" arrived in Sokoly, a Polish lawyer, Manikowski, organized a temporary town committee and militia. They requested that the Jews also participate in service in the militia, but they did not find any volunteers. In matters of economic administration, the Jews cooperated with Manikowski and contributed their share in organizing supplies, mainly in baking bread for the Jewish population, who constituted two-thirds of the town.

The Jews chose a committee that prepared an exact list of the people according to streets, and they rationed one-half loaf of bread (one kilo) per day per person. There was no change in the price of bread, which remained the same as it had been before the War. The bread was baked and distributed in three locations. At the beginning, long lines formed. As time passed, the distribution was organized, and there was enough for everyone.

Home for the Elderly

Twenty elderly people arrived in Sokoly. They had previously been moved by the Soviets from a home for the elderly in Bialystok to the landowner's palace in the village of Mazury, where they had arranged a pension for the elderly. Now, the Poles drove the elderly people out of the palace before the Germans had time to locate themselves. The old people arrived in Sokoly. Among them were some disabled and deformed persons. The Jews of Sokoly housed them in the *Beitar* Club and in the *batei midrash*. Every home supplied them with food, except for the portions of bread that were allocated to each person who lived in the town.

Most of the youths hid themselves, the boys from fear of being kidnapped for forced labor and the girls from fear of rape. Bearded Jews were afraid that their beards would be ripped from their faces along with the flesh.

Nissel Lapchinsky

Information arrived from Bialystok that Nissel Lapchinsky had committed suicide by hanging himself. In Sokoly, they thought this was crazy. All of them were amazed how a young, intelligent man like Nissel could allow himself to leave his young wife and six-year-old son. His wife was due to give birth in the near future. It is true that we can always expect dangers to life, but a living person has hopes of living through all the bad times.

Later, the Jews of Sokoly began to regard Nissel's act as one of courage and wisdom. This way, he prevented himself from the suffering and the atrocities that later visited the Jews of the town. He did not see with his own eyes how infants were pulled from their mothers' arms and shattered against the walls of the houses. He did not pass through the path of suffering on the way to the gas chambers. But only a few were able to do what Nissel did.

Rumors from Neighboring Towns

It became known that on the first day of their invasion the Germans, with the help of young Poles, seized 2500 Jews in Bialystok, imprisoned them in the great synagogue there and set it on fire.

While the synagogue was going up in flames, gangs of Germans and wild Poles kidnapped Jews from streets near the synagogue and threw them into the flames.

A rumor came from the village of Trzeszczyn [Trestin] that the Germans had gathered over 1000 young Jews who were able to work, and shot them to death. After two days, a rumor came from Bialystok that they had arrested more than 5000 Jews and sent them, apparently, to be killed. Among the 5000 Jews sent to be slaughtered were Yitzhak Morashkevitz, owner of a large ironworks factory on Surazi Street in Bialystok. His wife 'Sirkeh' [Sarah], the daughter of Moshe Hershel Seines, came with her children to her parents in Sokoly after her husband was exiled. The families of those exiled from Bialystok paid thousands of dollars and gold in order to find out where the exiled were sent, but these efforts did not succeed.

The heads of the Gestapo in Bialystok demanded that the *Judenrat* (the local Jewish council) supply five kilograms of gold, suits of clothing and boots. Following that order, the *Judenrat* began to gather gold rings and necklaces from the women in order to cope with these extortionary demands.

The *Kommandant* immediately demanded that he be provided with an additional, doubled amount of gold (ten kilograms) within three days; otherwise, all the Jews would be expelled from Bialystok. All these rumors caused enormous panic in Sokoly.

Organization of the *Judenrat*

Eight days after the Germans entered Sokoly, a German *Kommandant* and accompanying *gendarmes* arrived. The *Kommandant* immediately called for representatives of the Jews to come to him. A delegation was sent, headed by Alter Ginzberg. The *Kommandant* gave Alter Ginzberg the job of organizing a local Jewish council or *Judenrat* in Sokoly, whose task would be to meticulously carry out the Germans' orders. The *Judenrat* would bear responsibility for the actions of the Jews and would have complete jurisdiction over the local Jewish population.

In addition, the *Kommandant* demanded that a list be made of all the merchandise in the possession of the Jews. Gold, silver and jewelry must be given to the *Kommandancy*. The *Kommandant* warned that

23

searches would be made, and anyone found in possession of gold, silver, valuable jewelry and unlisted merchandise would be sentenced to death. The *Kommandant* also ordered the Jews, as well as the Christians, to hand in weapons, radio parts and other objects that were left behind by the Soviets. Any delay in fulfilling these orders would be punished by death.

Upon hearing these orders, all the Jews were seized by trembling and fear of death. In almost every house there were possessions that had to be immediately handed over to the *Kommandant*. What to do? Hand them in? There would be nothing from which to make a living. Not hand them in? This was the danger of death. Nobody knew what to decide. Life was in great danger in any case, and nobody would dare to declare what was in his possession and hand it over to the *Kommandancy*, especially when jewelry and valuables had been hidden.

The Jews established the *Judenrat* with great difficulty. Nobody wanted to take upon himself the dangerous responsibility. Slowly, the town's communal workers, led by Rabbi *HaRav* Yosef Rosenblum, succeeded in establishing a *Judenrat* at first comprising: Alter Ginzberg, Chaim Yehoshua Olsha, 'Aharki' Zholti, 'Lazerke' Rosenovitz, Zeidel Rachekovsky, Yechezkel Czerbonicz, Yisrael Maik, Yona Ginzberg, and Leibel Okune, owner of a fabric store. The Rabbi and scholar, *HaRav* Yosef Rosenblum was an 'honorary' member of the *Judenrat*.

Every member of the *Judenrat* had a specific task, and all of them worked energetically and with dedication, recognizing their responsibility under the difficult situation of the time.

Alter Ginzberg was appointed Chairman of the *Judenrat*. He owned a leather goods and shoe shop. His wife was a dentist. Alter was an educated, polite, and pleasant person.

Yehoshua Olsha was in charge of organizing professionals and workers for the construction trades, and the supply of materials and tools for work. He knew how to organize himself under the Germans' demands and to satisfy their wishes.

'Aharki' [Aharon] Zholti was a wood merchant and a relative of Judge Jeruzelsky. In their youth, 'Aharki' and Jeruzelsky were faithful friends and they always spent time together. As mentioned above, 'Aharki' had a large and beautiful house in Sokoly.

Yechezkel Czerbonicz and Yaakov Janowitz handled the matter of workers for unskilled labor. Yechezkel had previously been a witty fabric merchant, having energy and a quick mind. Yaakov (Avraham Borowitz's son-in-law) was the owner of a shoe store and well-versed in Torah.

'Lazerke' Rosenovitz and Yona Ginzberg supplied the Germans with various merchandise from Bialystok. Lazer was known for his overgrown mustache and straight posture, like a Polish squire. He owned about 30 threshing sledges, fields and large houses. He was the friend and advisor of Advocate Manikowski, the former mayor. Both of them conducted business of wide proportions. Rosenovitz supplied the bakers with flour and wood from his wagon, according to an official permit.

Yisrael Maik and 'Yankel' [Yaakov Janowitz] the shoemaker supplied leather and boots to the regime. Yisrael Maik was a watchmaker and goldsmith [by profession], and before the War, his wife Dina managed a hotel and a restaurant. Yisrael was intelligent and proud, and he was a friend of government officials, especially of the local courthouse judge, Jeruzelsky. He was accustomed to helping his friends and acquaintances with charity and mediation. Both Jews and Christians, in the town and its surroundings, liked and honored him. 'Yankel' (the second husband of Josefa Kanarczika) was a good and prosperous craftsman.

Soon, several others were added to the list of the *Judenrat* Committee:

Shlomo Rosachatchky (Meir Halpern's son-in-law and the owner of a haberdashery shop); Dr. Makowsky (the nephew of 'Little Alterke'); Zeidel Rachekovsky, who was a good speaker; 'Yankel' Surasky the blacksmith, a wise and enlightened man in public matters; and Moshe Lipa Shulmeister (David Borowitz's son-in-law), a student in the Volozhin Yeshiva, owner of a grocery, who loved to argue regarding political matters.

The Searches

After a few days, searches began. The first searches were conducted by *gendarmes* with the assistance of the translator, '*Zekankan*'. He was a Polish Christian with a sharp little beard, and that is why they called him "*Zekankan*" ['Little Beard']. Only a few of the residents of Sokoly knew that the *Zekankan* had previously lived in a small hut (a clay house) in the woods near a village close to Sokoly, and made house slippers out of rags to sell. His wife and children would gather blueberries or mushrooms and travel to the city to sell them. In September of 1939, when the War broke out between Germany and Poland, and after the first invasion of the Germans into Sokoly, the '*Zekankan*' accompanied the officers of the occupying German Army as a translator. He spoke fluent German.

At that time, the '*Zekankan*' brought a radio receiver to Moshe Maik to be repaired. He took the opportunity to tell Moshe that a few years ago he had been an officer in the Austrian army. He suggested that Moshe Maik turn to him for help if he needed anything, because he had a lot of *protektzia* [influence] with the Germans. But just then, Moshe did not need him.

A short time later, the Soviets entered and the '*Zekankan*' was no longer to be seen in Sokoly. When the Germans re-entered Sokoly, the '*Zekankan*' again appeared as a translator for the Germans and he accompanied the *gendarmes* on all their searches. They went from house to house among the Jews and took anything that they liked and put it with their personal things.

What Happened to Michael Maik

During these searches, a great miracle happened to Michael Maik, who was saved from death, thanks to the influence of the

Zekankan in gratitude to Moshe Maik for repairing his radio free of charge. What happened was as follows:

Before World War II, the brothers Yisrael and Michael Maik remodeled their old house, which they had inherited from their father. The War broke out just when the inspection of their new house had been completed. When the Soviets invaded Sokoly, they turned the Maik brothers' house into a hospital. When the Russians left Sokoly, Michael Maik installed a lock on the door of the house, out of concern that someone would seize the house, since Jewish property was subject to anarchy.

When the Germans came to search the locked Maik house, they were told that Michael Maik had the key. They called Michael and ordered him to open the house. During the search, the Germans found a picture of Stalin and various documents in the Russian language. The Germans began to suspect that Michael Maik, the owner of the house, was a Soviet agent. One of the *gendarmes* was ready to shoot him, but at that point, the *'Zekankan'* intervened on his behalf, arguing that he knew Michael well as an honest and respectable man. The Germans freed Michael Maik.

When the first searches were completed, many Jews told of miracles that happened to them during the searches. They were sorry that the Germans had taken valuables and possessions that they had inherited and that had been passed down to them through the generations.

Besides the ordinary searches, Jew-hating Polish informers also conducted searches. With their help the Germans found hidden merchandise, while simultaneously, criminals of the underworld carried out robberies and burglaries.

In addition to the above, there were imprisonments following denouncements. It was sufficient for someone to denounce a Polish Jew as being a Communist or active in a Soviet project, and the Germans would imprison the person. In this manner, dozens of young men and women were imprisoned and were expecting to receive a death sentence. This happened in all the nearby towns. Relatives of the prisoners were mourning their dear ones who had been sentenced to death. When they took 'Shmulke' [Shmuel] Weinstein, the painter, out from the attic of the Maik house on Bathhouse Street, his wife Rachel wailed spasmodic, heart-rending cries, until the German guards below took pity upon her and comforted her that soon they would release her husband. The fact that the Germans did nothing to the dozens of Jews whom they arrested was thanks to the 'Zekankan,' whom the Germans regarded as an important person.

During the German occupation, the 'Zekankan' moved from a small hut in the forest to a luxury apartment with splendid furniture—taken, of course, from Jewish ownership. The 'Zekankan' was also known by the name Marshlek. Even though the Jews of Sokoly regarded the 'Zekankan' as a German agent, he apparently was not antisemitic, but he did love to receive bribes.

In comparison with the 'Zekankan', it became evident at the time of the German occupation that the lawyer Manikowski, who had been the mayor of Sokoly during the Polish regime before the War and had then been regarded as a lover of Israel, was [really] a fervent anti-Semite. He drove many Jews from their apartments and installed Christian tenants in their stead. He threatened to prepare a ghetto for the Jews in the near future.

A short time after that, 'the 'Zekankan' was appointed as mayor of the town in place of Manikowski. The 'Zekankan' calmed down the Jews in Sokoly. All the Jews who had been sitting in prison for several weeks, and were already regarded as lost, were now freed, thanks to the 'Zekankan', the new mayor. Meir Charney (the son of 'Zusli' the tailor), who had been in danger of death, was finally freed from imprisonment.

When the order was issued that the residents must register in the municipality office and receive an identity card, otherwise they would lose the right to live in Sokoly, all the Jews returned from hiding at their friends' homes in the villages in anticipation of the entry of the Germans.

The *Judenrat* prepared a list of Jews who were able to work. Every day, the Poles would choose young Jews to go to work. The weak, or those who were granted special rights by the *Judenrat*, were sent to various other jobs as required. In the beginning, they sent workers to repair the roads. This time, they did not kidnap Jews for forced labor as they had done during the first few weeks, but rather employed them in easy jobs in the town and only for a few hours.

Nachum 'Trotsky'

One day a group of workers was sent to the Wysokie Road in a truck. When the workers were on their way home towards evening, the truck overturned on the slope of the road near the village of Mazury. The Jews were lightly injured, but one of them, Nachum "Trotsky", was killed.

Nachum Trotsky was an orphan, without a father and mother since his childhood. He would go from door to door on Fridays, together with his stepsister, who was called 'Pekka'. She was a fat girl who suffered from epilepsy. They went from house to house in order to collect food for *Shabbat*. Eventually, Nachum separated from his stepsister, and each of them would go separately from house to house.

Nachum 'Trotsky' supported himself by saying *Tehillim* at the side of the deceased before burial, from carrying the bier and covering, and from bringing these items back from the cemetery. On *Shabbat* and Festival eves, he would run through the streets and loudly proclaim, "Home owners to the bathhouse!" During a funeral he would run and cry, "*Mitzva* for the dead!" Mainly during the month of *Elul* and during the Ten Days of Repentance, Jews from the neighboring villages and towns would come to the cemetery in Sokoly every day (except on the *Shabbat* and Jewish holidays) to memorialize their departed ones. The people from Lapy also buried their dead in the Sokoly cemetery. 'Trotsky' and 'Pekka' would sit all day in a tent at the cemetery collecting donations from the visitors.

When 'Trotsky' grew up and had amassed a bit of money, he married a girl from Ostrow Mazowiecka where he was employed transporting milk for sale. 'Trotsky' did not adapt to his job. He returned to Sokoly after two years.

After the traffic accident in Mazury, 30 workers were missing from the list of workers. The Germans demanded that the *Judenrat* provide a large number of agricultural workers for the landowners' courts, such as Mazury, Recz, Stachowiczki, Krzywe, and more.

Jews were employed at the Kruczewo Train Station to load and unload coal, weapons, and ammunition; they widened the train track; cut down trees in the [nearby] forests; and worked in [forced] labor gangs in the city. All these jobs required a great number of workers, and the *Judenrat* was obligated to enlarge its list of those who were able to work. Until then, workers had been listed up to the age of 40. Now, the *Judenrat* was obligated to register workers up to the age of 60, and almost all the elderly and aged came to register.

Rumors arrived from neighboring villages that the Germans were killing the elderly, the weak, and the sick.

There was a disturbance in the *Judenrat* regarding unfair distribution of work. The *Judenrat* was accused of discriminating among the people. Some were sent to hard labor and some to easy jobs. One group of workers received an order to go to work every day, and another group worked only twice a week. There also were those who were privileged and were exempt from going to forced labor.

In this situation, Rabbi Rosenblum called a meeting of those who were fit to work. He reminded them that the situation was difficult and that saving our lives depended on our work. In other towns, the Germans had killed most of the Jews or, in the best instance, drove some of them into a ghetto. Therefore, it was obligatory for every able-bodied person to volunteer to work. It should be remembered that in exchange for work, a person rescues himself and his family from death, and as much as the amount of work increases, so does the chance of remaining alive. Whoever avoids forced labor should be fined. Whoever receives a notice from the *Judenrat* must appear immediately. The *Judenrat* will classify the workers into levels appropriate to their age and health and will take sole supporters into consideration. It is essential to support the families.

In the beginning, all the people summoned to work by the *Judenrat* would gather next to the home of Alter Ginzberg, the head of the *Judenrat*, where the names of the workers were read out from the lists. The secretary recorded the names of missing workers who were listed and did not show up, and afterwards the *Judenrat* conducted an investigation as to the reason for their absence. Whoever did not have a justified reason was fined. After the reading of the names, the workers were organized into groups. The first ones were the groups for hard labor and work in distant locations. The Christian work managers assisted in doing this.

Azorowski, who in the past had been the overseer of the railroad, along with his two sons and other work managers, would wait for the Jewish workers, and everyone they chose to work was obligated to listen to them and go. They sent groups of workers, most of them permanently employed, to the nationalized landowners' courts. Some of them would sleep in the locations where they worked, because it was difficult to go home every evening and come back the next day at dawn. The elderly and weaker workers were sent to relatively easy jobs in Sokoly.

About 200 workers from Sokoly would travel to the town of Lapy to work in the *Dapu* train factory. These 200 workers got up every morning before dawn and marched to the Kruczewo Train Station at 5:30 a.m. From there, a special train took them to Lapy and their workplaces. At 7:00 p.m. the workers returned home to Sokoly in the same train.

Once, while the names of the workers were being read out in front of Chairman Alter Ginzberg's house, a German came running and began to lash the groups of workers with a rubber whip on their heads and faces. In fear and panic, all the workers ran away in every direction. Chairman Ginzberg submissively turned to the German whipper and explained to him that according to the *Amstkommissar*'s orders, he was to organize the workers, divide them into groups by profession, and send them to their workplaces in accordance with the orders received. The German used the excuse that it was late and that the workers had to be at their workplaces to begin work at 6:00. The Chairman answered that according to the orders of the *Amstkommissar*, the workers were to begin at 7:00. The German whipmaster had no connection with the forced labor of the Jewish workers, but, being a bloodthirsty murderer, he could not bear to see Jews alive. When the German hooligan went away, the workers returned to Ginzberg, and the transport of the workers to their jobs was properly carried out. From that day onward, the workers assembled inside the *Judenrat* hall. After that, they found two apartments, belonging to Fraidel Golche and 'Yosha' Sarbrulow, to use.

At that time, additional decrees were issued against the Jews, among them: (1) requiring the wearing of a 'badge of shame' [a yellow marker to segregate Jews from non-Jews]; (2) expelling Jews from their homes; (3) confiscating furniture and household goods; and (4) raising taxes and special levies. These 'messages of Job' caused fear and trembling in every Jewish heart.

The 'Badges of Shame'

At the beginning, the Germans ordered Jews of both sexes, from the age of 12, to wear white ribbons on their right arms. After all of them had prepared the white ribbons, they were used only for a short time. After that, the Germans issued an order to change the badges of shame. Instead of round white ribbons, they had to wear two Jewish stars and write the word "Jew" in the center of each one, in black ink and in block letters. Any Jew who was caught without the 'badge of shame' was cruelly beaten and had to pay a fine of ten marks.

The right to expel a Jew from his apartment was given not only to Germans, but also to the Polish militia who served the Germans, to the local council, and even to any ordinary Christian.

The Christian shoemaker of Sokoly, Kanofka, an apparently quiet and innocent man, figured that, instead of always sitting on his shoemaker's bench and sweating out his work for a life of poverty, he could choose the life of a prince from Jewish booty. So what did Kanofka the shoemaker do? He left his shoemaker's bench and became a policeman in the militia. Yechiel Blustein's beautiful and comfortable apartment, with its fancy furniture, appealed to him. Kanofka had a document issued by the *Amstkommissar*, stating that he had the right to confiscate the apartment and furniture belonging to Yechiel Blustein and take them for himself. Yechiel was forced to ask another Jew to give him shelter and a roof over his head.

The Polish carpenter Dworkowski did the same thing. He was tired of carpentry work and desired the luxury apartment belonging to Mordechai Surasky the grain merchant (the son of the blacksmith Moshe Yitzhak Surasky). Dworkowski copied Kanofka. He became a policeman in the militia and had a document issued by the *Amstkommissar*, confiscating for himself Mordechai Surasky's magnificent and spacious apartment with all its luxurious furniture and utensils, including even the wood for heating. Thus, Dworkowski robbed Mordechai Surasky of everything he had.

Dworkowski the carpenter did even more than his predecessor Kanofka. He exploited his special rights to rob the Jews of abandoned property. He asked the *Amstkommissar* for permission to search the houses of the Jews in order to steal whatever appealed to him.

During one of his searches, at the home of a rag peddler who had received packages from his relatives in America before the War, Dworkowski found a box in a corner under a closet, full of hundreds of dollars that the peddler had saved to buy an apartment. The Germans had burned down the peddler's former house at the time of their first invasion in September of 1939. The peddler was dressed in rags and lived on a pittance. All his money and possessions fell into the hands of Dworkowski and his collaborators.

Polish militia police began to expel Jews from their apartments. The shop owners and craftsmen were not far behind them. Farmers forcefully entered Jewish shops, homes, restaurants, and cafes. After they drove out the owners, they stole the equipment and possessions.

Polish tailors, shoemakers, carpenters, and locksmiths drove the Jews out of their workshops and stole their livelihoods from them. A villager who worked in his youth as an apprentice to a Jewish milliner, but never dealt in the trade, did not hesitate to drive out his teacher, Yitzhak Koschevsky, and take his machines, the tools, and all the equipment and materials for himself. Koschevsky tried to compromise with the robber, and for a significant amount of money the villager agreed to concede the matter. It later became known that this Pole joined up with a Jewish milliner in another town for the purpose of carrying out a similar transaction with German approval.

Again, it is told that a village barber wanted to open a barbershop in Sokoly, and had his eye on the apartment belonging to Alter Ginzberg, the Chairman of the *Judenrat*. By scheming, the hooligan obtained written permission from the Germans to take over two large rooms and a shop, with all the equipment, in Alter's house. He stole the equipment for the barbershop, such as mirrors, chairs, and the like, from Meir Gozbonda the barber.

Thus, Polish laundresses, chimney sweeps, gamblers, robbers, the unemployed and simply reckless and irresponsible people settled in the homes of the Jews. They moved into comfortable and spacious Jewish houses, while those they expelled, along with their large families of many children, were crowded into single rooms. There even were cases of two or three such families being crowded together into a stable.

The Germans and the Polish police customarily conducted visits to the homes of affluent Jews, where they chose furniture and beautiful household utensils and confiscated them for themselves. Later, they forced the *Judenrat* to confiscate household items hand these over to them on a specific date and at an exact time. In case of refusal or delay, the Germans threatened to send the entire Jewish population to be killed.

The *Judenrat* supplied the four Germans who seized the large house belonging to the wealthy wood merchant 'Aharki' Zholti with the nicest furniture in town along with bedding, expensive curtains, kitchen utensils, and all kinds of objects. It is worth adding that before the War, in addition to the owner of that house and his family, other families had also lived there. During the Soviet occupation, senior officers and the military doctor had lived in the house with their families.

The Germans expanded the 'Aharki' house by demolishing the houses around it. Thus, the house that belonged to 'Itzele' [Yitzhak] Roseman, the son of Yisrael Roseman the beltmaker; the house and smithy of Tuvia Goldberg the blacksmith; the house of Yechezkel Morashkevitz, who owned a metal shop, and the cowsheds and warehouses that were in the courtyards around Aharki's house were all destroyed. Dozens of Jews were employed in the demolition work. After the demolition was completed, the Germans obligated the *Judenrat* to build a stable for their horses and large garages for their vehicles, and to enclose the entire area, including the new buildings, with a fence. The house had to be plastered. They built a tall watchtower on the roof, and Aharki's house became a palace. All in all, just four, single *gendarmes* lived in the house.

If that wasn't enough, not only the *Amstkommissar*, his secretary and his translator, who were living in the house of 'Lazerke' Rosenovitz, but also the three overseers of the railway, the Mayor Marshlek (the '*Zekankan*'), the manager of the dairy and the functionaries of the public railway had to be supplied with whatever they wanted. Occasionally, there were threats of death by shooting.

Boltz, a certain functionary of the Kruczewo Train Station was not sufficiently satisfied with the household utensils and expensive set of plates decorated with gold flowers that he received from the *Judenrat*. Boltz was boiling with anger and screamed horribly that they were comparing him to a Jew. How did they dare to serve rubbish to a Russian or a Pole?! The Chairman of the *Judenrat*, Alter Ginzberg, was so upset by Boltz's threats that he was afraid that the crazy German would shoot him.

The Germans' caprices were crazy. For example, they requested caracul fur, fox fur and seal fur, cameras, and anything they could think of. The *Judenrat* tried to obtain objects that were not available in Sokoly from the Bialystok Ghetto. The [community's] financial resources were not sufficient to cover the fantastic costs [of these items], and therefore the *Judenrat* was forced to raise money by taking all kinds of drastic measures, including searching houses where they thought people were hiding foreign currency. They asked for voluntary donations or sworn declarations that no foreign currency was being hidden.

As stated above, every Jew was burdened with taxes, according to the exact list prepared by the assessors under strict supervision. And so, our brothers, the sons of Israel, paid more than they were able to pay, each one doing so with the knowledge that with his money he was redeeming himself and his family from exile and death.

Besides ordinary taxes, the *Judenrat* required the monthly payment of a head tax and an apartment tax, whether the person owned an apartment or was only a secondary occupant. It was necessary to carry an identity card and a work card, for both of which a certain amount had to be paid. In this manner, the *Judenrat* acquired a fund that would enable it to fulfill the frequent demands of its oppressors, as well as independent management costs.

The Rumors from Neighboring Towns

Touching and saddening rumors coming from cities and towns near Sokoly disturbed the tranquility and contentment of our townspeople, towns where, during the first months of the Germans' entry, the entire Jewish population was exterminated. Groups of Jews were expelled from Lomza and Zambrow, and where they disappeared was unknown.

The most shocking and depressing impression upon our townspeople was made by the destruction of 'Tiktin' [Tykocin, about 25 kilometers from Sokoly]. In the beginning, the Jews of 'Tiktin' praised "their" Germans for the way they treated them. Suddenly, on 2 Elul (1941), the Germans ordered the Jews of 'Tiktin' to gather in the town square and line up in rows. The congregation of Jews, numbering about 3000 souls, including *Rav* Domta and the *shochet*, Shmuel Barish, filled the square. Each person was allowed to take a suitcase weighing up to 25 kg. At the gathering place, they were informed that they were being transferred, apparently to the Bialystok Ghetto. From the town square, the 'Tiktin' people were taken to the nearby village of Zawady, a place where eight Jewish families lived at that time. The Germans joined the Jews of the village to the Jews from 'Tiktin' and brought them all back to 'Tiktin', to the courtyard of the synagogue. There, they divided the Jews into groups and loaded them onto vehicles. The direction in which they traveled was toward the forests of Lopuchowo.

At that location, the robbers had prepared deep and wide pits well in advance. Poles from the area were informed to tell that the pits were intended to store kerosene. The "good" Germans of 'Tiktin' threw their victims into the pits of Lopuchowo. Some of them were shot to death, but most of them were buried alive.

The destruction of 'Tiktin' shocked all of us in Sokoly to the depths of our souls, after we had previously hesitated to believe general rumors about the mass murder of Jews at a location farther away.

Here, Dovka Goldberg was wailing for her sister and her family who had been murdered in 'Tiktin'.

Hershel the fisherman, a respected Jew from 'Tiktin', moved with his family before the War to live in Bialystok. There he acquired wealth and position. His sons and daughters acquired a high school education. Eight days before the destruction, Hershel returned with his family to 'Tiktin'. His two lovely daughters brought bridegrooms from Bialystok with them. On the day of the killing, the daughters went out arm-in-arm, as if to dance, with their young men, adding a tragic layer to the valley of killing.

The Jews of Sokoly knew, without a doubt, that they should no longer depend upon the promises of the "good and generous" Germans.

After the destruction of 'Tiktin', more rumors of bad news arrived in Sokoly. One rumor was more terrible than the next...

Refugees from Jedwabne and Radzilow arrived, who were coincidentally saved from death, and who saw with their own eyes and felt the hell on their flesh. With the help of local farmers, the Germans gathered the Jews of these places, with the Rabbi and leaders of the community at the front, in the market square. At first, they beat them cruelly and forced them to wrap themselves in their *tallitot*, to jump and dance, accompanied by singing. All this was done under an unceasing flood of lashes from cudgels and rubber whips. At the end, they pushed all the Jews, while beating and kicking them, into a long threshing house and set it on fire with them inside. This was the end of Jedwabne and Radzilow.

A deep and fearsome worry regarding the fate of the Jews of our town moved the representatives of the community to turn to the *Amstkommissar* and express to him their worry and fears with regard to the near future. The German, whose wishes were always satisfied by the *Judenrat*, promised with a wily smile that as long as he would be in Sokoly, nothing bad would happen to the Jews. He would not allow the Gestapo to harm them. His promises calmed the mood a bit, in opposition to the Angel of Death, who was frenzied and going mad. And again rumors, this time calming ones: "The mass murder will stop in all the districts on April 12th." Apparently Goering had said that the Jewish labor force should be exploited as much as possible.

Whereas this date was already behind us, we were entertained by the hope that a miracle would still occur for us and that G-d would have mercy on the sheep of his flock and send us redemption – and a downfall to those who hated us.

Of all the residents of 'Tiktin', a total of only 120 souls survived who had succeeded in fleeing to the [nearby] forests and other hiding places. Their Polish neighbors exploited the situation and robbed those who fled of all their possessions. After a certain length of time, when the searches for refugees from 'Tiktin' ceased, a few of them found temporary shelter in Sokoly.

In the town of Rutki Kossaki the Germans murdered 1,500 Jews and only 130 survived. Sixty of them worked in the Jezewo Quarry and the rest of them in various occupations recommended by Poles in Rutki. A number of survivors came to Sokoly.

In Wysokie Mazowieckie, which the Germans burned down back in 1939 and the Soviets partially restored, the Jews were locked into a Ghetto quarter. They believed that this would be good for them and that they would no longer be abandoned to anyone who wanted to scheme against them. It is interesting that they even supported the ghetto's establishment with their own money.

The economic situation was not so bad in the Wysokie Mazowieckie Ghetto. Our brothers learned to smuggle food from the villages, and the craftsmen were loaded with jobs ordered by the Poles. Grocery items were cheaper than they were in Sokoly.

There were people in our town who were former residents of Wysokie Mazowieckie and were familiar with the town. They would go there every day, a distance of 14 kilometers both ways, in order to smuggle in meat, oil and various food items that were sold there in the ghetto at very low prices.

Among the smugglers were Yerachmiel Weinkrantz (the son of Berish the *shochet* from Sokoly) and his four sons, some of whom were adults. Slowly the fear of being expelled from Sokoly and Wysokie lessened. Several weeks passed without any expulsions of major proportions. Here and there, cases of Jews being murdered were reported.

In Lapy, the Germans shot 13 dignitaries of the Jewish community, who were innocent of any crime and far removed from politics or the idea of Communism or even a hint of supporting it. Thus, Fishel Rachelsky, wise and respected in the community (the son of Shmuel Martzibur), his comely wife, his two, pretty daughters and his charming and intelligent son, all were shot to death.

Another victim was Frankel, a warehouse worker during the Soviet period, responsible for the export of products of the cooperatives in Lapy and the neighboring villages. Before the War, Frankel owned businesses. He was pleasant to everyone; he was good-looking and his deeds were as good as his looks.

The Germans also shot the intelligent Tannenbaum, a rent collector for the Soviets in Lapy.

The last ones of this group who were killed were Chanuni Asher, in whose house they found hidden merchandise; Yaakov Sarbrulow, an honest and innocent young man; Weinberg, the owner of a steam mill in Lapy, and his two sons. The list of victims on that day was completed with the owner of a shoe shop, in whose house they found a red scarf.

The barbarians threw their victims into swamps deep in mud. Over a period of time, the families of the victims were able to bring the bodies of their dear ones out of the swamps to Jewish burial in Sokoly. There was no Jewish cemetery in Lapy, and they were accustomed to burying their dead in Sokoly. The relatives paid a fortune for the transportation of the bodies.

After the recent events in 'Tiktin', while the blood of its victims was not yet dry, the murders in Lapy shocked every Jew in Sokoly. All of them knew the Lapy victims, who were cut down so suddenly and without reason.

Again, a few weeks passed, and a new decree was issued. The Germans in Sokoly commanded the Jews to dig a deep and very large pit in the cemetery. Horror and a deathly terror possessed our Jews. Who was wise enough to guess who was in line for annihilation this time?!

It is true that we worried that sooner or later the Germans would scheme against the elderly from the old people's home who had come to Sokoly from the Mazury court and were staying in the prayer houses. Someone remembered that some time previously, the elderly had been photographed and that something was "cooking." They also wondered about the need for a pit measuring tens of meters. From this grew the concern that we were facing mass murder.

On the Shabbat of Penitence, the rioters announced that the time had come to eliminate the elderly. In Sokoly, they especially mourned the fate of David, one of the 25 who were sentenced to death, a paraplegic who came from a very respected family in Bialystok, and another by the name of 'Yankel' [Yaakov], who was known already in his youth as a genius with a very sharp mind, learned in *Gemara* and the commentaries, knowledgeable in world literature and a "walking encyclopedia." In a learned community, he gave sermons on Torah matters interwoven with quotations from our Sages. When he spoke to the youth, he "shot out" quotations from Achad Ha'am, Sokolov, Max Nordeau, and others. There were a number of stories and anecdotes. He was accustomed to enter fixed places at specific times, in order to satisfy his hunger with a bowl of soup, for which he gave thanks with many blessings.

The *Judenrat* did not dare to warn the elderly and tell them to escape from the danger, because of fear of the Germans' reprisal. Nevertheless, information about what was going to happen reached a small number of young disabled persons, among them 'Yankel' [Yaakov]. Rabbi Rosenblum even showed him a place to hide for a number of hours, so that when the danger had passed he could be brought to Bialystok in a wagon.

'Yankel' ran to the women's section in the *beit midrash* so as to take his personal belongings, a small kettle and a package with a striped robe that he had received as a gift from someone. He guarded this package as if it were an expensive treasure (shrouds). He arrived near the *beit midrash* and immediately fell victim to the *gendarmes*. They threw him into one of the wagons that were standing some distance away. The Germans "calmed down" the unfortunates in the heap in the wagons as if they were going to travel to Bialystok, but 'Yankel' understood the situation and cried out, "*Torah, Torah, where is your protection? The Torah is life to those who keep it. Six times I learned the entire Gemara, the books of the Mishna and said the midnight prayers. Is this Torah and is this its wages? What is my crime and what is my sin that I should fall into the hands of murderers?*" Thus 'Yankel' wept and cried. In the cemetery, they shot him six times before he rolled into the pit. The Poles who watched what was being done even shed a tear and were shocked by his heart-rending cries. A Christian woman, Krinski, the wife of the electrician, fainted.

The Jews who had to cover the mass grave could not close their eyes for many nights, nor could they forget the terrible murder for even one minute.

Slowly, slowly, things calmed down and we went back to the ordinary daily routine we had become accustomed to many months ago. We accepted our fate, that we had been condemned to destruction. The Germans exploited us and our strength for hard labor and we suffered shame and a life of slavery full of degradation. They could manage to destroy the remainder of Israel a few minutes before midnight, before the end of the War, or as Hitler, may his name be blotted out, expressed it in one of his speeches:

The end of the War will come with the end of
the Jews in Europe; the miracle of Purim is over
and they will no longer celebrate it.

The Germans are confident that they are not
endangering themselves at all by exterminating
the Jews. Many countries will certainly be happy
to be freed of them and their eternal problem.
The nations of the world will not fight the wars
of the Jews and they will not bring the Germans
to trial for their deeds. It is a fact that England
has closed the way to immigration of Jews to the
Land of Israel, and even the United States is not
hurrying to open its gates to them.

Opinions of this kind characterized the speeches of Hitler,
Goebbels, Streicher, and others. Only a spark of hope remained to
the Jews that a miracle would occur and they would be privileged
to see the downfall of Hitler before he would be able to complete
his satanic program.

The Jews comforted themselves with these thoughts and regarded
the forced labor as a type of temporary life preserver and as the
only reason why the Germans had not yet completed their "final
solution." In our hearts resided the faith that G-d was watching
over our troubles, and us and that He would have mercy on his
flock and would send His good angel to help us.

Meanwhile, the Germans demanded that the *Judenrat* submit a list
of 250 workers for the *Dapu* railroad factories in Lapy. This was a
very difficult decree for us. First of all, one had to stand there
under rigid and strict supervision, bordering on cruelty, from
Germans and Poles alike. The great distance from home was likely
to cause delays that would endanger life. One had to work there
for eight hours and spend many more hours on the roads, traveling
back and forth. Only to be late for the departure of the train was
enough to be lost. There was no time left to rest, even a short
moment to relax, because before you got home you had to prepare
yourself to be up at dawn and give yourself over again to the claws

of forced labor and degradation. Clearly, there no longer was any rest on the Shabbat. Nevertheless, laboring through the auspices of the *Judenrat* was much easier. It was occasionally possible to pile up a bit of wood for heating and cooking, to be concerned a bit with running the home and somehow to supply oneself with food.

At this time, the situation got so much worse. We did not have any hot food, and the portion of bread was far from being enough to satisfy our hunger. The problem of clothing and footwear was very severe. How could we keep going under such difficult conditions? Our clothing was torn and patched, our boots were in extremely poor condition, and the road was long and difficult, through swamps and mud. And the season - it was autumn and rain was falling.

Considering the conditions I mention, and many, many others, it was difficult to compose a list of Jews who were slated to work at Lapy. Therefore, it was decided to choose representatives from all levels of the population, so that they would participate in composing the list and thus prevent endless, stormy arguments and grievances. It is understood that all kinds of arguments had accumulated. So-and-so is the sole provider of all the branches of his family; in another family, the youths are already going out to work. And more excuses, more or less justified. Where are justice and honesty?

The swords of the *Judenrat* rattled, and in every corner there echoed "…and they cried out." A number of times, it was necessary to change the list after it had already been completed. Finally, they succeeded in overcoming the tumult and the list was composed with the agreement of the representatives. Slowly, the cries of despair were strangled and became silent. In principle, men up to the age of 42 were included in the list for labor in Lapy.

At that time, the regime in Sokoly wanted to establish stables, cowsheds, shelters for wagons and warehouses of various kinds, and to build a tall watchtower in the courtyard of Aharki Zholti's house. The top of the watchtower had to be surrounded by a guardrail and it would be used to look over the surrounding area at a radius of several kilometers. For this purpose, they ordered the demolition of houses and buildings from two courtyards around the house, and the flattening and paving of the area. Many other jobs piled up at other points, such as the demolition of military buildings and a large clubhouse that was erected by the Soviets. Thirty carpenters worked on these jobs for four months.

For the *Amstleiter*, we were required to build a garage, a cellar for fuel containers, and a storeroom for wood and coal for heating during the winter. Further jobs were added, demolishing dilapidated, unnecessary buildings, and finally the jobs at the Kruczewo Train Station, mostly loading and unloading weapons, ammunition, and coal. We dug with primitive tools and before us were mountains and hills to level, weeding out of forest and woodland trees, quarrying of stone and paving of access roads.

The *Judenrat* had to provide 300 workers who were employed in these jobs every day and at precise hours. Up to the age of 42, the laborers worked seven days a week. Over that age, they worked only twice a week, and sometimes up to four days.

Good craftsmen had special privileges and rarely had to work at forced labor. There also were privileged Jews whom the Germans preferred as their personal servants and the like, whom they specially requested, such as mechanics, watchmakers, radio and electricity technicians, blacksmiths, saddlers, tailors and shoemakers. The *Judenrat* did not have any control over these workers and they were not able to include them in a list of those being sent to unskilled labor. Among these were 'Itzele' Roseman (the son of Yisrael Chaim, the beltmaker), who was a permanent servant in the *gendarmia,* and Chena Okune (son of Moshe) and his son, who were employed as wagoners. Chena was a wagoner before the War, transporting people to Wysokie Mazowieckie and the Wysokie Train Station.

During this period, life entered normalization. No hunger was felt. Besides the work for the Germans, the craftsmen worked by order for the farmers and private people. Many of the craftsmen had regular Polish customers, and in exchange for carrying out orders, they received plenty of food. True, the Polish needed to obtain official permits to order work from the Jews, but they did not do so. Because of certain difficulties and limitations imposed upon them, they turned directly to the Jews.

Here and there, the owners of large, as well as small, shops had some hidden merchandise from "the good old days." Now, they sold varied products, and they had many customers upon whom they could depend. Ordinary Jews sold their personal possessions, mainly from their own wardrobes or from packages that were sent to them from America by relatives. Any poor rag was regarded as merchandise, in exchange for which food could be obtained.

Youths, whose appearance did not raise the immediate suspicion that they were Jews, invaded the villages at dawn and did business with their acquaintances and various kinds of go-betweens. At that time, there were no expulsions, except for instances of uprooting people from their more spacious apartments into cramped and crowded apartments. Under these circumstances, many quarrels broke out between the women.

Searches of apartments and confiscation of private property began on behalf of the *Judenrat*. People were angered by these searches, even though they knew that the searches were conducted at the specific order of the Germans and that the confiscated property was to be given only to them, the Germans, who threatened death if their demands were not strictly carried out. On the other hand, the Jews understood that it would be a lot worse if the Germans themselves would search, and that they would steal everything from them, from a thread to a shoelace.

Nevertheless, everyone hated the *Judenrat*. Everyone was of the opinion that he was the only one they were pressuring, and that they were stealing more from him than from others. I must point out that the members of the *Judenrat* were sufficiently honest, and they certainly were no worse than their associates in other towns.

One of the victims who suffered directly from the Germans at that time was Chaim 'Itza' [Yitzhak] Fleer (the son of Leibel, the butcher), a wealthy Jew who owned property. One day Chaim found a Polish woman in his field who was gathering potatoes in a basket. He forgot what the situation was, and he raised a hand against the woman. The *Amstleiter* found out about the incident and Chaim was called to his office, where they beat him with whiplashes on his naked body and held him for a few weeks in prison, as well as fining him 2000 marks.

After a short time, Chaim's son took two old boards from a pile that was next to the *gendarmia*. The sentries saw him from the window, grabbed him and beat him cruelly, and fined his father 500 marks.

The third time, Chaim 'Itza' paid a fine because of Janina Palkowska, an active member of the *N.D.K.* well-known in Sokoly. She made a lot of trouble for the Jews and it is worth describing her image, which will reveal a grim chapter in the life of the Jews of Sokoly during the period before the War and until November 2, 1942, when the Jews of Sokoly were sent to total annihilation.

Janina Palkowska

In her youth, Janina Palkowska became friendly with Jewish girls and was a visitor in their homes. She would frequently come and go, not as a guest, but like an actual daughter of the house. Janina knew everyone in town, young and old alike. She spoke fluent Yiddish as if she was Jewish by birth, and she also knew all the customs. She spoke smoothly, politely, nicely, and sweetly, with noticeable flattery. No one saw in her even a speck of anti-Semitism. On the contrary, everyone saw her as a fervent friend of Israel. She established faithful friendships that her friends returned with heart and soul. People were not careful about speaking in Janina's presence about any subject, and she even entered into confidential conversations regarding personal and discreet matters.

But everyone knew one thing: Janina was jealous of the life of the wealthy Jews. She was especially jealous of the owner of a large fabric store – Yaakov Kaplansky.

Janina was accustomed to frequently enter the store, in order to buy something or just to talk with Masha Kaplansky, whom she regarded as her friend. Then she would investigate, with seven eyes, the considerable proceeds of the store and trace the organized and abundant weekly supply of fabric from Warsaw and Bialystok.

A few years before World War II, there was an especial growth of antisemitic movements, specifically the *Endatzia* (*N.D.K.*) in Warsaw. Boycotts, pogroms and persecution of Jews were daily occurrences. In this situation, Janina decided to exploit the hour of opportunity. She obtained a very large storeroom and filled it with fabrics of every kind, even more than there were in Kaplansky's store. For this purpose, she sold one of her two farms that previously had belonged to her husband, and she accumulated an enormous amount of money, with which she was able to purchase the large storeroom, a shop and a stock of merchandise. She knew how to exploit go-betweens, Jewish delivery clerks and wagoners, to her own advantage, and with their help she found sources of fabric in Warsaw and Bialystok. Janina succeeded in buying fabrics at a lower price than the Jewish merchants, because she paid in cash and not with notes. After she completed all her purchases, she began to busy herself with advertising.

She ordered the printing of thousands of advertisement sheets, with the addition of an antisemitic proclamation to the Christians, under the headline: *"Saboie du Sabago"* (Give Birth to Your Own), which stated:

> It is forbidden to buy from the Zhids, who are deceivers and haters of gentiles. Good Christians are obligated to buy only from the new Christian firm that has now been established in Sokoly. There you will find a large selection of fabrics of all kinds, and wonderful, exacting service. They will no longer cheat you in the Jewish shops!

Janina Palkowska's husband rode his bicycle through all the villages surrounding Sokoly and distributed the antisemitic advertisements. Immediately, a real fair began at her store: the streets leading in the direction of Palkowska's shop were filled with farmers' wagons from all the villages in the area. They came to buy from her new Christian firm. Every day, dozens of farmers stood in long lines in front of the entrance to her store and patiently waited for their turn to buy the wanted goods. Even so, Janina was afraid that in the end the farmers would discover that the same merchandise was being sold in the Jewish stores for prices lower than hers. For this purpose, Janina became close with a group of empty-headed wastrels, card-players, robbers, burglars, and members of the underworld, and organized them into a gang of 'pikatniks' whose purpose was to go around with cudgels and clubs in front of the Jewish stores, and not allow any Christian customers to enter them. This continued for a long time.

Many of the farmers were afraid to enter a Jewish store because of the *pikatnikim*. It is true that there were some who were bold and were not afraid of the *pikatnikim* and argued that no one had the right to force them to buy merchandise at an expensive price, when the same merchandise could be gotten at a cheaper price. The *pikatnikim* did not want to hear arguments and answers. They made scandals, beating the rebellious farmers with clubs and cudgels, and ripped up and trampled the merchandise that they bought from the Jews. The wounded farmers turned to the police to intervene, but the police were bribed by the *N.D.K.* shop owners and took the *N.D.K.* party into consideration, knowing that the government of Poland supported harassment and pogroms against the Jews. The *pikatnikim* received whisky and regular wages from the *N.D.K.* shop owners.

During the Soviet occupation, Janina Palkowska was worried that the Jews would denounce her and that she would be sent far away to Russia. Therefore, when the Soviets first entered Sokoly, Janina Palkowska packed up her merchandise and all her furniture, household utensils and property, and brought all of it to the villages to her relatives and good friends. She hid everything in safe places. Palkowska, her husband and her two children traveled to Warsaw, where she learned a bit of German. She hired special German teachers for her children, until they were sufficiently fluent in the German language. When the Germans re-entered Sokoly, Janina Palkowska returned with all the members of her family to her home; then she found a good opportunity to enrich herself from the destruction of the Jews, with the help of the German Nazis.

First, she became close to the German *gendarmes* by luring them with alcoholic drinks, cakes and delicacies. She introduced them to her daughter, who loved to show off and who spoke fluent German. The soldiers of the *gendarmia* visited her home every evening and spent the time until midnight in debauchery, drunkenness, song and dance. One officer even fell in love with Janina's daughter and brought a piano that they took from a landowner's palace to her room. Palkowska wanted to beautify and decorate her house, and the police sent her Jewish carpenters and painters to do all the repairs and remodeling, until her house turned into a fancy palace. All this did not cost her a cent.

After that began the affair of how to squeeze from the Jews the money she needed in order to enlarge her business. For this purpose, she used guile. She told the Germans that at the time she fled from the Soviets, she had left potatoes in the cellar of her house and the Communist Jews had stolen the potatoes. For this, she demanded 1000 marks. The *Judenrat* was forced to impose a tax of 10-20 marks upon every Jew who was more or less established, in order to give 1000 marks to Palkowska the same day.

After that, Palkowska chose a few Jews against whom she carried a grudge from past years. First of all, she decided to take revenge against Shlomo Jaskolka, with whom she had a feud. She slandered him by saying that he had destroyed her fruit trees, which bordered on his garden, during the time she was absent from Sokoly during the Soviet occupation. In compensation, she demanded 300 marks. The *gendarmia* summoned Shlomo, cruelly beat him with dozens of lashes, and forced him to pay the 300 marks to Janina.

Then, with the help of the *gendarmes*, Palkowska demanded 500 marks from Chaim Itza Fleer and two Jewish blacksmiths, because, according to the testimony of a Christian neighbor, they had destroyed her board fence during the Soviet occupation.

Besides the above, Palkowska sent Germans to conduct searches at the homes of a few Jews and beat them severely. Thus, Shlomo Jaskolka, Chaim Somovitz (the son of 'Yechielke', the baker) and the blacksmith, Pesach Tabak, Janina Palkowska's "*Moshkim*," [*i.e.*, Jews, sons of Moshe] were cruelly beaten.

In spite of Palkowska's anti-Semitism, she had a few Jews with whom she had a "great friendship" in order to exploit them for her own selfish purposes. When a Christian needed to enter a Jewish house at that time, he had to sneak in through the back door and look around lest they would see him entering. But Palkowska felt free to enter directly into a Jewish house belonging to her apparent good friends. That is how she openly and publicly entered the home of Dina Maik, who had been her faithful, loyal friend in heart and soul since their youth.

At that time, with Dina as a go-between, Palkowska obtained various types of valuables for herself. Dina Maik had connections with all the merchants and agents in Sokoly. She also was familiar with the entire Christian community in the Sokoly area and she knew who could be trusted completely. Dina was certain that in times of trouble, Palkowska would protect her from all harm.

Palkowska's son also did not detest occasionally entering a Jewish home when he was able to exploit them for his own benefit. Thus, he would come and go from Michael Maik's house in order to learn photography. He made friends with Moshe Maik and sometimes invited him to his home. In general, it was then regarded as a special privilege for Palkowska or a member of her family to enter a Jewish home, on the assumption that in times of trouble, this would help them. But Palkowska and her family only knew how to exploit the right time to enrich themselves from the destruction of the Jews.

In such a way, Palkowska took a good living away from her Jewish neighbor, Moshe Tzvi [Seines], who until then had been a friend of hers. Moshe had machines for spinning wool yarn. Palkowska wanted his factory. The *gendarmes* immediately fulfilled her request, and since she herself did not know how to take care of the machines, she hired their owner Moshe Tzvi as a technician, at a forced laborer's salary of one mark per day. In order to obtain the knowledge and experience to manage the factory, she secretly hired Moshe Tzvi's son, 'Yankel' Seines. She promised to give him, in addition to his official salary, a certain percentage of the profits from the food products business, in cash. In this way, Moshe Tzvi and his family would regard themselves as partners in the factory until Palkowska would acquire the experience and knowledge needed in order to manage the factory and the business.

After a few weeks, Palkowska drove Moshe Tzvi out of his oil factory. With the help of the *gendarmia*, she took over the other three oil factories in Sokoly that belonged to Naftali Plut, Alter Goldin and Shlomo Jaskolka. Palkowska was not sufficiently satisfied with that, so she denounced the poor, robbed Moshe Tzvi by saying that before the War he had managed a business selling the farmers' homemade fabrics, and that he had hidden some fabrics. Searches began along the entire length of Bathhouse Street, where Moshe Tzvi lived.

The searches happened to take place on *Shabbat*. At the time of the searches, morning prayers were being held in Rabbi Rosenblum's house. There were about two *minyanim* [20 people] of worshippers in the Rabbi's house, which was across the street from the public bathhouse. The house was built before World War I, by a wealthy Jew from Manijenie-Novogrod who was born in Sokoly and came back at the end of his life to live in the city of his birth. He donated a lot of money to build the Rabbi's house and a brick fence with a shelter around the new cemetery, and to remodel the bathhouse according to a modern plan.

At first, Rabbi Avraham Epstein, of blessed memory, lived in the house. During the Soviet occupation, Rabbi Yosef Rosenblum, of blessed memory, moved into the house and lived there with the widowed *Rebbitzen* Epstein. During the German occupation, Rabbi Rosenblum prayed there.

On that fatal *Shabbat*, the worshippers saw from the windows that the Germans were preparing to enter the Rabbi's house. Most of the worshippers, together with the Rabbi, fled through the back door. One *gendarme* by the name of Czepkin entered the Rabbi's house from the front and found a few Jews who hadn't managed to escape. A *Torah* scroll was open and lying on the table and many *talitot* were around it. The *gendarme* was surprised at the sight and the Jews explained to him that they were conducting prayers. The German honored the old Jews with whiplashes on their heads.

A second German entered through the back door, where he met up with Moshe Novak, the son of Avraham Dov, who lived in the Rabbi's house with his sister Devosha. Moshe Novak was running with two packages in his hands, because he was afraid the Germans would steal them. In flight and confusion, Moshe dropped a package of silverware. The German called out "Stop!" in a loud voice. Moshe stopped and stood at attention. The German asked him what he was carrying. Moshe showed him what was in the second package, notebooks with writing in them. The German took the package of notebooks away from him, along with the package of silverware he had dropped, and honored him with a few blows on his head.

After that, the second German entered the Rabbi's house and both Germans began to search the rooms. They beat the old *Rebbitzen* Epstein for not wearing the 'badge of shame' on her dress. In vain, she justified herself and showed them that she had a badge on her coat, on her sweater, and on all her upper clothing that she wore when she went outside, saying that she did not know that she had to put one also on her housedress. In addition to beating her, they requested a fine of 15 marks. After that, the Germans opened a cupboard where they found velvet bedspreads, blanket covers and tablecloths that the *Rebbitzen* had prepared as a wedding gift for her sister's son. The Germans took everything that they found in the cupboard and took the *Rebbitzen* to prison.

After that, they went back to the Rabbi's house. They found the Rabbi and arrested him as well. The Rabbi had already fallen into the barbaric hands of the Germans when they kidnapped him to work cleaning their vehicles, and then pulled off half of his beard along with the skin and cruelly beat him. The Rabbi felt that they were leading him to be hanged in martyrdom for the sanctification of G-d. The Germans brought the Rabbi into their office and demanded that he tell them where Moshe Tzvi [Seines] hid his fabrics. The Rabbi, in his righteousness, promised them that neither fabrics nor any other merchandise were hidden in his house and asked them to search the entire house. The Rabbi was soon freed, but the old *Rebbitzen* was held for a few more hours. When they did free her, she had to lie in bed for a number of weeks, ill from beatings and fear.

After searching the Rabbi's house, the search continued in the bathhouse and in cracks in the attics and cellars. They opened the cowsheds and storerooms around the bathhouse and grabbed anything that was more or less of value.

The Rabbi believed that according to *gematriot* [numerology], the Redemption would come in the near future, on *Chanukah*...

The workers who had been traveling to work in Lapy said that they had heard from Christians and workers from Bialystok about radio broadcasts reporting large losses to the Germans on all fronts. They had also heard from the Christians that there were bomb shelters in hidden places. This information was comforting and encouraging. One of the distributors of this encouraging news was Chena Finkelstein, Daniel's son. Most of this news about German losses on the fronts was imaginary and exaggerated. They simply wished to find some comfort for all the trouble and distress and hoped for a miracle from Heaven.

The Hidden Shelter

Michael Maik's son, Moshe, who was a radio technician by profession, would go from time to time to visit a Christian farmer by the name of Stanislaw Kalinowski, who lived in a settlement near the village of Bruszewo. There, Moshe prepared a radio receiver hidden in a bunker. In this hiding place, it was possible to hear radio broadcasts from London and Moscow. It is true that at that time no good news was to be heard, either from London or from Moscow. The Rabbi and Moshe Lipa Shulmeister, who knew about the radio, asked Moshe Maik and his father every day whether they had heard anything encouraging. Since there was no special news, they thought that the Maik family was afraid to reveal what they had heard, lest the farmers would find out about the radio and denounce them.

Moshe Lipa Shulmeister was learned in *Talmud*. He was a former student at the Volozhin Yeshiva. Before the War, he was a wealthy shopowner, well-versed in politics. He reported everything; he was a walking telephone for news about what was going on in the town. He knew about weddings, circumcisions, intimate matters, disputes that broke out and arguments. He was the first to know the news about everything and was interested in every detail, which he passed on to his friends and good acquaintances. In conversation, he knew how to apply parables. He was blessed with an exceptional memory for people's names.

Moshe Lipa was a *gabbai* in the large *beit midrash*. On *Shabbatot* and holidays, he would call people up to the *Torah*. He was not born in Sokoly, but settled in Sokoly as the son-in-law of David Borowitz; nevertheless, he knew and remembered the names of everyone in the town, from the youngest to the oldest. He knew how to give the appropriate nickname to each one. Those who were ordinarily called "Alter" or "Zeidel" he called by Hebrew names when they went up to the Torah. For example, "Zeidel" became "Reuven;" "Alter" became "Shlomo." Some of these men were called to the Torah with two names, the way they were named at their circumcisions. For example, Moshe was called to the Torah as "Moshe Yitzhak." Shlomo was called "Shlomo Zalman." Moshe Lipa remembered the names of every one of the hundreds of Jews of his acquaintance, and he never had to ask them their given names, or the names of their fathers.

The Local German Regime in Sokoly

That winter, the local German regime in Sokoly was changed. The regime up to now of the local army was exchanged for an administrative civilian leadership. At the head of the local regime was *Amstkommissar* Wagner from Vienna, and he was a comparatively good German. However, he was quickly replaced by another *Kommissar* named Wassel, an old, lean redhead, a hard, strict man, with furious eyes surrounded by large eyeglasses; with his yellow mustache he gave the impression of the Angel of Death. We called him the 'Yellow Satan.'

From the beginning, he threatened to establish a ghetto in Sokoly. There immediately arose a tumult, after which the matter was hushed up. This "*Chad-Gad-Ya*" [chain of events] was repeated a number of times, until the masses in Sokoly stopped being afraid of rumors regarding the *Amstkommissar*'s decisions and accepted the threats of the 'Yellow Satan' as a means of squeezing the *Judenrat* for more gifts and bribes.

Before the *Pesach* holiday, the *Kommissar* was good to the Jews. He gave the steam mill permission to grind grain flour for *matzo* and the Jews of Sokoly bought black-market *matzo* for *Pesach* from the *Judenrat*. During the first days of Passover the Jews did not feel so bad, and when, during the *Seder* service, they came to the prayer "Next Year in Jerusalem," every one prayed with special concentration that G-d would grant them freedom from Hitler's hell and that they would be privileged to see the building of the State of Israel.

During the intermediate days of the holiday, a worrisome rumor spread. The *Judenrat* sent a message to every Jewish house, saying that every man who was fit for work, no matter his age, must come at eleven o'clock in the morning to the street in front of the *Judenrat*. Confusion and panic set in. Everyone knew that in all the towns and villages, this kind of order from the *Amstkommissar* ended, for the most part, in mass murder. There were some optimists who comforted us by remembering the town Wysokie Mazowieckie, where the [their] *Amstkommissar* also had gathered all the Jews in the street and made a speech to them full of threats, and in spite of it all, their fear was for nothing. As proof of the correctness of their estimation, they based themselves on the assumption that if the *Amstkommissar* was intending to kill or expel the Jews of Sokoly, he would also order the women and children to gather in the street. Apparently there was a different reason behind the matter.

Before eleven o'clock in the morning, a few hundred Jews gathered in the plaza in front of the *Judenrat*, but it was obvious that only half of the Jews of the town had come. Exactly on the hour, the 'Yellow Satan' appeared accompanied by a German official from the railroad dressed in a Nazi uniform with a swastika on his arm. The Chairman of the *Judenrat*, Alter Ginzberg, approached the *Amstkommissar*, bowed, and removed his hat in welcome. The *Amstkommissar* asked the Chairman why so few men had showed up and slapped Alter Ginzberg in the face. He then looked at his watch and proclaimed, "Within 30 minutes, every Jew in the town must be here. Otherwise, the entire *Judenrat* will be shot." He finished his proclamation and left.

Panic arose in the *Judenrat*. All the leading members of the *Judenrat* and their messengers began to run to all the Jewish houses. They went from house to house and drove all the people into the street with warnings that anyone who evades the call and does not show up at the public gathering will be severely punished; the lives of the *Judenrat* members depend on a few who will be missing and the Germans were likely to shoot all the members of the *Judenrat*. After 15 minutes, the street in front of the *Judenrat* was crowded. Jewish men organized everyone into three long rows.

Precisely one-half hour after his proclamation, the *Amstkommissar* reappeared, accompanied by the railroad official, and ordered all leading members of the *Judenrat* to stand in a row in front of the gathered Jews. The members stood in front of the *Amstkommissar*, who inspected the long rows. He counted all the men. He commanded Alter Ginzberg to bring him a stool. The *Amstkommissar*, accompanied by the railroad official, went together with the Chairman to see exactly which stool would be appropriate. Such a stool was found in the Polish cooperative store. After a few minutes, all of them returned, the Chairman carrying a round stool with a screen that was used to scrape and clean shoes.

First, the *Amstkommissar* commanded the Chairman, Alter Ginzberg to bend over the stool and reveal his bottom. The railroad official immediately brought out a rubber whip and whipped the Chairman's bottom and head with 15 lashes, with all his strength. The next member of the *Judenrat* was Yona Ginzberg, who also received 15 lashes on his bottom and head; the third was the watchmaker Yisrael Maik, who received the same portion of lashes. After that, in order, were: Yaakov Janowitz, Yechezkel Czerbonicz, and Zeidel Rachekovsky. All these received only 12 lashes, because the whipper was already tired and sweating. After them came 'Yankel' the shoemaker, who pleaded with the whipper. The shoemaker was forced to lie down and be whipped, during which he cried, without stopping, "Enough! Enough!" The whipper lessened the number of lashes he gave Yokil, compared to the number he gave to the rest of the members of the *Judenrat*. It is possible that he already was tired out from the beatings. Aharki Zholti, Leibel Okune, Eliezer Rosenovitz, and Chaim Yehoshua Olsha were not whipped.

Dr. Makowsky was severely reprimanded for giving out too large a number of sickness permits to the *Dapu* railroad factory workers in Lapy, in order to free them from work for a day or two. At the end, the 'Yellow Satan' slapped Dr. Makowsky in the face until his hat fell off. He was told to leave Sokoly and its surroundings within three days.

Before the *Judenrat* was whipped, the *Amstkommissar* made a short speech: The Jews are not properly fulfilling his orders: (a) A lot of hidden merchandise has been found. In spite of the warnings, their owners did not inform the government about them. (b) According to the list, workers for labor in Lapy are missing. (c) When Jewish citizens are requested to gather in the street in front of the *Judenrat*, a lot of them evade the order and the *Judenrat* is responsible for all of them. However, the longer the War will continue, the more severe the laws will be. For sabotage, the *Judenrat* will be subject to the death sentence. However, since this is the first time, the punishment will be lighter: whippings instead of death. The next time orders are not obeyed (sabotage), there will be no further warning, and the death sentence will be carried out immediately.

After the flogging, the *Amstkommissar* commanded the seven beaten members of the *Judenrat* and Leibel Okune to stand in line, and took them, in pairs, off to jail. A tumult and wailing began in the town. It wasn't enough that they had insulted and degraded the representatives of the Jews in a deplorable manner. They had flogged them in the middle of the marketplace, in full view of the Jew-hating *goyim,* and imprisoned eight members of the *Judenrat.*

G-d knows what more awaits them! At first, it was hoped that they would hold the prisoners for a day in the jail and then release them. But when the first day passed and they were not released, the families of the prisoners began to worry about their fate.

The next day, the German railroad official—the 'Whipper'—entered the jail and beat the prisoners again. This time, the Whipper did not have mercy for Leibel, upon whom the *Amstkommissar* had taken pity the first time because of his poor appearance. The four members of the *Judenrat* who remained free were afraid to go to the *Amstkommissar* to try to release their companions, lest he become angry and imprison them as well.

The first one to attempt to help the prisoners was Selina, the wife of *Judenrat* member Yona Ginzberg, who had been a teacher in the Polish public school. She had special privileges with the Germans from the local council, because of her younger sister Lutka, who spoke fluent German with a pure German accent and was personally acquainted with all the local Germans. Lutka went to the railroad official – 'the Whipper' – bringing him a gift of an expensive gold watch, and asked him to free her brother-in-law, Yona Ginzberg, and his companions. He promised to free Yona, and ignored the rest of the *Judenrat* members. Yona Ginzberg was indeed freed the next day.

The well-established families of the rest of the *Judenrat* members prepared gifts, and on the third day they all were released. They also made a recommendation in favor of Dr. Makowsky, saying that he was a wonderful doctor, loved by all the local residents, Jews and Christians alike. The *Amstkommissar* permitted him to stay

59

in Sokoly, on the condition that he would not continue to give medical permits to workers so as to free them from their jobs.

The *Amstkommissar* wanted to enlarge the list of *Dapu* railroad factory laborers in Lapy from 200 to 250. In addition, he demanded another 50 laborers for Jezewo and a number of workers for chain gangs in Budziska and for cutting down trees and arranging them in piles. Again there was panic in the *Judenrat*. It had been difficult to prepare the list of 200 railroad workers in Lapy, and how could they add another 50 workers for Lapy as well as workers for stone quarries, cutting down trees in the [nearby] forests and digging in chain gangs? But there was no choice. They had to fulfill all the demands, no matter what. Thus, men who had special privileges, who up to now had worked in Sokoly, volunteered to be registered for railroad work in the *Dapu* factory in Lapy because they were afraid that the *Judenrat* would send them to Jezewo to quarry rocks. There, the work was more difficult, and it was hard to come home every night to sleep.

All the skilled workers up to the age of 40 were employed. Those who were older, or the sole supporters of a family, did not at all want to voluntarily register themselves for labor. The affluent ones suggested that the *Judenrat* hire poor workers at their own expense. The *Judenrat* called all the craftsmen with special privileges. Older men were also requested to register for work three times a week, and were told that their lives depended on the matter. After a great deal of effort and work, the *Judenrat* succeeded in sending only 220 workers to Lapy, and the 30 workers needed in order to complete the list were still lacking.

Michael Maik volunteered to register for permanent daily work on the railroad. The *Judenrat* took the opportunity to point him out as a wonderful example. Michael Maik, 54 years old, who had never in his life done physical labor, was prepared, of his own good will, to travel every day to labor on the railroad in Lapy. The *Judenrat* requested that all the men between the ages of 40 and 50 follow Michael Maik's example and register for work, without exception. The *Judenrat* agreed to register the craftsmen for work only three times a week, and to have two workers share one card. Thus, the list was completed within two hours.

They succeeded in completing the list for labor in the stone quarries of Jezewo without special difficulties. The work in Jezewo was not permanent. The workers did not have to sleep there. Every morning, a special vehicle took the workers to work, and towards evening it returned them home. Every day different workers travelled to Jezewo.

Labor in Lapy

The laborers who worked in Lapy had to wake up at 4 a.m. Awakening so early was torture for the younger ones. Their mothers could no longer sleep at night from worrying that their sons would be late for work and be beaten. On the way to the Kruczewo Train Station, the workers usually met groups of other laborers marching to work like soldiers, with packs on their shoulders and canteens in their hands, an inheritance from the Soviet soldiers.

Near the train station, the workers divided themselves into groups according to types of work. They would talk among themselves about different subjects: work, the *Judenrat*, the community, good and bad work managers, and eating, as opposed to everything else. When the train arrived in the station, all the workers hurried to get a comfortable place in one of the cars, even though there always were enough seats.

Once on the train, all the workers took their packs off their shoulders and took out their food, which included for the most part bread, soft cheese and a bottled drink or water sweetened with saccharine. Those workers who had the means would eat bread and butter with eggs, and drink milk or tea sweetened with sugar. Others would eat bread with jam and drink sweet tea or beet or vegetable soup. After they ate, the workers would smoke a cigarette rolled from newspaper. There were pious workers who brought their *tefillin* and a *siddur* in their packs, and they would pray every day before they ate breakfast.

Upon arriving in Lapy, every worker presented his work card to the German guard next to the Lapy Train Station. Whoever forgot to bring his work card had to pay for a train ticket, as well as a fine.

When they arrived at the *Dapu* railway factory for work, a siren was sounded at exactly 7 a.m. and each worker would hurry to the office to which he was assigned. There were certain permanent workstations where the workers were not required to go first to an office, but rather, they checked in by means of small, numbered pieces of tin.

One of the labor offices was called Ozorowski. When the laborers arrived at the office, two Poles would come out. One, Ozorowski, was old and tall, and had angry eyes like a robber. The workers called him the 'Grandfather.' The second Pole was young. His name was Wiczenowski. They would line up the workers in two rows, Wiczenowski reading off their names from a list. When his name was called, each worker would answer, "Present." If someone was absent, Wiczenowski marked his name on the list. After the names were read, the 'Grandfather' divided the workers into groups. A group of 12 men was sent to carpentry; a group of 8 was sent to the transportation department, and a third group of 10 men was sent to the train station to repair the tracks. The 'Grandfather' divided all the remaining workers from the first three groups between three Polish work managers for loading coal, unloading freight cars, and paving plots of ground and streets. Each manager chose his group of workers and brought them into a shed with various tools. Each worker took a tool. The workers were again lined up, this time in pairs, and marched in pairs after their managers until they reached the locations where they would work.

The Work Managers

Suzin, the work manager, had been a functionary in the Magistrate's Court before World War II, with the task of collecting fines and implementing evictions according to the judgments of the Court. Now, he had become a beggar for contributions from the workers in his group. For example, the workers supplied Suzin with bread and butter, honey, cheese, and eggs. In exchange, he did not hurry them at their work, he allowed them to rest as much as they wanted, and even allowed them to leave work when they wanted. There were workers who came in the morning to register with him and afterwards they would leave for the entire day, to trade with workers from Bialystok and Lapy. The men from Sokoly traded with the men from Bialystok for food, clothing, shoes, fabrics, and leather smuggled from the Bialystok Ghetto. The smugglers would earn tens and hundreds of marks in a day from their trading.

The majority of the workers in Suzin's group did not work very much. Every one of them held a spade or a hoe in his hand on the pretext that he was working. When a *"Krok"* (German *gendarme*) was relieved from guard duty, they began to work energetically. Suzin himself took care not to be tripped up by the German supervisors. When he saw at a distance a German or the 'Grandfather', who came from time to time to supervise the work, Suzin would immediately shout, in Polish, *"Kalopczi, wada!"* ("Boys, water!"). Everyone understood that now they must work intensively for a few minutes.

Whoever wanted to smoke would go into the toilet, because it was forbidden to smoke during working hours.

The group that fell into the hands of the work manager Tashikelski did not have the relief that Suzin's group had. Tashikelski had been a cashier in the tax office before the War. Now, he urged the laborers to work harder and pressed them to hurry, but the fellows had already gotten used to his *"Nu, Nu"* and they scorned his stiff demands; they would hide in the toilet to smoke and pass the hours of the day.

Work manager Jarmulowicz's group was similar to those of Tashikelski and Suzin, the only difference being that Tashikelski and Jarmulowicz did not ask for contributions like Suzin did. They did not ask the workers for bread and butter, although occasionally they begged somebody to roll a cigarette for them, and regarded themselves as friends of every one of the workers.

In Lapy, besides the office of the 'Grandfather', there was Gidrowicz's office, which sent Jewish workers to hard labor under the supervision of Nazi inspectors. Among these was a German who was an evil dog...a whipper and a sadist. The workers called him the *'Pahtcher'*. Every day, this evil-hearted German joined groups of workers from Gidrowicz's office at their workplaces. He would hide under a fence, supervise from the sands, peek through the cracks to see if someone dared to rest for a brief moment from his labor, or if someone exchanged a few words with a friend. Then the *'Pahtcher'* would run from his hiding place and cruelly beat the workers. He beat them until the blood flowed. If the work was urgent, the *'Pahtcher'* stood next to the workers, who labored for long hours, forcing them to exert themselves and work beyond their strength, quickly and without pause, unable to breathe. Sweat would cover the worker's body; the *'Pahtcher'* would accelerate the rhythm until the soul left the body, and even then, he would still stand there and beat his victim with his whip.

Every two weeks, Gidrowicz's office would disqualify the weaker workers and send them back to Ozorowski's office. Ozorowski would send stronger workers in their place.

Michael Maik was assigned to Gidrowicz's office. Coincidentally, on one Shabbat Michael Maik's son traveled to work instead of his father. Moshe was a young, healthy lad, so the 'Grandfather' sent him to Gidrowicz' office to work. In any case, Michael Maik remained registered as a worker with Gidrowicz.

On his first day of work, Michael Maik had to carry boards in the Gevizrona lot, through which the train tracks passed. Every day, dozens of freight cars of boards went out and came in. The Jewish workers would load and unload the cars of boards, carry them on their shoulders, and transfer them to a place where they sorted them according to type and quality, length and width. They carried and moved the sorted boards to destinations determined in advance, where they would set down the boards according to a certain order.

That day, the '*Pahtcher*' happened to be on vacation. The supervisor who took his place was a quiet German who spoke in a low voice. He did not hurry the workers, but he also did not allow them to stand with empty hands or enter the toilet for a long time to smoke and talk with friends, as the workers in Ozorowski's office were accustomed to doing. The workers called the quiet German '*Marok*' ["the Silent"]. The Polish work managers were strict. The Jews worked nine hours per day, until 4:30 p.m., and they had to carry 2-3 boards at a time, that were 3-4 meters long and 2 fingers thick. A pair of workers would carry the boards on their shoulders. All the workers prepared cushions at home, so that their shoulders wouldn't hurt from carrying the heavy boards every day.

The manager took pity upon Michael Maik as he was an older man, and put him to work next to the holding racks, to receive the boards from those carrying them and to lay them down one by one according to order. Work in the area of the holding racks was a lot easier than carrying the boards a long distance. Here, no work manager could hurry the workers, because the boards must be laid on the holding racks with extreme precision. It was possible to rest occasionally, because one had to wait for a new board until the previous one was placed in its row.

Half an hour before work ended for the day, a true taste of hell was felt. They grabbed all the workers, from the board carriers to those standing next to the holding racks, and forced them to transport heavy pine beams, the type that ten healthy and strong men would be able to carry only with difficulty. For this job, they did not depend on the '*Marok*' but appointed a violent, strong, strict, evil and cruel German as supervisor. Instead of ten men, he commanded that only six men carry the heavy, long beams, and four men for the shorter beams. He hurried us by screaming: "Tempo! Tempo!" The Jews encouraged their companions by saying: "Gather all your strength! Don't stop, or they will kill us on the spot! Help 'Old Maik' to take back the heavy burden, otherwise the burden will fall and crush us and we will be killed under it!" It was a miracle that men were found who were able to lower their heavy burden and help 'Old Maik'. Even though the

German was evil and cruel, he did not interfere with helping old Maik. Thus, the work in Lapy continued, day after day.

A Story about Cows

When you travel to work for the entire day, you forget general troubles, but when you return home, there is news and your own worries, besides those of neighbors, relatives and friends. Again there is distress in the town. One day has passed quietly with difficulty; again a story of trouble, this time regarding cows.

The 'Yellow Satan' ordered the confiscation of cows from all the Jews in Sokoly — cows that they owned, and that until then had been in their possession. One fine day, they put out an order to gather all the confiscated cows in the marketplace, to bring them to the Kruczewo Train Station and load them into cattle cars.

The cows had been a source of livelihood for the Jews. When there is a bit of milk in the house, there is something to feed the children, and adults can also be fed. There is something with which to prepare a meal, and when a few liters of milk are sold, there is money to buy bread or potatoes and you don't have to suffer hunger any more. The family cow is dear, and is considered a member of the family.

From dawn until dusk, the members of the family are busy worrying about their cow. At four in the morning, they take it out to pasture. At noon, they bring it home, milk it, and take it out again to pasture. Towards evening, they bring it to the cowshed, give it fodder, and milk it again. The family members take turns caring for the cow; every two or three hours they change places. These days, the Christian herder refuses to take care of cows belonging to the Jews, and that is why the Jewish owners have to pasture the cows themselves and pay their Christian neighbors for using the pastures. When a cow gives birth to a calf, there is happiness in the house – a child is born.

And suddenly, such a decree! It is not difficult to imagine the tumult and pain caused by the decree to confiscate the 90 cows belonging to the Jews of Sokoly. The small children ran to the train station behind the cows, their eyes streaming with tears, crying, "They are taking our cow away and it won't be ours and with us any more." As the Jew brings his cow to the barbaric Germans, he feels distress in his heart: "We are very sorry for you, our beloved cow. Up to now, we took care of you like a treasure and now we are forced to bring you with our own hands and turn you over to the murderers…this was decreed from Heaven…who knows if soon they won't expel us to be slaughtered as well?!"

When the cows belonging to the Jews of Sokoly were confiscated, a few Jews put themselves in danger. They did not give their cows to the Germans, and they caused themselves a lot of problems. This is what happened to Pesach the blacksmith (the son-in-law of Yisrael [Goldberg] the blacksmith), who had a family of 8 souls and did not give his cows to the Germans, but deposited them with a Christian acquaintance. One of the Christians denounced him, and Pesach suffered a murderous beating. In addition, he had to pay a cash fine and in the end, he had to bring the cows to the German *gendarmia*. But Pesach's troubles did not end.

Janina Palkowska, the infamous anti-Semite, who was Pesach's neighbor and held a grudge against him, now found an opportunity to denounce him for having many hidden possessions that he had accumulated from the Soviets. Even so, they had not conducted any searches of his house.

After the matter of the cows, the *gendarmes* descended upon him again. They arrested him and his wife 'Sarachi' [Sarah] and his ten-year-old son, 'Moshele'. They tied Pesach's hands and feet and he lay that way all day in jail. They beat his wife with a rubber whip on her entire body, which turned blue from the beatings, and she was unable even to touch any one of her limbs. They also beat their small son 'Moshele', aged ten, with murderous blows. The Germans wanted to pressure the prisoners by torturing them, so that they would tell them where the Soviet possessions were hidden. Pesach's wife was unable to bear the torture and she went to show them a hiding place. The Germans dug out a few suitcases. They were not satisfied with this. They continued to beat and torture the prisoners, until Pesach's relatives started to try to intercede with the *gendarmia*, with the help of Chaim Yehoshua Olsha as intermediary. For a bribe of three blankets, three sheets, three covers and a few more items that the relatives were forced to buy and give to the *gendarmia*, they succeeded in freeing the tortured prisoners.

Stealing Employment from Jewish Blacksmiths

After the confiscation of the cows from Sokoly's Jews, the Germans began to take away all the blacksmith shop equipment and working tools, materials and coals. They gave the blacksmith shops to Christian apprentices who had learned their trade from those very same Jews and had coveted their masters' property. The apprentices were jealous of their masters' wealth and desired their workshops.

The new owners of the Jewish blacksmith shops did not know enough about their work; they only knew how to make simple repairs. They needed the previous owners for any job that was more or less complicated. Now, they exploited the opportunity and easily bought large shops without sufficient knowledge.

Among all the Jewish blacksmiths, the one in Sokoly who felt the terrible blow most was the wealthy blacksmith Yisrael Goldberg. He could have competed with all the rest of the blacksmiths in Sokoly, because he had money. The blacksmiths bought wagons, for the most part on credit, and this cost them dearly.

Yisrael Goldberg was industrious. From his youth until his old age, he diligently and tirelessly worked 14 to 16 hours a day. He was tied to his job, and was wholeheartedly devoted to it. He had what are known as "golden hands" and worked quickly and efficiently.

Yisrael worked with his sons, who were as industrious as he was. His wife died at the young age of 40, leaving him with nine children. His four daughters got married. He employed his sons as assistants from the time they were small.

The oldest son, Mordechai, worked with his father for a few years.

The second son, 'Avrahamle', left his father's blacksmith shop and went to work as a carpenter. After a short time, he succeeded in his profession, traveled to Warsaw, and worked in firms there. He was superior at his job.

The third son, Yaakov, went to learn in a yeshiva and became well known as a genius. He was ordained as a rabbi and was regarded in our area as the greatest of scholars. Rabbi Yaakov, the son of Yisrael the blacksmith, married in Zambrow and was appointed to the rabbinate in a small city named Kozloszczina near Slonim. The War began a short time later. During the occupation, *Rav* Yaakov learned ritual slaughtering and worked in Jablonka [east of Zambrow] as a *Shochet*

The fourth son of Yisrael the blacksmith was Zalman, who worked with his father. He was drafted into the Soviet army and was killed in battle at Rostov in Russia.

Yisrael Goldberg was left with his youngest son, Chaim 'Yudel' [Yehuda], who had previously learned in Lithuanian *yeshivot* and was an excellent *Talmud* student. One *Rosh Yeshiva* wrote in a letter recommending Chaim 'Yudel', "I promise that he will be a great man in Israel." During the War, Yisrael employed his young son Chaim 'Yudel' as an assistant. Yisrael's son Rav Yaakov was unable to watch his father's continued isolation and found him a wife from Zambrow. Yisrael Goldberg remarried.

Now, the source of the blacksmith's income was ripped from his hands, along with that of the rest of Sokoly's blacksmiths.

Dov (Berel) Krushevsky

When the matter of the blacksmiths in Sokoly was over, the town became agitated again. At the center of the event was Berel Krushevsky, a 40-year-old man. In his youth, Berel had been a partner with his three brothers in a business selling furs and fabrics.

A few years before the War, Berel started to buy rags and scrap iron from small peddlers. He sold the rags to textile factories and the scrap iron to casting plants. Little by little, he succeeded in competing with other merchants in this field, mainly with the heirs of Pesach Brill, of blessed memory. Berel set up storerooms and erected a large shed in his courtyard, which he bought from 'Alterke' Makowsky. The shed had previously served 'Alterke' as a hostel and restaurant, after his first house, which he bought from Dina's 'Leishke' [Leah], burnt down. When his new, three-story house was completed, he sold the four-room shed to Berel Krushevsky.

As the owner of three spacious storerooms, Berel managed his business on a significant scale. He prospered more every day. He employed young girls to sort the rags at a low daily wage.

When he saw that his business dealings were expanding and were very profitable – he had invested a few cents and made a profit of hundreds of *zlotys* – he invested all his money in the business. He was not satisfied with that, so he went and got interest-bearing loans as well as charitable [interest-free] loans. His stock of rags and scrap iron filled his storerooms to overflowing.

Berel would frequently send freight cars loaded with sorted rags to the factories, and the emptied spaces in the storerooms would immediately get filled with new merchandise. The new house where Berel lived and all the buildings in his courtyard were built with money sent to support his mother-in-law Beila Rachel by her wealthy sons in the United States. Berel's family numbered six souls: himself, his wife, his mother-in-law, and his three children.

On the day that the War broke out, twenty freight carloads of rags and scrap iron were in Berel's storerooms. During the Soviet occupation, Berel was able to sell these to government factories at good prices, but because he was worried that he would be cheated, he decided to keep them until after the War, in the hope that he would be able to enjoy his property in the future. Meanwhile, he was given a position by the Soviets as an agent in his profession, and he felt himself to be qualified and honest. Thus, he lived in contentment until the Nazi occupation.

In the spring of 1942, the *Amstkommissar* of Sokoly, who was known as 'the Yellow Satan', happened to walk by Berel Krushevsky's house, and he heard the clucking of geese from the courtyard. He entered the yard and commanded that the chamber be opened. He immediately saw a number of geese. He also found an English-style scale and a number of bicycle parts. After discovering these things, he ordered the storeroom and other buildings to be opened, among them the long shed. In amazement and rare satisfaction, he found all Berel Krushevsky's treasures.

The 'Satan' ordered all the geese to be brought immediately to his own house. Soon after that, he sent Polish policemen, headed by a German *gendarme*, to conduct a thorough search of Berel's house.

During the search, they found fabrics, women's winter shoes, and galoshes in Berel's basement under a pile of potatoes. They immediately confiscated everything and took all the merchandise that they found for themselves.

The *Judenrat* was requested to send 100 workers to empty the rags and scrap iron from all the buildings and to sort them under the supervision of the police, in order to determine whether there was any hidden merchandise. The *Judenrat* immediately drafted all the young women and old people to work, because most of the people of the town had already been sent to their permanent jobs at forced labor.

It took two to three days until all the rags and iron were removed from the storerooms and sorted into piles. Three weeks went by in total silence, and they did not bother Berel any more. Nobody came to harm him. Berel thought that the Germans would not take any more rags away from him. Why would they want rags?

After three weeks had passed since the search in Berel's house, a train of empty freight cars arrived at the Kruczewo Train Station to take the rags away. The *Amstkommissar* drafted 100 farmer's wagons to transport the load to the train. Again two weeks went by, in silence. Occasionally, Polish policemen came to Berel's house. They checked to see if he was at home, but they went away as they came, without saying anything.

During that time, Berel [Krushevsky] went around in the nearby villages, continuing to conduct his business with the farmers he knew. Once in awhile, orders would come from the *Judenrat* for him to go to work at forced labor, but his wife knew how to arrange things and would send a needy lad in place of her husband for two marks per day. Berel's son would travel every day to his regular work in Lapy. Berel and his family were very concerned that their possessions, by means of which they had hoped to reestablish themselves after the War, had been taken away from them. But what could they do? In these crazy times they gave praise and thanks to G-d every moment that He was allowing them to live.

A week before the holiday of *Shavuot*, the 'Yellow Satan' again agitated the Jewish town. He suddenly ordered the *Judenrat* to gather all the workers in the marketplace and to stand them in rows one by one according to professions: tailors, shoemakers, carpenters, builders, painters, locksmiths, blacksmiths, and bakers. He requested that they immediately report to him how many workers among them were in each profession and where they worked. For example: how many workers are employed in chain gangs in Budziska, how many in cutting down trees, how many in clearing stones, etc.... At the end, he wanted to know how many workers were employed at the train station. He warned that all of them were obligated to be present to be counted and it was forbidden for anyone on the list to be absent.

This was the second "public gathering" in which the *Judenrat* was tested, bitterly and painfully like a beaten dog. They smelled the danger of death threatening the Jews of Sokoly. There was no choice but to carry out to the letter the murderous orders of the 'Yellow Satan'. He personally followed up after every group that was organized in the marketplace. While searching among the rows he determined that Berel was not present.

Berel returned from the village at sunset, and in his heart there were conflicting thoughts. His possessions and capital, upon which he had hung rosy hopes, had been confiscated. If so, he was a qualified proletariat and was prepared to present himself for daily labor among the other workers and poor people of the town.

Suddenly, his meditations were cut off when Yanchenko, an officer of the Polish police, entered his house. He informed Berel in the name of his Honor the *Amstkommissar* that he had come to arrest him.

Berel Krushevsky thought that this is probably in connection with another investigation regarding the hiding of merchandise. Naturally, he was afraid. Trembling seized him as he worried about being beaten and about the cruelty of the Germans and Poles who would force him to admit whatever they would accuse him of doing. The previous search had been very strict and they had taken everything away from him. What could they be expecting to find in addition? He tried to comfort himself with the hope that they would keep him in prison only until the next day and would then release him.

Early the next day, the 'Yellow Satan' came running to the *Judenrat* and ordered them to immediately send workers to erect a gallows with a long rope in the marketplace, opposite the *Judenrat* building. He presented them with a plan how the gallows should be built.

The town shuddered under the shadow of death. G-d knows who will be the victim this timel; maybe the members of the *Judenrat*. Maybe it is only to frighten us? Recently, 'the Yellow Satan' had not bothered anyone and sometimes he was even friendly to those who came to him. Everyone fulfilled his requests with exactitude and, to his satisfaction. Many were of the opinion that this was only a crazy prank on the part of the evil one in order to press harder and frighten the public into doing additional deeds to satisfy his appetites, which, in spite of everything, were not satisfied. That the gallows was being prepared for Berel did not enter anyone's imagination, and certainly not the imagination of Berel himself.

Shavuot eve. Into the jail cell came Yanchenko, the Polish police officer, accompanied by a number of *gendarmes*. Berel jumped up in joy, thinking that they had come to release him after they had not found him guilty of anything. On the contrary – all his possessions had been stolen from him and they had impoverished him. The *gendarmes* brought Berel outside, saying that he was being summoned to the *Amstkommissar* who was standing near the *Judenrat* building. A spark of hope arose in his heart. He thought that no evil would come to him; and certainly in the presence of the representatives of the Jews, he would be protected from being beaten, and perhaps he would even find someone who would protect him.

In the street, Berel took off his eyeglasses, wiped the lenses, and put them on again. He walked, accompanied by the *gendarmes*, at a normal pace. Suddenly he saw the gallows. Horror took hold of him!!! What is happening here? For who is the gallows intended? What if it is for him? Here, no trial was held and no judgment was made! He doesn't even know what they are accusing him of!

Berel Krushevsky did not have time to evaluate his unfortunate situation. 'The Devil' ordered Berel's hands to be tied behind him. One *gendarme* was sent into the *Judenrat* to call a few more Jews to come and help hang Berel, but no one was found there because they had all run away in panic. The *gendarme* brought Berel to the gallows, put the rope around his neck, and pulled him up to the top of the gallows. The victim kicked his feet and then remained hanging in the air in the noon sunshine, while the blue skies spread over his tortured head.

Berel's wife, who was present, wailed tragically and fainted. The children cried and trembled, calling, "Our dear *Abba, Abba*, the crown of our heads, *Abba, Abbale*. What did they do to you and to us? Woe to us, woe to us!"

The despicable murderer, the 'Yellow Satan', commanded that they leave Berel Kreshevsky hanging there on the gallows for 24 hours.

All the people of the town were in shock, and the shadow of the cruel and sinful murder accompanied every Jew in Sokoly for a long time.

On the first day of the *Shavuot* holiday, the 'Yellow Satan' allowed the body to be removed from the gallows and to be properly buried in the cemetery.

The Victim in Lapy

On the day that they hanged Berel Krushevsky, another victim fell in Lapy, from among the 250 slave-laborers from Sokoly who worked in the *Dapu* railroad factories.

The victim was a young man from Kobylin who had recently come with his mother and sister to live in Sokoly after the Germans had wiped out the small community of Kobylin.

In order to receive a work card, he voluntarily registered for work in Lapy. Tragically, on his first day of work, they immediately sent him to Gidrowicz's office. On the first two days, he was sent to work in a group of 12 workers, including the elderly Maik. The group loaded and unloaded scrap iron from lathes. This work was especially difficult, because the scraps were stuck to each other and were covered with rust – making it necessary to separate them with blows from a special axe. Only then was it possible, with the aid of a rake and shovel, to pour the scrap into a crate and bring it in a wheelbarrow to the freight car that stood nearby. As already mentioned, this labor was difficult. The supervisors were constantly rushing them to fill the freight cars, and they did not allow the workers to go home until they finished loading all the freight cars that had been prepared. In general, they demanded that the work of two days be completed in one day.

The young man from Kobylin was quiet and serious. He was not careless with his work and he did not push hard work off on others. He never argued with the other workers, his partners in labor, about the quality of the work. When they told him to strike with the axe, he rained unceasing blows on the hard scrap metal, and when they told him to carry heavy crates, he carried them. He was not accustomed to rest after he carried two crates as did his companions.

On the third day he was sent with a group of six workers to unload a freight car filled with crates of glass. At the outset, the workers were happy, thinking that they would have an easy day without supervisors. Slowly, they started to slide one crate after another on the boards of the unloading ramp. After they slid each of the two crates off the unloading ramp, they sat and rested until they had to unload another two crates. It was eleven o'clock in the morning.

Suddenly they saw that the train engine was coming closer in order to hook up to the car that had carried the glass. The workers began to hurry to unload the last two crates from the car. Two workers stood above, inside the freight car, and four stood below, on both sides of the car. In the haste, or carelessness, of the two workers above, one crate pitched sideways and started to fall. Three workers succeeded in jumping aside and were saved, but the young man from Kobylin felt responsibile for the crate and was afraid that the glass would break. He, alone, tried to save the crate and was crushed to death. The weight of the crate was 600 kilograms.

It was an everyday occurrence to be injured in working for Gidrowicz's office. Thus, Shmuel Krushnansky, the son-in-law of Tuvia Baran the butcher was seriously injured. This happened a few weeks after he was married. Once he was sent to work in Lapy and it was his misfortune to work lifting heavy loads with a special machine. Shmuel Krushnansky's job was to attach and release metal chains on the loads. Once a heavy load fell on him and broke his spine. His lungs were crushed and they swelled up. His sight was also damaged, and he was sent to the hospital in Bialystok. Krushnansky was so broken up and crushed that no doctor believed that he would live. He did remain alive, but only because of his strong heart. After six months in the hospital in Bialystok, he was sent home, broken and crushed.

Another yeshiva student, Betzalel Malach, aged 40, the son-in-law of Yaakov Leib Perlowitz, was injured by an iron wheel and his leg was broken.

Light injuries were customary. After the *Shavuot* holiday, the working conditions in Gidrowicz's office became much worse. The *'Pahtcher'* came back from his vacation and continued, as was his custom, to beat the workers with murderous blows. He cruelly beat a strong, healthy young man, 'Yudel' (Yehuda) Lehrman from Ostrow Mazowiecka. For several months his face was so swollen that his eyes, red with blood, could hardly be seen. The *'Pahtcher'* had a unique, sadistic appetite for injuring handsome youths and making their faces so ugly that it was difficult to recognize them. In addition to this, he would distribute such strong, dry blows that the pain was felt for weeks afterward.

Among the workers from Sokoly was a young man from Lapy by the name of Weiner. His father had been a supplier of goods to the Polish government. His mother had been a teacher in her youth. His father was sent to Siberia by the Soviets and his mother remained in Lapy with the Germans, working as a secretary in the *Judenrat*. Her only son was gentle and spoiled. Before the War, he lived in luxury. They had special nurses for him. The *'Pahtcher'* had a hobby: every day, he would give Weiner, the only son, 20 slaps on the cheeks, ten on each side. Weiner had to stand up straight. Sometimes, in addition to the slaps on the cheeks, the *'Pahtcher'* beat him until blood flowed. Weiner, a handsome lad, had no one to complain to because the Jews were outside the law and their lives were worthless. Any German could do whatever his heart desired to the Jews.

Once, the Sokoly workers in Gidrowicz's office spoke about trying to bribe the *'Pahtcher'* with a nice gift so that he would stop beating the workers. Two of them who knew how to speak German took it upon themselves to talk with the *'Pahtcher'*. One of them, Rubenstein, was the owner of a print shop and a store that sold paper and writing instruments in the city of Ostrowlenka. The Sokoly workers decided to donate a pair of deluxe boots to the *'Pahtcher'*, the likes of which were very hard to find at that time. Every worker obligated himself to contribute his portion of a certain amount. A delegation headed by Rubenstein turned to the *Judenrat* with an urgent request to help them obtain the boots because their lives depended on it. They would no longer have to bear the suffering and the murderous beatings of the *'Pahtcher'*. The two intermediaries explored bribing the *'Pahtcher'* with a nice gift and he did not hesitate to take it. The robber expressed this by giving them permission to measure his feet.

The local *Judenrat* immediately provided leather of superior quality from before the War. An excellent shoemaker from Sokoly made an extraordinary pair of boots for the *'Pahtcher'* which cost over 1,000 marks. Rubenstein humbly gave the boots to the cruel German who, by the way, was extremely pleased.

The workers were happy and thought that rescue and an end to their torture at the hands of the oppressor had arrived. But they surely erred in their calculations. The cruel one was glorified in his new boots like a peacock in his feathers, but he did not improve his attitude toward the Jews at all. On the contrary, he became worse and hardened his heart to torturing them with suffering. Until then, he had been accustomed to supervise the work only sometimes, and now he stood and oppressed them during all the hours of the day, almost until the soul left their bodies. Men became deformed. Occasionally they fainted and collapsed under the crushing burden of labor. Many of them cursed the day they were born and preferred to die rather than bear the suffering.

As if it weren't enough for the *'Pahtcher'* to remain in Gidrowicz's office, the boss Delmayer added more trouble, in the form of a tall, fat German from Koenigsberg, who also tortured us with whips and scourges. We honored the new oppressor with the title *'Dzhabig'* ('crane' in Polish).

He was a brave type, had a great deal of physical strength, and was able to lift heavy loads. He had a jaw like a Britton dog and a voice like a wild animal. The *'Dzhabig'* was in charge of the lumberyard like his predecessor, the *Marok*. He also supervised the work in other branches, and he did not allow anyone to relax for a moment. He spread his terror everywhere he went, such as in the office of the 'Grandfather', the *Halla Saniterna* [inner *sanctum*] of the Goltz firm, and more. They feared him like the Angel of Death. He would stand next to a pile of boards, a thick pole in his hands, and with wild screams would hurry pairs of workers to move boards five meters long while running without pause. After a day of eight hours of work, the workers were worn out and injured from the lashes meted out by the evil one with his whip on every part of their bodies. Once in a while he would leave the place for a short time in order to bother the workers in other locations. These moments were very precious and were used to take long breaths and wipe off the sweat. As soon as the *Dzhabig* came back, the beatings resumed.

He would release the workers ten minutes before the train was to leave Lapy for Sokoly, whereas in other places the workers were released half an hour before their trip, even though the distance to the Lapy Train Station was longer by over one kilometer than it was, for example, from the Gawizdowa area. The way to the station led over a high bridge of railway ties, which had to be crossed quickly in order not to miss the train trip home. It sometimes happened that older or weaker men reached the train at the last minute, breathing heavily or completely worn out, and then the railroad official obstinately did not allow them to board the train. The poor fellows were forced to walk home, a distance of 16 kilometers to Sokoly.

Sometimes, when the train had not yet reached the station, the official found an opportunity to amuse himself with the Jews and treat them brutally, as an addition to the daily hard labor. He would line up the 250 men from Sokoly in three long rows with an exact distance between them and order them to slap each other in the face. Whoever did not slap hard enough, received a double dose from him. After the slap-in-the-face game, he ordered them to compete in running races and other games, all for the purpose of wearing out and tiring the workers after a long day of hard labor.

In the morning, when the workers arrived at the Lapy Train Station to report for work, the Nazi devils would stand there and ambush them. One of the Nazis, called 'Gelev' would check if they had properly shaved. If someone was not cleanly shaven Gelev would take his work card away and force the worker to shave at noon in order to get it back. Another Nazi supervised the 'badges of shame' to make sure they were in order. If someone did not wear the 'badge of shame' on his clothing he would be beaten and fined. Other Nazis searched in the workers' packs and in their pockets, and felt all over their bodies looking for choice merchandise. Experienced smugglers would bribe the 'Kroks' (the German *gendarmes*) in advance with gifts, so that they would not search them. Occasionally the *Kroks* conducted searches of the workers in the railway cars on the way from Sokoly to Lapy and back.

From time to time, the *Amstkommissar* of Sokoly would suddenly come to the station before the train would leave in order to check whether workers on the list for Lapy were missing. For this purpose, he would command all the workers to stand in line and be counted. Of course the fear of death fell upon all of them. When he punished the members of the *Judenrat* with beatings, he threatened that if the offence would occur in the future, the members of the *Judenrat* would be shot without advance warning. One of the biggest offences to him was the absence from labor in Lapy of the required number of workers.

Once, he started to count the workers at a line-up 15 minutes before the train arrived. One group arrived late for the lineup and he did not allow them to get on the train. He recorded their names and informed them that from today, they would work for a few weeks in the stone quarry at Jezewo. He immediately sent them to the *Judenrat* to be transferred to Jezewo. The workers were happy that the shadow of death had left them–they were not afraid of hard work.

The *Judenrat* sent 50 workers in wagons to Jezewo every day at 4:30 a.m. and brought them back home in the wagons at five o'clock in the afternoon. The work wasn't that hard, but riding around in crowded wagons for four hours a day in addition to the work was hard enough. Every day, the *Judenrat* changed the [slave-labor] workers for Jezewo, so that the younger men would also not have to travel more than two to three times a week.

Recently, a group of workers from Bialystok ran away from the labor in Jezewo, because they were hungry. In Jezewo, there was no public kitchen so everyone had to bring his own food from home. The Bialystokers did not travel home every day because of the great distance and therefore they suffered from hunger and were forced to sleep on a hard floor. The conditions were such that dozens of workers ran away from the place.

At the outset, the boss from Sokoly placed the guilt for the flight on his *Judenrat*, but they were justified in explaining that they could not bear the responsibility for workers from other places and that the problem of feeding the workers was a matter for the Bialystok *Judenrat*.
I do not know how they punished the workers who ran away and how they related to the matter in Bialystok, but in Sokoly they requested, in addition to the ordinary 50 workers, an additional 20 workers to strengthen the group in Jezewo as well as an arrangement for supplying their food. Besides the Jezewo contingent, 50 workers were requested for digging in the chain gangs in the village of Budziska to supply fuel for heating stoves.

Many other jobs were added at the Kruczewo Train Station where freight cars arrived filled with stone to be pulverized and crushed with mixers on hand to be used for this purpose. Because of a lack of men for the work force, young women were sent to do these jobs. Some worked at digging for cabling in Budziska and the rest in the gravel jobs and in the kitchens that had been set up for the workers.

The shifts were changed at the cabling job once every two weeks, whereas for the gravel job, the shifts were three days a week. Clearly the yoke of slavery was lighter upon those who were employed in Sokoly than it was for those who worked elsewhere.

The outside [slave-labor] workers did not taste the rest of the Shabbat and were subject to constant persecution at the hands of tyrants, murderers, and sadists such as the *"Pahtcher"* and the *'Dzhabig'* in Gidrowicz's office and *Azaf* at the Goltz firm.

There were cases where poor workers were hired for labor in place of wealthy ones, for a payment of ten marks a day. Thus, a job market was created and lads aged 13 and 14, who did not yet appear on the lists because of their young age, were employed. Such youngsters sometimes worked in place of their relatives. Among them were those who were alert and aware of everything going on around them, and they made a profit in business and in smuggling goods of all kinds. Poor workers were even sent by the *Judenrat* to work in place of others, for a reasonable payment. These poor workers were paid two marks for a full day of work.

Rumors Regarding Mass Murders

During the last summer, rumors reached us regarding the mass murder of Jews all over Lithuania and White Russia. In Vilna, Slonim, Baranowicz and Minsk, the Germans destroyed the entire Jewish population with the assistance of gangs of Lithuanians and White Russians. In the small towns surrounding Vilna and Minsk, thousands of Jews simultaneously were killed, and all their money and possessions were stolen. Since these shocking rumors originated in relatively distant places and no live witnesses had arrived, people did not pay sufficient attention to them, in spite of the fact that for a long time we had known that a enormous amount of killing had taken place no farther from us than 'Tiktin', Rutka, Myszyniec, and Jedwabne. In Sokoly, they comforted themselves with the hope that time would bring better days and that the Good L-rd would not desert us. As mentioned before, the consideration was that the Germans needed the work force for purposes of the War, and we hoped for their defeat in the near future.

The days passed; the rumors stopped and were slowly forgotten in the whirlpool of events and the difficult life. The economic situation improved relatively during the last months before the destruction of our town. People no longer suffered from hunger in Sokoly. Jews sold their possessions without hesitation and without making deep calculations. What do you live for…if the world will continue to exist, it will be possible to buy new things, maybe even nicer and more expensive ones, and if, G-d forbid, it won't, then there is no reason to have any attachment tor them; it is better to live for the moment, in other words, to sell them and eat, because they will fall into the hands of our murderers in any case.

Jews had accustomed themselves to existing and living close to the local Germans and *gendarmes*. Through the *Judenrat*, they supplied the Germans' needs for clothing, footwear, furniture, jewelry, and everything good. When the Germans were satisfied with everything, they stopped conducting searches in the houses and they ignored transactions between the Jews and the Poles.

Even the 'Yellow Satan' was calmer, especially after the hanging of Berel Krushevsky. In his talks with the representatives of the *Judenrat*, he found it correct to point out that he, and only he, is keeping alive and trying to keep alive, the ghetto in Sokoly, at a time when ghettos have been eliminated in other places and he is the only one to thank for that. To the extent that his attitude toward the Jews was stricter and more rigid, the greater would be the benefit that would be brought to them. There was a period when they were going to transfer the 'Yellow Satan' out of Sokoly. It was a paradox that so many Jews were sorry about this, since they were worried that they were losing their only protector and defender. They calmed down only when it became known that the 'Yellow Satan' would remain in the town.

Despite the specific ban on the sale of wood for heating and cooking, somehow the Jews managed to obtain this necessity in all kinds of ways. It was permitted to go out to the nearby forest and gather dry wood, twigs, and branches, which were regarded as ownerless. Thus, women, young boys and girls, and the elderly went out with sacks and ropes in order to equip themselves with wood. In the vicinity were the Kruczewo Forests (forests that previously belonged to Leibel Dinhas), Wysokie Forest, Jamiolki

Forest, Idzki Forest, Bruszewo Forest, Bialystok Forest, and the Dworkie Forest.

During this period, the [nearby] forests swarmed with crowds of Jews. Everywhere, you would see them carrying packages, pulling beams with ropes, or transporting wood in wagons. The larger the family, the larger the amount of wood with which they equipped themselves, for the entire winter and even for the entire year. Those who worked in construction or other places where there was scrap wood brought home a supply for heating. Craftsmen who worked privately for Poles received wood for heating from them. The Poles even supplied wagons of wood to the Jews during the hours before dawn, in order not to be seen.

At that time, a group of technicians from the *Wehrmacht* arrived in Sokoly to exploit the broken vehicles and tractors that had been left behind by the Soviets on all the roads. They demanded that the *Judenrat* supply them with Jewish workers to help dismantle the vehicles. This work also provided the workers with another opportunity to obtain wood scraps.

During those last days, fearful rumors spread again about the mass murder of Jews. This time, the rumors arrived from the area surrounding Warsaw. Every single day during the entire summer of 1942, the Germans rounded up thousands of Jews from Warsaw and its surroundings and sent them in boxcars to Treblinka, a place where the Germans had built a giant slaughterhouse for killing Jews by both electrocution and strangulation with gas. Exact details as to how they killed the Jews were not yet known, but it was known that every day dozens of boxcars loaded with Jews arrived at Treblinka. First, they were shoved onto special platforms and after that they were supposedly taken to a 'bathhouse'…they were ordered to undress; everyone was given a piece of soap and a towel. After that, the doors were opened to an empty room, into which the victims were sent. When the room was filled with people and so crowded that there was no more space, the doors were locked, and in a few minutes they suffocated. Every five minutes, new transports of Jews were sent in there, and they immediately were turned into dust. Other Jews from Poland,

Lithuania, Ukraine, White Russia, France, Belgium, Holland and other European countries also arrived in full trains at Treblinka, where they were murdered.

At the beginning, the Germans deceived the Warsaw *Judenrat*, telling them that they were sending the Jews to labor camps...there even were Jews who hurried to register with the *Judenrat* for work in Treblinka. There were some who gave the *Judenrat* certain sums of money so as to be registered as soon as possible for Treblinka. After a few days, it became known that they were not sent to Treblinka to work but to be killed.

The news from Warsaw completely broke our hearts. The disappointment and discouragement grew. We knew that the Holocaust was coming nearer and nearer to us, and that we would not be prevented from suffering the tragic fate of Polish and European Jewry. Our sentence had been sealed, and even so, the instinct to live did not let us surrender to accept it. It was hard for us to imagine that we already were standing on the threshold of destruction.

There were still optimists among us who fed us deceptions, such as: Hitler is separating the Jews of the Third Reich and the Jews of the General Government, and we, who belong to the Third Reich, will enjoy special privileges... In any case, the optimists were comforted by vain hopes that a miracle from Heaven would occur, and as long as we were alive it was forbidden to be discouraged. One had to eat, drink, and take care of his household.

The Days of Awe, of *Rosh Hashana* and *Yom Kippur*, were approaching, and after that, the long *Sukkot* holiday, *Shmini Atzeret* and *Simchat Torah*. The Jews bought food for the holidays - chickens and fish. They baked *challot* and cakes, as they had done in the good years. On *Rosh Hashana* of 1942, the elderly of Sokoly prayed in the Rabbi's *minyan*, because the *batei Midrash* and the synagogue in Sokoly had been taken over by the Germans since the first day they entered the town. The Germans used the large *beit midrash* and the synagogue as storehouses for crops and potatoes. The Germans made the new *beit midrash* into a carpentry shop and the tailors' *beit midrash* became a storeroom, so that the only place where the elderly Jews of Sokoly could pray on the holidays was in the Rabbi's *minyan*. A few Chasidim, headed by Shlomke Olsha, who prayed according to the *Sefardi* custom, established a *minyan* for themselves in an empty room at the back of the buildings belonging to Zalman Yachnes. All the *Rosh Hashana* and *Yom Kippur* prayers were held in secret. They were very careful and kept looking out the windows to see if any Germans could be seen. Children stood watch outside.

On *Erev Yom Kippur*, the *Judenrat* warned those who worked in the *Dapu* railroad factories in Lapy that on the holy day they would have to travel as usual and that no one should delay his travel, because his life depended on it. The *Amstkommissar* was likely to investigate whether there were workers who did not show up for work. The *Judenrat* members reminded everyone that on the Monday of the previous week, 'the Satan' had come to the Kruczewo Train Station to see the workers before they left for work, because he had made a mistake in his calculation and *Yom Kippur* was actually a week later than he had thought.

In spite of the warnings, dozens of the Lapy railroad workers stayed home on *Yom Kippur*. At the outset, all of them came to the train station, but during the last few minutes before the train left, when they saw that the *Amstkommissar* did not come, dozens of workers returned home. It was *Yom Kippur*, a holy day for fasting and praying, the Day of Judgment…'the Satan', did not come, a sign that it would all pass quietly. At most, the Germans could make them pay a fine of a few marks.

At noon on *Yom Kippur*, freight cars that were to be loaded with stone for gravel arrived at the Kruczewo Train Station. The *Judenrat* called the young men out from the prayer services and sent them to the train station to work at loading. The Rabbi ordered the congregation to take an intermission in the prayers for half an hour so that workers could be chosen as commanded by the *Judenrat*. He explained that danger to life takes precedence over the *mitzvot* of the *Torah*.

After the *Sukkot* holiday, there were terrifying rumors that in a few towns around Warsaw, such as Kaloshin, Shdaltz and Wenagrod, the Germans expelled all the Jews, young and old, infants and women, and sent them to Treblinka. A few refugees who had escaped from the boxcars succeeded in reaching Sokoly. They told that they fled to the villages around their towns, but gangs of robbers had spread in all the villages, attacked them, and chased them day and night. The refugees told that the robbers pulled the boots and shoes off their feet and took their clothing, money, and jewelry. The robbers left them naked and barefoot. Thus, they wandered in the forests and the villages and asked the farmers for bread to break their hunger. They slept outside until they reached Sokoly. They had heard that there still were Jewish settlements in the Sokoly area. The refugees told us that in the cities of Sokolow and Wenagrod, the young Jews showed strong opposition to the Germans at the time when the ghettos in those places were being eliminated, and that they had even killed a few Nazis.

The Sokoly *Judenrat* took care of the needs of the refugees who arrived from the Warsaw area. They supplied them with food, clothing, footwear, and a place to sleep. They established a kitchen for them and took care to include them among the workers and to hide their illegal presence in Sokoly. They enabled them to travel to work in Lapy with work cards belonging to others.

At that time, a Christian woman from Warsaw brought a seven-year-old Jewish girl to the *Judenrat* in Sokoly. She told them that the girl was from a wealthy and distinguished family and the Germans had killed her parents, and she had taken pity on the poor girl who had suddenly become an orphan. She liked the girl, who spoke Polish and was pretty and intelligent. The good woman thought that Christian parents who had no children should be found to adopt the girl, so that they could hide her Jewish origins. She had found a wealthy family who were prepared to take the girl in as their daughter and give her a warm home and an education, but the girl refused to remain with Christians. She cried and begged them to bring her to the Jews. The girl understood her situation and what had happened to her parents and to other Jews in the area.

Following a brief consultation, the *Judenrat* accepted the orphan, who was given into the care and education of an appropriate woman, for proper payment.

Shocking stories from the refugees increased the fear and depression arising from a concern that terrible, fateful days were drawing near. No longer was there any doubt that our turn for destruction would arrive sooner or later and that we were standing at the edge of the pit. We estimated that the elimination would start in Bialystok and gradually spread to the areas in its radius. The consolation was that the present situation was still continuing, and would continue, since there were many factories in Bialystok necessary to the Germans, whose workers were mainly Jews. They manufactured felt shoes there for the army, who needed them for the bitter winter cold on the Russian front, in the war against the Russians. Shoemakers, tailors and many other professionals of all types and all kinds were employed in Bialystok. The factories and workshops were working at full capacity. It is estimated that the Jewish population of Bialystok in 1942 reached 60,000 souls. The labor of the Jews was exploited in every factory, and as long as they were needed, they would not hurry to kill them. These thoughts occupied the minds of the Jews of Sokoly, but at the same time, they knew this was nothing but self-deception.

During the last weeks, the workers from Sokoly tried to contact Jews from Bialystok in order to find out what the situation there was and whether the Jews expected to be expelled. Understandably, those they asked were unable to give any answer, because "what are we and what are our lives?" They even appeared to be content and calm, being regularly employed at work that almost never stopped.

One clear morning, the *Amstkommissar* suddenly informed the Bialystok *Judenrat* that they should prepare an exact list of the elderly and the small children for him. There is no way to describe in words the panic and heartbreak in every home. The *Judenrat* evaded preparing the list, and even expressed the opinion that no one would consent of his own will to be separated and distanced from his dear ones. No Jew could be found who would not defend himself and who would hand over his children or parents to be killed, even though the *Amstkommissar* hinted that perhaps the listed persons would only be brought to a safe place.

The confusion lasted a few days, until it finally ended with the cancellation of the order. It was not hard to understand that this was a lowly plot on the part of some Germans, in an attempt to obtain additional bribes for themselves.

A Tragic Incident in Lapy

One Sunday, a very tragic incident occurred in Lapy involving the workers from Sokoly. On Sundays, they generally worked half a day, until one o'clock in the afternoon. Whoever completed his task before that time had permission to leave. In any case, at 1:00 p.m., all the workers were free to leave. The problem was that there was no transportation to Sokoly, and it was necessary to wait until six in the evening for the train to come.

On their way to the train, the workers were accustomed to go into the Dworkie Stare Inn, where they could order complete or light meals. The Inn was a kind of trade and smuggling exchange where trade transactions and commercial agreements were carried out.

On that fatal Sunday, ten workers from Sokoly and Bialystok sat in the garden in front of the restaurant, talking with two of the young owners. Suddenly, a warning call was heard from one of the workers that 'Six Feet' was approaching. This was the nickname of one of the *gendarmes*, who was always accompanied by a large German shepherd dog.

When they saw the danger of the unexpected and unwanted meeting, they quickly ran to a storage shed behind the restaurant. It was their bad luck that the German saw them running away. He followed them and arrested them all.

It was clear to the German robber that he had nothing of which to accuse the men, because they had done nothing wrong. They simply ran away from him in fear, which in those days was in the

89

hearts of all the Jews because of weakness and the inability to protect themselves against the hard fists and constant threats to their lives on the part of the Germans, who were brutal to them whichever way they turned.

All of them were in order with regard to their work. They had finished what was required of them and were waiting for the departure of the train from the Lapy Train Station.

In the shed, the German discovered two sacks of flour. The owner of the shed denied that the flour belonged to him and stated that he had no idea how the sacks had been brought into the shed.

'Six Feet' took the ten Jews to a prison camp in the town of Knishin, where they were shot. Among the murdered were those who were their parents' only sons and their sole support. One of them was the only son of Berel Krushevsky, who had been hanged only four months previously on the eve of the *Shavuot* holiday. This was an additional tragedy for his poor mother, who could not be consoled.

'Yudel' Gritczak, a lad of 14 and the son of 'Velvele', was another victim among those ten. His grandfather, Yaakov Moshe, from Kobylin, was a Gerrer *Chasid*, a merchant and an intelligent and honest Jew. The third victim from Sokoly was Moshe Barbinsky, who filled his family's cup of poison. Moshe was the son-in-law of Chaim Baruch Goldwasser and his wife 'Rashka'. In the summer of 1942, he worked every day in Lapy and would return worn out and crushed by the difficult labor. Towards evening, his two daughters, tots of 3 and 4, would run out to meet him with innocent, childish happiness, and with shrieks of joy they would fall upon their father with unending kisses, telling him about everything that had happened to them that day and how they missed him. The people who witnessed these meetings were moved to tears by the happiness of the tots and their father. Who could have guessed that by going to the storeroom of the Dworkie Stare Inn, Moshe Barbinsky would bring destruction upon him and his precious family?

Self-Defense

A few weeks before the Jews were expelled from Sokoly, a group of youths decided to organize self-defense for the purpose of not allowing the Germans to bring us like sheep to the slaughter.

A number of youths conferred in secret and selected five members who would constitute the operating committee of the protective underground. These members were: Shlomo Plut, 'Yankel' Seines, Mordechai Moshe Blustein, Shmuelke Maik, and Moshe Maik.

At the first meeting, they worked on a plan to organize all the youths and train them for actions against the Germans. We heard from other places that the day before the expulsion (*Ausweisung* as the Germans called it), the murderers would inform the *Judenrat*, by suggestion, of their evil intentions. If so, then every movement should be followed and an ear be turned toward what was happening in the vicinity to obtain any information regarding the expulsion of the Jews. Members were assigned to stand at various locations and on the roads on the fateful day, and if they detected the movement of elimination squads, they would immediately inform the rest of the group. A number of actions were determined:

The moment it will be known that there is a movement of Germans towards Sokoly, each fighter will set his house on fire with all the possessions inside, and thus Jewish property will not fall into the hands of the oppressors. Some of the organized youths will throw grenades at the approaching members of the Gestapo, and the others will open fire on them with pistols. It was easy to guess that in this battle many of the fighters would be killed and the chances of remaining alive were slim, but it was better to fall in battle, knowing that by your death you also eliminated a German.

The meeting took place under the slogan, "My soul will die with the Philistines." This was a plan made by the youths, who were determined to die a hero's death. The spirit of battle was awakened in them. In these moments of exhiliration, they also thought of shelter for the few who might succeed in escaping from the heavy gunfire. Meeting places in the surrounding forests were determined so that, at a later stage, they would be able to make contact with the partisans.

The plan was already drawn in general terms, and now they began to prepare to carry it out. The most difficult and urgent problem was obtaining weapons - at least fifty pistols and hand grenades.

The young Moshe Maik had a Polish friend who was one of the heads of the *A.K. (Armia Krajova)* underground. He lived not far from Sokoly, and there was a hidden cellar in his house where the organization's stock of weapons was stored. When the committee's meeting ended, it was decided to send Moshe Maik to that very Pole to negotiate obtaining weapons from him. The members waited impatiently and worriedly for their messenger's return. Moshe returned with news: "The Pole promised to supply us with seven pistols and 12 grenades at the price of 200 marks per pistol and 100 marks per grenade."

The committee met a second time and discussed ways of obtaining money to purchase the weapons. Shlomo Plut and Mordechai Blustein were given the task. 'Yankel' Seines volunteered to search in the nearby forests for an appropriate place for bunkers. It also was decided to contact the youth from Wysokie-Mazowieckie. There were rumors that the Jews from Wysokie had organized and succeeded in maintaining contact with the Soviet partisans in the Mazury Forests.

Shlomo Plut and Moshe Maik took the task of contacting the youth of Wysokie. For this purpose, Moshe applied to the *Amstkommissar* for permission to purchase materials needed to fill batteries built of nickel and iron plates, which could be gotten only in Wysokie-Mazowiekie. Since the local pharmacy no longer had these materials, permission was granted and the two youngsters, Moshe Maik and Shlomo Plut, went out to their destination immediately, on foot. In meetings with people there, it became clear that the Jews in Wysokie Mazowiekie had not actually organized yet to defend themselves. However, they promised to contact the youths of Sokoly in any case, and to take steps toward effective action in opposing the enemy and making contacts in the forests.

Very unfortunately, the youths of Sokoly began to organize themselves too late; also, financial donations did not stream in as they hoped. The workers in Lapy, who were the initiators of the defense organization, decided to postpone their payments to the organization until they had received their wages from Lapy.

In spite of the tension, many were of the opinion that it would be a few more months until the expulsion, because the eyes of the Jews of Sokoly were on Bialystok, which was "in line" before Sokoly, and there still were no obvious signs [of expulsion] in Bialystok; work in the factories continued at full speed. There were even opinions that the higher echelons of the German leadership had promised the Bialystok *Judenrat* that the ghetto would exist for a long time under conditions that were not so bad. As long as no danger to the *metropolia* existed, the Jews of the surrounding area regarded themselves as relatively calm. As a result, the self-defense organization was run lazily, and the total contents of the fund amounted to a mere 150 marks.

And suddenly, on Shabbat, October 31, 1942, 200 farmers were drafted from Wysokie-Mazowiekie, along with their horse-drawn vehicles, to come to Sokoly on Monday, November 2, at six in the morning. The farmers themselves revealed that they were drafted for the purpose of transporting the Jews of Sokoly to unknown destinations. In spite of everything, there were some optimistic Jews to be found who did not believe the farmers and were of the opinion that they had been drafted to transport trees that had been cut down in the forests.

Meanwhile, another rumor was spread that 150 farmers from Lapy, with their vehicles, had also been drafted for the same day, that is, November 2, at six in the morning. One of the Jews from Bransk said that 300 local farmers from there had also been drafted for the same date.

A messenger was sent to Bialystok on behalf of the Sokoly *Judenrat* to investigate and verify what the situation was there. The representatives of the Bialystok *Judenrat* were of the opinion that "they wouldn't touch them" in the near future. Thus, it became clear that the expulsion would begin in the neighboring towns, contrary to all estimations and necessitating, from now on, extra caution from the danger. In any case, all these terrifying rumors caused panic among the Jews of Sokoly, who were comforted only by a spark of hope that the farmers of Sokoly had not yet been drafted.

Towards evening on Shabbat, between the *Mincha* and *Maariv* prayers, many Jews gathered in the *shteibel* of the *chassidim* in a rear alley of Sokoly, in order to hear words of encouragement and revival from the local rabbi.

He opened with words of comfort, and the congregants immediately perceived that these were words of parting. He said:

> Perhaps it will be our fate to die as martyrs and in sanctification of G-d's name. We must prepare for this in our thoughts and preserve spiritual tranquility, as much as possible, because everything comes from G-d, the Creator of the world. Nothing in the world is done without Him. 'A person doesn't hurt his finger unless it is decreed in Heaven.' Therefore, every Jew has the obligation to accept everything with love and fulfill the commandment of 'and you shall love the L-rd your G-d with all your heart and all your soul,' even if He takes your soul... We must not ponder the attributes of G-d. We will never be intelligent enough to understand the ways of the Eternal. We must believe that the Master of the World is merciful.

> It is the fate of the completely righteous to bear suffering; this apparently appears contrary to the attributes of G-d. Nevertheless, we must understand that G-d is conducting His world towards high, elevated purposes, bringing us

closer to complete redemption, the coming of the *Moshiach* and the revival of the dead.

The Rabbi wanted to explain everything according to the belief that our world is only an entrance to the World to Come, and that we should accept the sacrifice that the L-rd requests of us, willingly return our souls to its Owner, and say, with all our hearts, 'I deposit my spirit in Your hand'...and the main thing is the World to Come.

The next day was November 1, 1942. From the morning on, Sokoly was quiet. The farmers' wagons had not been ordered, as they had been in the neighboring towns of Lapy, Wysokie, Zambrow, Bransk, and others.

As yet, during the hours of the afternoon, wherever you went and whomever you met, no signs of fear or panic were to be found. Everyone appeared to be content and calm and no one imagined that we were standing at the mouth of the pit. At three in the afternoon, the situation changed drastically and turned into panic, based on rumors going from one to another, that the farmers around Sokoly indeed had been drafted for the known and expected purpose.

When I came in from the street and told my wife, 'Tsippa' [Tsippora Maik], who was an optimist by nature, how the people felt, she said, "My heart tells me that if G-d wills it, nothing bad will happen to us...and meanwhile, I am very worried that we don't have any bread in the house."

I ran to the bakery, but I did not get any bread. They said there would be bread in another hour. I ran there a second time and a third time, but there still was no bread. My wife worried because I had not eaten anything since the morning and there would be no bread tomorrow to take to work in Lapy.

Our son 'Moshele' and his friends shut themselves up in another room and conducted secret consultations. In the first room sat my wife, waiting for me to return and for the youngsters' consultations to end. Eventually they did and Moshe's friends left the house.

Moshe told us that the *Judenrat* in Sokoly already knew that the 'Yellow Satan' had ordered 400 farmers' wagons. At the same time it was known that it was calm in Bialystok and the general opinion was that the expulsion would begin in the outlying towns. Moshe told me that he had to run immediately to one of the villages on an important errand for his friends.

I suggested that he take his mother with him and find her a hiding place in the village of Lapy because, apparently, I would be traveling as usual there. I also requested that before leaving for Lapy, he should take the small amount of money and jewelry out of the hiding place inside the wall, along with as much clothing and underwear as he could carry, as long as there was comparative calm and no one would suspect anything. Tomorrow, in the panic that was likely to ensue, it would be too late to think about movables. Mainly, I asked him again and again to take his mother with him.

However, Moshe Maik was caught up entirely, body and soul, with public affairs and the task his friends had given him. He had to run to Lapy village as quickly as possible, bring back three pistols, and return tonight to Sokoly in order to distribute them. Not much time remained; the sun was already starting to set. The village was an hour's walk away, and if he took his weak mother and many possessions, he would not be able to fulfill his important task. Covering the distance of five kilometers to the village under those circumstances would take an inestimable amount of time, which, at this moment, was so precious. Finding a hiding place for his mother would cause the complete failure of his plans.

Moshe briefly said to me, "There is not enough time to discuss these things now, and at this moment it is impossible for me to deal with anything other than supplying the weapons. Also, there is no reason to worry about our gold when the world is burning. If we remain alive and the world will be rebuilt, we will acquire new gold, and if, G-d forbid, we will perish, what do we need gold for?"

And regarding *Imma* [Mother], said Moshe, first he would prepare a suitable place of refuge. He asked me to go out with his mother and take along clothing and underwear, and join the groups of Jews who were going out tomorrow to the forests. In any case, he would try to meet us in the forest and provide whatever we lacked.

"Tomorrow might be too late! What if we have to run away in the general panic? Your mother is weak and it is better for you to take her with you before it is too late."

My wife Tsippora Maik returned just then from the bakery. When I asked her to change her clothes and go immediately with Moshe to Lapy village, she answered, "Where will I go and where will I turn to in a strange place in the middle of the night? I have a stomach disorder and am likely to immediately suffer stomach pains."

Moshe did not respond to his mother's arguments because he was worried that he would not have enough time to fulfill his task and his holy obligations to his organization. He went into the kitchen and burst into tears. After he calmed down, he came back, wiped his tears, and kissed his mother and me, reminding us to wait for him in the Idzki Forest where we should go together with our neighbors. If Abba [Father] goes to work in Lapy, he will meet his mother and find her a safe place.

Moshe refused to take clothing and boots with him. He immediately ran off to the village to obtain the weapons. When he left, I could not restrain myself and I complained to my wife that the problems of others are closer to his heart than worrying about his parents in times of trouble and need, when the sword of the Angel of Death is at our necks. The people close to himself ... and he is worrying about buying two or three pistols, which in any case have no value, compared to the large number of soldiers armed with modern automatic weapons and the help of the Polish police, who are also well armed. It also is doubtful whether the Pole will want to sell the pistols at a time of calamity and general confusion.

But my wife, excitedly, and with a mother's love, defended her son, saying, "Look, how our son's heart shrank and he cried bitter tears like a baby. No! You can't complain about our son 'Moshele', may he live and be healthy! He loves his parents and they are very precious to him. He was ready to take me with him, even though I would make his way more difficult and bother him in his errand for the honor of *Am Yisrael*. I myself refused to go the five kilometers with him, because I have a stomach disorder. Moshe is a wonderful boy and the task that was given to him, and that he willingly and responsibly accepted, is holier in his eyes than anything else in the world. It is also doubtful whether he would have succeeded in finding me shelter with the Christian. You know that even the lives of the Poles are in danger if a Jew is found in their homes. It is better for Moshe to first explore the situation in the village. Both of us can trust our son. He will not leave us in need. He is good-hearted and innocent, and there isn't another among thousands as righteous as he is."

I decided to immediately pack the most necessary possessions and, to accompany my wife and the rest of the neighbors to the Idzki Forest at 4:00 tomorrow morning, before dawn. After Moshe [Maik] will find us, I will be able to join the group of workers going to Lapy. These workers had almost no concern for their lives, because they were of the opinion that they wouldn't be harmed, since they were an efficient part of the War machine. This was also the opinion of the excellent craftsmen, who were employed on a regular basis by the *gendarmia* and the administrative management. This is exactly what happened in Rutki and other towns; the Germans left the professionals and the Jews that they needed in place, while the expulsion of the rest of the Jews was carried out with maximum cruelty.

Therefore, and, also on the advice of the Rabbi and the *Judenrat*, the Lapy workers decided to go to work as usual and gather at the exact time at the Kruszewo Train Station.

A few tailors, whose job it was to sew suits of clothing for the *gendarmes* and the *Amstkommissar*, did not close their eyes all night, so as to finish their work before morning. Among these were 'Zussela' Charney and Zeidel Berliner, who thought that their dedicated work would rescue them from the Angel of Death. There were Jews who thought that after the panic of the expulsion would quiet down, the Gestapo murderers would leave the town and it would again be possible to somehow continue to live under the auspices of the local Germans, who would no longer harm them.

The watchmaker Yisrael Maik, his wife, his 18-year-old son 'Shmuelke', his 16-year-old daughter 'Teibele', and his relative Hinda [Czernetzky] (who was educated from childhood in Yisrael's house) were busy for three hours packing their possessions to hide them in the home of a Christian neighbor who lived in the last house on the same street, the son-in-law of Kuczlaber, Janina Palkowska's lame sister's husband.

The Pole himself took the trouble to move the possessions from the home of the rich Jew Yisrael Maik to his own house. Every five minutes, he would return with an empty sack in order to fill it with more possessions. Gradually, everything was moved to Kuczlaber's house. The Pole made an effort to hide his joy that he had suddenly become the inheritor of the property of an established Jew. As they say, "without a stomach ache or a toothache." He certainly scorned the Jews' hope and their innocent belief that they would remain alive. There is no doubt that at that moment, he felt himself the owner of everything good – in his possession.

The gold in the valuables, including gold watches and various kinds of jewelry, whose total weight reached several kilograms, Yisrael deposited in the hands of the notorious antisemitic oppressor, Janina Palkowska. Dina (daughter of Sarah), Yisrael's wife, had a life-long and intimate relationship with Palkowska. They spent day and night together, in unequalled friendship. It was not surprising, at this fateful moment when their lives were in the balance, that Dina Maik placed her faith exclusively in her good friend and gave her a suitcase filled with gold jewelry.

Dina even believed that they would never conduct a search at Janina's house and that it was a safe place for the expensive items. Palkowska was friendly with the *gendarmes* and no one would even think to suspect her of hiding capital. Dina agreed to leave her daughter 'Teibele' [Yona] at Janina's house for at least one day until a place could be found for her in the village.

After the Maik family made these arrangements, they locked the door of their house, where the furniture, wall clocks, bedding, kitchen utensils, and more still remained... it was impossible to take care of these because of a lack of time. The family started to walk towards the nearby village of Idzki, to the home of an old Polish friend by the name of Wilk, with whom they had a fraternal relationship. Yisrael was certain that Wilk would receive him with open arms. He knew that Yisrael was a wealthy man and that it would be worthwhile for him in every respect, as they would pay him for every service. Meanwhile, as agreed, Maik's daughter Yona remained at Janina's house. The son 'Shmuelke' had to travel to work in Lapy with the group of workers who had decided on their own to do so.

In this way, it appeared to Yisrael Maik that the temporary arrangement would somehow succeed, at least for a number of days until the Gestapo would leave the town and the local Germans returned to normal. They needed a watchmaker and goldsmith such as himself, and proof of this was the fact that to date he had worked for them and he was loaded down with unlimited work. So Yisrael Maik hoped and dreamed.

The neighbors were secretly jealous that Yisrael had many Polish acquaintances who were prepared to give him their full assistance and receive him and his entire family.

After the Maik family had left, their son 'Shmuelke' came to my house and told me, with despair and bitterness, that he could already have been in the Land of Israel for four years, as he had wanted with all his heart and soul, but his parents had been influenced by the advice of their relatives and had prevented him from going. His heart had prophesized to him that terrible days were coming closer, and there was no reason to remain on Polish soil.

I answered him that four years ago, nobody could have imagined that what was happening in Poland would happen and that the destruction of its Jewry would occur. I explained to him that his parents and relatives did not think it was right to allow him to go to the Land of Israel at a time of riots and bloodshed by Arab gangs. Every day, they heard about murders and Jewish victims there, and of course, the economic situation was also difficult and there was a crisis in the Land of Israel.

"You, 'Shmuelke', were then in an excellent situation, and your friends were able to envy you, because you learned the weaving profession in a short time and your father immediately bought you an electric loom. As a lad of 14, you already were independent; your parents were established and you lived a life of luxury. It is no wonder that people thought you were crazy to leave bread and seek crumbs, to leave a life of wealth and suffer hunger. In any case, no world Holocaust was seen on the horizon, nor was it foreseen that Hitler would complete his satanic plan to destroy the entire Jewish nation."

'Shmuelke' told me that in today's secret meeting of the youths, it had been decided that part of the Lapy workers would gather in the threshing house belonging to the baker 'Yechielke' Somovitz and the rest at Yosef (Mendritzka) Blustein's house on Mountain Street. All of them would stand guard. In the event that they would see a Gestapo vehicle coming towards the town, they were to disperse quickly and escape to the forests. If everything would go quietly until five in the morning, they would all go as usual to the Kruczewo Train Station, so as to travel to work in Lapy.

'Shmuelke' asked me to use only the back door, because his father had barred the front door with an iron bar, and added, "If my uncle stays in the house to sleep, please be very careful, because

101

outside, the Poles are running around in all the Jewish courtyards for the purpose of stealing everything they can."

When Shmuel left, I consulted with my wife whether it was worthwhile to transfer some valuables, clothing and underwear to Janina Palkowska.

At that very moment, Janina passed by our window. I ran to ask her if she would allow me to leave some possessions with her? Janina answered that if I don't want to become impoverished and remain a "*Dazhad*" (beggar), it would be best for me to remain in the house and guard my property, because "nothing will happen…and to preserve the peace and quiet." In any case, she was not prepared to take responsibility for watching the property of strangers.

After Janina left, the Polish police officer Yanchenko came in. He hinted to me that I should go into the next room and lock the door, as if he wanted to reveal a secret. He said that he knew that my family and I were preparing to flee, because it was clear to the Jews what awaited them tomorrow. He, Yanchenko, would not prevent or interfere with any Jew from fleeing as they wished. But he had a request. He heard that a week ago, my wife wanted to sell four meters of women's dress fabric, and he wanted to buy the fabric and pay "something" for it, because tomorrow they would take everything away from the Jews. My wife answered the Pole that the fabric was sold a few days ago, because she had urgently needed the money. Yanchenko immediately left the house, without saying another word.

We closed the shutters on the windows so that no one outside would be able to see what was done inside the house. It began to get dark. In the streets of the town, all the traffic stopped and silence reigned. The shutters of the surrounding houses were closed and the doors were locked. Everywhere it was as silent as the cemetery. Most of the Jewish population had already fled to the forests.

We decided to bring some of our possessions to a Soviet doctor [Claudia Volosvitza] who had remained in the town and was one of our son Moshe's friends. We packed clothing and the items that we needed the most, and snuck out of the house so that the Poles would not see us with bundles on our shoulders. We walked through dark, deserted alleyways. It was permitted to be outside until eight in the evening. Here and there, gangs of Poles were running around, robbing the homes of those Jews who had already fled and had left some of their possessions behind.

My wife and I did not manage to bring all the bundles we had packed to Dr. Volosvitza. I found it necessary to go to the *Judenrat* to get back my labor card, which I handed in every Sunday morning so as to be able to send someone else to work in my place for payment, as was the accepted practice.

Not a single clerk was to be found in the *Judenrat* office. The Rabbi and a few Jews sat there and read letters from the Jews of Bialystok that had arrived via workers who worked in Lapy. In these letters, people advised their relatives in Sokoly to carefully preserve their lives and escape as far as possible from the hands of the murderers by fleeing to the forests, so that they would later be able to succeed in infiltrating the Bialystok Ghetto, which, at present, apparently would continue to exist.

On my way back home, I saw gangs of robbers in all the courtyards. They fell upon abandoned Jewish property like wild animals on their prey.

Their owners had locked most of the houses. Sick elderly people, the disabled and such, who trusted in G-d's loving kindness, remained in only a few houses. They did not have enough physical, and perhaps spiritual, strength to run in panic in the darkness of the night to an unknown place, to destruction. They worried about life in the forest, hunger, poverty, cold, and suffering. They would accept the judgment decreed on them in Heaven. They felt there was no other choice.

When I crossed the threshold of my house, a few Poles burst in after me with the excuse that they had left watches to be repaired with my brother Yisrael and they wanted them back. Since the door at the entrance was barred, they asked to enter through my kitchen, which bordered my brother's house. I tried to threaten them that I would complain to the *gendarmes* against them for breaking into a house in the absence of the owner. With a great deal of effort I succeeded in getting rid of the robbers and I immediately locked the door. We were afraid to go out of the house even though it was only 7:30 p.m. We had wanted to take some more of our possessions to the Soviet Doctor.

It remained for me to carry out my decision to wait with my wife in the house until four o'clock in the morning, bring her to the forest, and then return to the group at the Kruszewo Train Station leaving for work in Lapy. We dressed in a double layer of clothing from the best we had, and thus we lay on the bed in order to get a bit of rest before leaving the house.

We left behind clothing, shoes, bedding, underwear, furniture, radio parts, and various tools used by our son Moshe. I had to abandon my library, numbering hundreds of holy and educational books in different languages, writing supplies, and some works of art, including expensive items that I had inherited and which had been passed down in the family for generations. Every single item in every corner where I looked seemed to beg me not to abandon it and to take it with me. All these possessions seemed to say, "You were accustomed to be glorified by us, and now what will our fate be? In the hands of the defiled ones, we will be regarded like the dust of the earth."

We got up at three o'clock in the morning. I lit a candle and we took packages in our hands. At four o'clock, with the dawn, we left our house, locking the doors behind us. We walked in fear and looked carefully in all directions to see if, G-d forbid, anyone was following us. Maybe somebody was standing behind the house and would follow our footsteps. We quickly crossed the street and entered the courtyard of 'Yechielke' the baker. 'Shmuelke' Maik had hinted that a group of workers would gather in the threshing house of 'Yechielke'. I looked inside, but the threshing house was empty.

We walked over to a window in 'Yechielke' Somovitz's house and stood next to the shutter in order to hear if there was a sign of life inside. We heard a whisper. Speaking through the shutter, I asked them to open the door. They opened it quickly and we went in where we found Yechiel, his son Chaim, and [Yechiel's] son-in-law (Chaya Rivka's husband). 'Yechielke' the baker's young daughter, Chaya Rivka, lay sick in bed after arriving recently from Bialystok with her husband and two young children. Besides the members of the family, several neighbors were also in the house. The men ran worriedly from corner to corner. I asked Chaim Somovitz if his family intended to go to the forest. He answered that he was confused and was unable to decide because Chaya Rivka had not recovered properly. How could they take her to the conditions in the forest?

We then went to the house owned jointly by my brother and me. Three families lived there: Zeidel Kubaner (the son-in-law of Tuvia's 'Yudel'), Pinia Shmogler and Sotilichs' daughter.

We wanted to join up with other people who were going to the forest because we feared the gangs of robbers on the roads. Our tenants looked at us in amazement that we had taken packages with us. "The Poles will immediately attack you and rob you of everything, and they will even leave you naked in the middle of the forest."

We went back to our house, left the bundles, and immediately went outside again to the street. We met up with a group of workers going to work in Lapy. I turned to my wife and said to her that I wouldn't have time to accompany her to the forest and then go to the train station. I asked her to join the neighbors or our tenants and go with them and that they should hurry to the forest. I was sure that our son Moshe was waiting for her and would find her immediately. With a heavy heart, I left my wife and went in the direction of the train. After half an hour, Yechiel the baker sent his son-in-law to give me a kilo of bread. He told me that my wife had arrived and had sent the bread for me.

We waited at the Kruszewo Train Station until six o'clock in the morning. We thought that the train was late as usual.... .

Exactly at six o'clock, we saw three vehicles moving toward Sokoly on the road that crossed the train tracks. We understood that these were the demons. Our hearts began to pound. They moved straight in the direction of the town and did not stop at the train station at all. We continued to wait for the train to come, with a prayer on our tongues that the engine would appear as quickly as possible and that the quick journey from Sokoly would save us.

After a quarter of an hour, we saw a vehicle at a distance coming back from Sokoly towards us. We instinctively felt that we were in grave danger and without waiting we dispersed and began running in different directions, with all our strength, into the fields with the intent to reach the forest. Through the morning mist, I was able to see rows of country wagons hitched up and undoubtedly intended to be used for the expulsion of the Jews from the town.

When the Gestapo murderers saw us fleeing, they opened fire, but due to the morning mist and the farmers' vehicles, dozens and perhaps hundreds of which were moving in from every direction, the Gestapo lost aim and none of us were injured. We heard shots behind us and sped up until we were breathless. Once in a while we lay down on the ground; and when the shooting stopped again, we continued running even after we had reached the nearby forest. We wanted to get as far away as possible from Sokoly to a place where, relatively speaking, the danger would be less.

After hours of running, I reached the end of a thick forest. On the way, my feet stumbled and I almost stopped breathing – I did not believe that I would reach the forest alive.

The [Idzki] forest, closest to Sokoly, was located six kilometers from the town. I counted about 100 Jewish souls, many of them having arrived in the darkness of the night from forests closer to town, afraid that the Germans would comb the forests. I sat down to rest under a tree, and my conscience immediately began to bother me.

Why had I left my wife alone and in mortal danger? How stupid I was to leave my 'Tsippa' at the mercy of the neighbors! It hadn't even been the neighbors' intention to flee to the forest! Did not Chaim Somovitz specifically say that he would not leave his ill sister alone in his house?! It must be that my wife has fallen victim to the German murderers!

The more I thought, the more my heart broke into pieces… This was not only folly on my part, but an actual crime! I had recklessly left my wife, who was faithful and loyal to me with all her soul and might … and what reason does my life have without her? I cried and wailed over my dear wife who was certainly a victim in the hands of the cruel murderers!

From moment to moment, the crowd in the forest grew larger, the forest serving as a type of way station. People rested a bit and continued on their way. Groups of people moved into the depths of the forest, trembling and afraid of every sound – even the sound of a falling leaf and the whispering of the trees. The distant echo of a moving vehicle, the sound of horses' hooves, or even the barking of dogs caused trembling in the hearts of the fugitives. What if they start combing the forests outside Sokoly and quickly discover us there, or the other possibility, that we would be attacked by gangs of Polish robbers?

I saw a few of my neighbors among the crowd of fugitives in the forest, including 'Yechielke' the baker's son-in-law. He told me that Chaim Somovitz had not moved from his house and had remained there with his ill sister and her children. The man cried bitterly that he had abandoned his poor family and left them to fall into the hands of the murderers. Now he was convinced that it would be better to die together with his young children, who were more precious to him than anything else. He saw his four-year-old son, a beautiful child – like an angel – and his sweet daughter 'Michaleh', aged three, stretching her arms out and looking at him

107

with her beautiful eyes, as if she were begging him not to go away from her. If strangers were excited by and loved the tots, how much more so did their father love them with a passion? It was sad to see the man burdened with his heavy tragedy. I was surprised how he could continue to exist and overcome his misfortune.

I saw 'Shaya' Seines, the son of Chava and Moshe Tzvi among another group of fugitives. He did not stop talking, praising and counting the attributes of his 2½-year-old daughter 'Rivkele' – how she talked and understood everything that was said to her and how much she loved her *Abba* (father); how she would hug him with both arms when he came home from working in Lapy, saying, "*Abbale*, my dear, good *Abbale*, I missed you all day and waited for you to come back to me!" 'Shaya' did not stop talking about his daughter; his heart weeping within him.

Fugitives continued to stream into the forest, each one with his own deep pain for his relatives, his dear ones who were not with him and for their bitter fate.

Slowly the basic question began to rack our brains: What will happen to us and what will be our fate? It is true that we were able to escape from the initial fire, but where will we go? Where is the corner where we can go and the stone upon which we can rest our heads...? This way or that, we are lost and doomed to die. It is forbidden for us to be seen by those who are waiting to threaten our lives. How long can we wander in the forest?

In everyone's opinion, the murderers will conduct searches for us, and it is already the autumn season with its rain and cold and snow. The winter, with its intense frost, will be crueler to us. Above all, what worries us is the question of provisions and clothing.

But we must be realistic. It is not the right time to think about the future. We must only think about today and our life at this moment.... .

Members of families were cut off from each other. Parents were in one forest, and their children, in the best case, in another forest. The Lapy workers had run from the Kruszewo Train Station into the forest. Others had already fled the day before from the town, dispersing in all four directions wherever their feet took them. Some had fled today before dawn. Many remained in Sokoly and fell into the hands of the murderers.

Of the entire crowd, only a few were familiar with the forest and its surroundings so these few became guides for the others.

I joined a group led by Neta Chernievsky, the son of Leibel and 'Sarake' (Sarah). Neta intended to reach his family, who had fled the night before to the Jamiolki Forest. This forest bordered the Bruszewo Forest, towards which my son Moshe (Maik) had gone yesterday. I hoped I would meet him there.

There were a number of men with their wives and children in our group. One of them was a learned rabbi from the *Gemara* study group, Rabbi Shimon Bar, who had recently come to live in Sokoly from Wysokie-Mazowieckie. He fled to the forest with his wife, son, and daughter. Another was the *Rebbitzen* [Rosenblum] from Sokoly with her five-year-old daughter 'Chayele' and son 'Yankele', a tot aged three, who was a "wonder boy" and knew prayers and sections of the *Chumash* from memory. The Rabbi's three daughters, aged 10, 12, and 14, had fled with their friends the day before to another forest. The Rabbi's oldest child, his 17-year-old son Berel, a genius in Torah, remained in one of the Lithuanian *yeshivot*. The Rabbi himself did not flee; he remained in Sokoly and certainly fell into the hands of the wild animals.

Neta Chernievsky saw that the group accompanying him was too big – with old people, women and children who were likely to frustrate his plans to reach his family so he tried to evade them. I saw that he was not happy with the situation. I tried to walk at a distance from him, always keeping him in sight because I felt that I could only reach my son with Neta's help. On our way, we came across other groups of Jews.

Suddenly, we heard the sound of a vehicle. Fear gripped us all. We thought that the Germans were combing the forest and had discovered us. In a second, we dispersed and hid behind bushes and trees. While doing so, I and a number of people from Neta's group found ourselves among another group of people, who were being led by Kalman Jaskolka, son of 'Shlomke'.

Neta Chernievsky took advantage of the confusion and quickly disappeared. Thus, he was freed of his unwanted companions.

When I found out that Jaskolka and his group were going in the opposite direction, my heart almost stopped I had no money with me. Moreover, I was afraid and trembled at every shadow lest it be a German or a Polish robber who would take everything away from me and leave me naked. Rumors spread that in all the villages the Germans posted signs warning the residents not to hide Jews in their houses. Any Christian caught hiding a Jew would be shot.

When the shadows of evening approached, my discouragement grew. New groups were no longer arriving from Sokoly. The few people who had arrived in the forest during the afternoon met up with Jaskolka's group. They told us that the Gestapo had shot a few Jews. The pharmacist and his young wife were among the first of these. This happened when they fled from the pharmacy owned by the Christian Kolesh on Kusczelna Street (*Tifla Gass*). The Jewish pharmacist thought that working in the Christian quarter in a pharmacy belonging to a Christian would save him, but he found out that the officers of the Gestapo were also searching for Jews among the Poles. He fled with his wife, carrying his infant daughter, up to the Christian cemetery, and from there they continued on towards Leibel Dinhas' forest [Kruszewo Forest]. A German lookout on the tower next to the cemetery saw them fleeing and shot and killed them. The baby fell from her mother's arms and was thrown into a farmer's wagon, which brought her, with other Jews, to be killed.

Two workers who arrived at the Kruszewo Train Station to go to work in Lapy arrived too late to flee with us and were shot. They were Avraham Lapchinsky, the son of Leibel the blacksmith, and

Hershel Schweitznik, the son of Tova Devorah the hat-maker and the grandson of 'Mosheke' Neiberg the butcher.

They told us that the Gestapo, with the assistance of the Polish police, had rounded up several hundred Jews, among them the Rabbi and Shmuel Leib the *shochet* as well as superior craftsmen, such as 'Zeidke' Berliner Sokoly's excellent tailor with his wife and two children. Zeidel did not sleep all night, as mentioned above. With all his remaining strength he tried to finish sewing a suit for the *Amstkommissar* so he could give it to him at six in the morning. Zeidel was certain that if he would be at the mayor's house with the suit in his hand at the fateful hour, the German would take pity upon him and his family and would not hand them over to the murderers.

The brothers Alter and Yisrael Sarnivitz, mechanic smiths, thought the same. They were the sons of 'Avrahamke' the blacksmith. They worked and slaved every day for the *Amstkommissar* and the *gendarmes*, who could not relinquish them because of their great efficiency at their work. They believed that the *Amstkommissar* would protect them and allow them and their families to remain in the town. The 'Yellow Satan' did indeed receive all the jobs that he ordered from the smiths, and immediately afterwards he handed his expert workers and their families over to the murderers.

Among the victims that first day in Sokoly was 'Shmuelke' Maik, my brother's 18-year-old son. At five o'clock in the morning, 'Shmuelke' was on his way to the Kruczewo Train Station, in order to join the workers going to Lapy. When he passed his parents' house he felt that he should peep in to see that everything was all right. He immediately saw that one of the shutters had been burst open and broken. He crawled inside and saw that bedding and other large possessions, whose absence was obvious, had been stolen. In his anger at the robbery, he forgot for a moment in what world we are living. He stayed there and began to interrogate the Christian neighbors. The Gestapo saw him and arrested him on the spot.

On the first day of the expulsion of the Jews from Sokoly, the Germans gathered 500 Jews with the help of the Polish police and brought them in farmers' wagons to the infamous military camp of the Tenth Division near Bialystok.

These were the "greetings" from Sokoly on the first day.

I searched among the fugitives for people going in the direction of the village where my son Moshe had gone. All of them answered that they were not familiar with the roads and paths and therefore were not going in any specific direction. If that was the case, how could I go by myself to my son when I did not even know the way? What fields and forests would I have to pass through, which paths should I tread, and which ones should I cross? From which Christian stranger should I ask the way, and from which one should I hide?

I was depressed and discouraged. In addition to my own situation, I also suffered from the people around me. The youths were impertinent and had long tongues...without a trace of politeness. Everyone was poor. Only three out of 25 people had an amount of 25 marks with them, a few had five marks each, and I had only four marks in my pocket. All the rest of the people in the group had no money at all.

On the first day, the people somehow managed to eat the portions of food that they had taken with them. I had the one kilogram of bread that my wife had sent to me at the Kruczewo Train Station. On that day, people ate almost nothing, because they were so upset by what was happening. The youths were very thirsty, but they had nothing to quench their thirst. A number of times the youths ran to the nearest settlement and drew water. At first, they drank plenty and filled bottles with water to bring back to the forest, but they did not stand up to the test and emptied them completely, returning to the group with empty bottles.

As Kalman Jaskolka was wandering in the Budziska Forest at the head of the group, he met 'Yossel' Malon's son. Malon used to sell to the residents of the surrounding villages. Both of them decided to enter a village near the house of a Christian acquaintance to find out what had happened to their families. They assumed that he might know something about them. Jaskolka and Malon turned aside and whispered in secret. The group understood that their guides were planning to elude them, because they had become an obstacle in their path…All their hearts were filled with despair…where will we go without a guide? Now we will be like sheep without a shepherd!

One of the workers in the group, a young man from Czyzewo named Buczka who had recently arrived in Sokoly, stepped forward and announced:

"Friends! It is forbidden for us to be left without Kalman Jaskolka! Without him, we will be lost in the depths of the forest like young lambs, since no one knows the paths. Where he goes, we will go!"

Without any discussion, everyone agreed with Buczka. When Kalman came back from consulting with his friend, he informed us that he wanted to enter the village to get news about his parents and family. Then Buczka turned to him and said, "Listen, Kalman! It is forbidden for you to leave an entire community at such a very difficult and fateful hour for all of us. You are the only guide! As long as we do not have another leader, please do not abandon us!"

Kalman answered, "How can so many lean on a single person and make it difficult for him when he longs to meet with his family, or when he has the possibility of finding a Christian acquaintance who will give him a bed in his house, or will be prepared to hide him during these difficult days? Does he have to sacrifice his life to a group of people?"

Buczka answered, "We will not make it difficult for you and we will not, G-d forbid, bother you if you find a refuge, but do not leave us until tomorrow. We hope to find another guide in your place and release you from the yoke that is too heavy for you, as you have said."

After arguing back and forth, it was decided to send three representatives from the group to accompany Kalman and Malon to the village: Buczka, Chaim Tzvi Rachekovsky and the son of Beila Gittel Djajeh, one of two brothers who were in our group.

Buczka had only settled in Sokoly in 1942. The Germans had expelled his wife and two children with the Jews of Czyzewo. Buczka himself escaped to his sister in Sokoly. He was a blacksmith – not educated, but an intelligent, serious young man with a talent for organization. In his childhood, Buczka had lived in a village. He was attached to the company of the *goyim* and the life of the farmers. He spoke Polish with a farmers' accent. In addition, he had the talent of fascinating any villager with his conversation and interesting him in such a way that he immediately became his loyal and faithful friend.

Chaim Tzvi Rachekovsky spoke pure Polish with literary expressions. However, he was far from being able to engage a villager in conversation. Only Buczka could do that.

The five of them, with Kalman Jaskolka at their head, entered the village and headed toward the Christian acquaintance's house. The owner of the house informed Jaskolka that the members of his family had indeed passed through the village that morning and had rested for a short time before continuing on their way. He said that he did not know any other details about his family. Regarding the situation in Sokoly, the farmer added that the *Amstkommissar* had a list of several hundred Jews who had fled from the town and apparently searches could be expected in the entire area.

Notices had been posted in all the villages – warnings to the residents that anyone hiding a Jew would be punished by death. Notices were also sent to each head of a village council (*Soltis*), stating that every farmer was obligated to inform the *Soltis* about where Jews could be found and to reveal the places where Jews were hiding. Anyone who handed a Jew over to the regime would be awarded a prize, and anyone hiding information about the location of Jews would be punished severely.

The warnings spread panic and fear among the farmers. Even close friends who had been prepared to help the Jews in their trouble were afraid of endangering their own lives and the lives of their families.

After our delegation returned from the village, everyone lay down to sleep behind thick bushes in the forest.

At about four o'clock in the morning, everyone awoke and rose from their forest "beds" in order to move further into the depths of the forest, far from the roads and far from people. After walking for a long time, the company sat down among the shrubbery to rest.

But then the problem of food arose because the bread they had taken with them for the trip was completely finished. On that fateful Sunday, the day of the expulsion, there had been difficulty in obtaining food in Sokoly, and people were not equipped with a sufficient amount of bread for more than one day. There had been some Jews who ate all their bread the previous night and had no more in their packs.

Buczka from Czyzewo now became the leader of the group of fugitives. All of them had regard for him and respected him. He was our representative when it was necessary to negotiate with a farmer about ordinary matters. He did this with the talent of an outstanding mediator, and in our eyes, every farmer was an officer or a senior official.... . Everyone in our group voluntarily obeyed Buczka's orders. When the problem of food was discussed, Buczka suggested that the people who were familiar with the paths should go first to the village so as not to get lost and fail their mission – which was our mission.

Accordingly, Jaskolka and Malon were sent to the nearby village for the purpose of buying as much bread as possible, because both of them had acquaintances there. At the same time, a number of youths were sent in a different direction through the forest to search for food in another nearby settlement.

After two hours, Jaskolka and Malon came back equipped with five kilograms of bread at the price of two marks per kilogram, double the price of bread in Sokoly on the day before the expulsion. The second group did not succeed in buying anything, but a kind-hearted farmer had given them two kilograms of bread free of charge.

It was difficult to divide the small amount of bread into 25 hungry mouths. Youths, as well as adults, pushed themselves in so as to receive larger portions. Noise and grabbing began, like in a pack of hungry wolves, and Jaskolka's and Malon's five kilograms of bread barely satisfied 12 people. The others had to wait for the second group, and their bread was divided into very small portions.

Buczka ordered the youth to knock on doors of the villagers and ask for bread. He thought that the people of the village would not refuse to give them bread, and that even the worst person would give a helping hand to the hungry and homeless lads. A few of the youths took Buczka's advice and spread out towards the villages. But the gentiles are not "merciful ones, the sons of merciful ones," and don't know the reasoning of a hungry boy who is fleeing from death. The lads returned, bringing with them only a few raw beets that they had started to eat in order to drive away their hunger pangs.

Again, the question arose of what now? What possibility would we have of living in the forest without a roof over our heads during the rainy days of autumn, with the storms and frost of the approaching winter, without any money?

What chances remained to us at all, at a moment when the Germans were preparing to make thorough searches and every villager was afraid to give shelter to a Jew, or at least to allow him to sleep one night in his threshing shed? Many of the people I was with dreamed at first of joining the Soviet partisans in the forest and fighting shoulder-to-shoulder with them against the common enemy – the Germans. Of course, they would not lack anything because the partisans are organized and they have hidden bunkers in which they have everything, including many weapons. That dream evaporated quickly because it became clear that the Soviet and Polish comrades-in-arms were nothing but gangs of robbers who, with their weapons in their hands, were attacking deserted, homeless Jews and pursuing them to death. They stripped the clothing from their poor victims and left them naked and barefoot in the heart of the forest.

This news reached our ears from Christian acquaintances who told us about the fate of a number of Jews from Sokoly who had been robbed in this manner by gangs of Polish "partisans" including a number of armed Russians. The gangs pulled the boots off their victims' feet, stripped them of vests and coats, and stole everything they had. There were some robbers who still had a spark of conscience and gave their victims rags to wear in place of the stolen clothing.

When they heard these things, the members of Buczka's group plotted how not to draw the attention of robbers to their "good" clothing. A few of them ripped out the seams of their clothes so they would appear worn-out and tattered; others sewed patches on the backs and sleeves of their clothes. They covered their boots with mud and rolled their pants over the boots to cover them. The rest of the people did not have to take these actions, because their clothing was worn and torn in any case, such that the entire group appeared miserable and pitiful.

While it was still daylight, a number of young Polish *goyim* appeared who apparently came in order to check whether it was worthwhile to "deal" with us. They looked at each one of us, measuring us from head to toe. As was his custom, Buczka immediately entered into a conversation with the uninvited visitors. He spoke to them in a friendly way, reaching a point in the conversation where he asked how to find shelter and whether it was possible to join the Polish partisan camps. The conversation continued for over half an hour. At the end, one of them asked if anyone had any cigarettes, and one of our people pointed to me. I was lying curled up under a tree, but I gave a cigarette to the one who asked. He made an effort to inspect me up and down, but since all our people looked worthless and the few *goyim* did not feel strong enough against dozens of us, they left us alone and politely went away.

We immediately left the place where they had found us and went deeper into the forest, worried that the lads would come back accompanied by armed robbers.

After walking a number of kilometers in the direction of the village Wienda, we sat down to rest a bit. A few of our lads ran with bottles in their hands to the nearby village in order to draw some water. They returned with their vessels full of fresh water and told us that on the way they had met Rachel Leah from Wienda with her entire family and other women and children. Jaskolka, Malon, and a few others from our group ran to meet the women in the hope that they might hear something about the fate of their families.

Rachel Leah from Wienda was born, educated and grew up in the village. She was married in Wienda and there gave birth to three sets of twins – all sons. A few years before the War broke out, Rachel Leah moved to Sokoly with her family. She ran a haberdashery business and her clients were the many villagers that she knew. During the German occupation, she dealt in smuggling food items from the country to the town. She was a superior businesswoman and knew how to mentally compute complicated accounts, even though she did not know how to read and write. She supplied all kinds of merchandise to the villagers and filled their needs. She looked like a typical village woman and spoke Polish with a country accent. This made it easy for her to go around in the villages without arousing suspicion that she was Jewish. Her first four sons were vigorous and talented boys.

After the expulsion from Sokoly, Rachel Leah was in the forest with her family not far from the village of her birth – Wienda. Her husband Meir from Wienda took care of the two infants, the twins, who were lying like chicks on feather pillows and covered with cushions. They nursed from bottles containing a mixture of milk and water. One of the sons tended to their only cow, which they had succeeded in bringing to the [Budziska] Forest. The cow had previously been among the herd of cows in Sokoly. Rachel Leah foresaw what would happen so she had brought the cow to her village before the Germans took the cows away from the Jews of Sokoly. Her older boys helped their mother sell the merchandise that remained to them from before the expulsion, and the middle son helped his father take care of the babies and carry them everywhere. Meir from Wienda had a large *siddur* that contained Psalms and daily selections from the Bible, *Mishna* and *Talmud*, and he studied it when the babies fell asleep or lay content, or in those moments when he was free of all work.

Women and children accompanied Rachel Leah in the forest. They ate her bread and the cooked food that friends in the village had prepared for her and which her sons had brought with them. The boys went there unhesitatingly and without fear, because they had grown up with the village lads and every corner was home to them.

With regard to the weather, I managed to endure the cold during the first two days of the expulsion, even though it was the end of the [Hebrew] month of *Cheshvan* [November]. Rain had not yet fallen.

When Jaskolka and those accompanying him met with Meir from Wienda, a continuous rain began to fall. Meir tightened the cushions around the babies. He did not have any news for us other than what we already knew.

I asked him to advise me how I could get to the village where my son was. He warned me not to dare to do that, because the Germans and Polish police were swarming around in all the villages near Sokoly, not to mention spies! And so, what could I do?

I envisioned rescue only if I could meet up with my son Moshe, but how could I do that when I had only four marks in my pocket which would barely be enough for bread for two days?! If I went out on a long trip to seek my son, where would I go? And with whom would I go, if nobody was going in that direction?

Jaskolka and his companions went out to the village again on the second evening, to find out the fate of their families and maybe to check out the possibility of finding temporary shelter for reasonable payment. However, this time they returned empty-handed. Every Christian was afraid to endanger himself with a death penalty. In any case, the possibility of finding shelter for many people could not be imagined. Once again, we all slept in the forest.

On Wednesday, November 4, Buczka evaluated our financial situation. Concerned that we should not suffer from hunger, he and Chaim Tzvi Rachekovsky asked everyone in the group to participate by contributing an amount of money so that they could order a stock of bread for at least one week and pay an acquaintance in the village to prepare hot food once a day. It became clear that the amount of money the comrades gave him was not enough and would suffice only for one day's food. Buczka and Jaskolka went alone to the village to make contact with a trustworthy person who would be willing to sell them food and cook for them. Rachekovsky and Malon went in a different direction for the same purpose.

Buczka and Jaskolka saw a farmer standing near his straw barn. They slowly approached and called him aside into the woods to talk. The man talked to them pleasantly and in a friendly manner, and they suggested the bread and food transaction to him. Buczka convinced the man that the matter would be completely secret and would not be seen by anyone. They would signal him, and then he would put the food under a certain bush. They explained that he would not be in any danger and that he would earn a nice amount of money every day.

Our friends further suggested to the good farmer that he allow our people to sleep in his straw barn, while taking special precautions. We would enter during the late hours of the night, when everyone in the surrounding area was asleep and leave before dawn. We would return to the forest at four o'clock in the morning. Of course the farmer would be paid in exchange for all these actions on our behalf. After a short hesitation, the farmer agreed. But he could give us a final answer only towards evening, after he consulted with his wife. In any case, he did not have any prepared bread, but food could be prepared within an hour.

Meanwhile, Rachekovsky and Malon returned, bringing with them five kilos of bread for 25 hungry mouths. The bread was divided into small, but equal portions.

After a short time, all the people in our group walked in the direction of the farmer's house and stopped some distance away. Our two leaders approached the bush, took the pot, and ran to meet us. We sat down on the ground, expecting to taste some food and enjoy a meal after three days of wandering. The food contained potatoes and mushrooms, and was sparse. When Buczka saw the contents of the pot, he immediately understood that it could not satisfy the hunger of 25 people, and he took care that it would be distributed as exactly and rightfully as possible.

The farmer was not prosperous and his family was small. The cooking pots in his house were the size his family needed. It was clear that the food did not satisfy us, but instead, over-stimulated our appetites. We went back to the forest hungrier than before. After the noon meal, we went deeper into the forest and again we sat down to consult each other and survey the situation.

Buczka made it clear that we did not have any choice but to split up into smaller groups, because there was no chance of convincing any farmer to provide shelter for 25 people for one night, and even more so for a longer period. Rain, snow, and frost could be expected any day, and it would be difficult to endure without a roof over our heads. On the other hand, a small group of people has a better chance of squeezing into some warm corner if they would come across villagers with some human heart.

Therefore, Buczka suggested that the youths and older men whose families had fled to other forests should leave tomorrow morning in order to reunite with their families. Who knows what awaits them on the way? But there is no choice! They will have to go from one group to another that they meet on the way. They will ask and investigate in order to find signs and directions to the place where their dear ones are.

Everyone realized that Buczka was right and that his opinion should be considered. But how could we go without a guide? Would the present guides, Jaskolka and Malon, go together in one direction?

Towards evening, Buczka came to the village farmer who was asked whether we could sleep in his straw barn.

He answered that he was willing to endanger himself and accept five adults, but Heaven forbid, no children because they are accustomed to chatter and run around, and this is extremely dangerous. However, he did agree that all of us could sleep there one night on condition that we arrive after ten p.m. at night, lie down quietly, and cover ourselves with heaps of straw. No chatting, coughing, or snoring and no living soul in the straw barn after four o'clock in the morning.

At ten p.m., we stole one by one into the straw barn in absolute silence, following the villager's instructions. We were careful not to say a word nor make the slightest sound. At four o'clock in the morning, when total darkness still reigned outside, we left the barn and returned into the depths of the forest.

Buczka informed us that he could no longer worry about all the people in the group and suggested that everyone worry about himself with regard to food and a place to sleep. Of course, everyone felt depressed and discouraged and saw no way out. In Buczka, we lost a friend who was concerned about us. We lost a leader and representative, a planner who carried out his plans and awakened hope and confidence in all our hearts. Now, he joined up with the two guides and two others, the most well-to-do comrades, who formed a group of five. Apparently, they had spoken previously with the farmer, and we knew that they would sleep permanently in his straw barn and be under his protection.

On Thursday, November 5, 1942, the fourth day of wandering in the forests, seven more members of our group left us, all former neighbors. They decided to go from forest to forest in the direction of Sokoly in order to look for their families. They entered one village in order to supply themselves with bread and by chance they met up with former Jewish neighbors who gave them complete and exact information about where their relatives were.

Other members of our group joined Rachel Leah from Wienda and her entourage.

That afternoon, an old, widowed, Christian woman who lived in a remote cottage, approached those of us who remained in the forest and asked for a Jewish boy to work for her as a shepherd. She promised to take good care of him and to provide him with everything. There was a nine-year-old boy, the son of Beila Gittel Djajeh, the grandson of Meir Gedalia the builder, who spoke Polish well and looked Christian. With him in the group was his bar-mitzva aged brother. The boys' father was living in America.

Buczka did us one more good service before he left. He spoke with the old widow and convinced her to take five more lads into her home; that is, the boy's brother and four of their friends. The woman asked where the boys' parents were from, and it turned out that she knew them well. From Feivel Lev, father of 'Baruchke', she was accustomed to buy groceries; from the parents of 'Shmuelke' Rabinek she bought leather goods, and Yisrael Kapitovsky made shoes for her.

Buczka also did not disappoint me. "His" farmer agreed to take me at sunset to the village of Bruszewo – to my son Moshe Maik. What remained was to take care of three 12-year-old boys. 'Chaimke' Goldin was the grandson of 'Moshele', a quiet boy, his parents' only son, handsome and successful. The other two were the sons of the shoemaker Todras from Wysokie-Mazowieckie who came to Sokoly when the War broke out. Buczka spoke to the boys and told them that they should follow the farmer who would take me to Bruszewo. On no account were they to let him know that they were there. When they got closer, they would go on their own because they were familiar with the area.

The boys liked the idea. 'Chaimke' said that he knew the forest near Sokoly well, and that in Bruszewo there were people he knew who frequently came to his father's oil-press. A Christian farmer by the name of Macziewski was a close friend of his parents and lived in Bruszewo. 'Chaimke' himself had visited Macziewski's house a number of times. The Todras boys reasoned that from Bruszewo they could get to the Ros and Mazury Forests and that there they might meet people from Wysokie-Mazowieckie whom they knew. They also knew hundreds of Christians there as well as the paths. Again and again, Buczka reminded the boys to keep their distance from me so that the farmer would not sense their presence. At the same time, they were to watch out so as not lose sight of me.

I asked Buczka how much the transportation would cost, emphasizing that I only had two marks in my pocket, along with two packages of tobacco from Curacao (the price of each of these being four marks). Buczka comforted me that everything would be all right and I should not worry. I handed over the two packages of tobacco to Jaskolka.

The farmer arrived at five o'clock in the evening. Buczka asked him the price and he said he wanted ten marks for his trouble. Buczka convinced him to take five marks from 'Old Maik', because he was poor and without any more money. The farmer agreed because five marks was still good earnings. I must point out that he was a wonderful, good-hearted man, who wanted with all his soul to help the persecuted Jews. There were few like him among the Poles, and it is very regrettable that I do not remember his name.

My benefactor, the farmer, requested that I walk about a hundred paces behind him so that no one would suspect him because his life depended upon it. When we had distanced ourselves from the place, suddenly the three boys got too close to me. I begged them not to interfere with me, not to endanger the farmer with their presence, and that they keep their distance. They promised that as soon as we reached Bruszewo they would disappear from my horizon like the night and go their own way. It is already dark, they said, and no one will see us, so we will walk closer to you in order not to lose your footsteps.

Despite all the warnings, the farmer caught sight of the boys and explained to them how great the danger was to him and to them. The boys begged him to have pity and not drive them away and that they would soon go their own way.

The farmer, my guide, would occasionally stop and with trepidation look around in every direction. The boys angered him because they broke their promise by not keeping their distance from us. There were moments when he wanted to get out of this dangerous situation and go home. He talked to himself and cursed the day that he had agreed to such a crazy adventure that threatened him with death. He became confused and went around in circles... The straightest line to Bruszewo was about five kilometers. The farmer had estimated that it would take us about two hours to get there, yet here we were, already walking for three hours and far from our destination.

We saw lights in the distance. When we came closer the farmer told me to wait while he went to see where we were. It turned out that this was the village of Jamiolki. German guards were standing next to the bridge at the entrance to the village... . The farmer came back, trembling and frightened. It was a great miracle that they did not see him. We went in another direction, and again saw lights, only this time it was from the village of Piszczaty, which is near Bruszewo. For safety's sake it was necessary to enter the village from the side. In order to prevent any suspicion, my benefactor said that he was looking for a shepherd from Bruszewo who had been recommended to him. We finally, arrived in Bruszewo after walking for five hours. Even in peacetime, you could not find anyone, even the neediest person, to travel 15 or 16 kilometers for a wage of five marks. I saw the man as an angel who was sent from Heaven to rescue me from distress.

We reached the edge of the village and the farmer asked who would pay him for his trouble? I answered that I had given Jaskolka two packages of tobacco for him and I added ten cigarettes. The man parted from me amicably. He was willing to bring me to the center of the village, but it was already ten o'clock at night and he had a long way to travel to reach home.

The Todras boys put on a very pitiful show for me. They did not let me alone for a minute which could have caused our plan to fail. I advised them to spread out and go to the homes of their acquaintances, as they had already agreed to do, and ask for bread and permission to sleep in their barns. Tomorrow they could continue on to the Idzki Forest where they might find their parents. I added that they would not improve their situation by following me, because it was unimaginable that anyone in the village would agree to take care of all four of us and that during the course of events and carelessness, they were likely to bring destruction upon me and upon themselves. My words did not convince them.

Meanwhile, the dogs began barking more and more every minute, until there was a whole chorus of barking. Hearing this canine symphony, people started coming out of their houses to see who the visitors who had arrived were. Maybe they were robbers? In the midst of all the confusion, the boys became emboldened and entered one of the cottages to ask for some water. The farmer was worried because they had come inside his house so he brought a pitcher of water outside. He warned that Germans were walking around in the village.

At that moment I approached the farmer to ask him where the Kalinowski farm was located. To my great happiness, the man was a confidant of the villager at whose house my son Moshe was staying. Both of them belonged to the *A.K.* underground organization.

The man knew me personally, but I did not know him at all. It became clear that he had been accustomed to buy schoolbooks for his children and sometimes a Polish newspaper from me.

With a friendly smile, he said to me, "Mr. Maik? Good evening! It is good that I met you. I will bring you to your son. Ho! Ho! Your son will be very happy. He already knows that they took his mother away; at least he has one of his parents!"

He put his arm into mine and pulled me forward, but he sensed that the boys were following in our footsteps. He whispered that I should send them in another direction. Staczek is very careful and it is best that no one should suspect, Heaven forbid, that a Jew is under his roof. No one in the village would even think about hiding Jews, except for Staczek's faithful friend. He is certain that because of the boys, his friend will not open his door to me. I hid my anger and quietly turned to the boys:

"What's with you, they won't let me enter the house either, and this will not bring you any benefit. Try to knock on the doors of your parents' friends, where you have a better chance. The man who is hiding my son is endangering his life; he is very careful and is afraid of any slight sound. You see that my son wasn't even able to save his mother."

The Todras boys did not want to listen to what I said. They threatened that if I would not allow them to come with me, they would cause such a scandal that my son would be driven out and his hiding place exposed to everyone.

The Christian farmer interrupted and told the boys that they should not cause any harm to Mr. Maik. He told them to go to the home of Staczek's brother, not too far away. He promised them that the owner would not refuse to let them sleep in the barn.

Chaim Goldin, a lad who was calmer than his two friends, tried to reason with them, saying that they really would not benefit from all this and that they were just putting an obstacle in the way of 'Old Maik'. Whereas my pleading with the boys did not help, the brief words of Chaim Goldin did. Without saying goodbye, the youngsters turned away from us and went in the direction of the farm belonging to Staczek's brother Palek.

The Christian farmer complimented me and introduced himself as Antony Maczuszko. After walking a short distance, we reached Kalinowski's farm, where I was supposed to find my son.

We entered the house. Kalinowski, the 70-year-old owner of the farm, had retired for the night. Maczuszko sat down next to him on the bed and introduced me, adding a few warm words about the difficult times, troubles and consolations. I asked Kalinowski where his sons were. He told me they would come back in a little while.

I sipped water. I had not eaten for 36 hours, but to ask for some slices of bread was beneath my dignity. I drank more water from thirst, hunger, fatigue, nervousness, and tension. I sat on a bench and waited. I sat there for hours, but Kalinowski's sons did not yet return. Maczuszko had gone home a long time ago. The old man suggested that I lie down on the bench and put out the kerosene lantern.

In the darkness, I pondered the miracles and wonders that G-d had done for me, sending good angels in the images of two Christians to light my way, which was planted with thorns and thistles. One, who brought me along a difficult and dangerous path in exchange for two packages of tobacco; and the second, Maczuszko had come out of his house late at night to give water to the boys. He recognized me and agreed to bring me here. Without these miraculous events, I would have died from hunger and thirst in the forest. By nature, I am fearful and lack confidence. I would not have been able to take the initiative to reach my son Moshe Maik on my own.

I grew tenser every moment; I was very excited about meeting my son. When would he come already? Where was he now? At four o'clock in the morning Kalinowski's youngest son, Palek, came in.

I asked him, "Where is Staczek?"

"He is not home, he will come back later. Meanwhile, you have to go to the forest! It is very dangerous these days for a Jew to be in the house!"

I asked Palek to show me a place to hide until Staczek came because the forest near the house was relatively small and the trees were too sparse to hide there without being found. But Palek answered me angrily:

"It is not my business to hide Jews and I cannot show you every place on our farm. It is forbidden for you to stay in our house another minute!"

As I got up to leave the house, Kalinowski's oldest son, Jozef, arrived at a run. He was a good friend of mine who lived at some distance from there. He made a lot of noise and tumult, and told me that before midnight, some Jewish boys had knocked on his door when his family was asleep and said that they had arrived together with 'Old Maik' from Bruszewo, and that Maik went to Kalinowski's house to meet his son.

Jozef raised his voice and yelled at his father, "How could he give permission to Staczek to hide a Jew in their house? If the neighbors know about it, the Germans will immediately know about it too and they won't hesitate to destroy us and burn down our farm. From the moment that those boys came to me, I haven't closed my eyes!"

In anger, he grabbed a pole and fell upon me to beat me. He screamed: "Get out of here as quickly as possible; otherwise I will break your head open!"

Like an arrow, I fled from the house. My heart was beating very fast. I hid behind the cowshed and looked through the cracks, prepared for and expecting the arrival of Staczek, who would take me to my son Moshe's hiding place.

Jozef went outside to the yard to see where I had gone. He saw me, and I had to flee further away. To my joy, Staczek just then arrived. Apparently they had regard for and respected him, and the proof of this was that as soon as he had arrived they calmed down and were quiet.

Staczek took me to the nearby forest and explained to me politely that he could not take me to meet Moshe who was hidden in a safe bunker which could not be approached during daylight hours. He pointed to a place dug out in the ground and told me to lie there without fear until dark. He added words of encouragement and promised to bring me some food. If one of the shepherds should happen to pass by, I should hide in the bushes on the side. The shepherds would not cross the woods that day. I unhesitantly followed Staczek's instructions. I lay in the pit all that day, curled up and trembling from every leaf that fell and every shadow. At noon, Staczek brought me cooked food and a large slice of bread.

After a fast of two days, the food revived my soul and sustained my heart. I waited impatiently for nightfall, with praise to G-d that I had merited the yearned-for meeting with my son. With great emotion, Moshe and I recounted everything that had happened to us in recent days from the moment we had parted.

We were still talking when Staczek stopped us, saying, "*Nu, nu*, it is enough for today that you have met and you told each other enough about everything. Now 'Old Maik' must return to his hiding place in the forest, where he came from, and you, 'Mushko' [Moshe], must return to your bunker."

"No!" said 'Moshele'. I will not leave my old father alone and without support. He will be next to me wherever I am and wherever I go. If you refuse to allow *Abba* to stay with me in the bunker, you will force me to find another hiding place."

There was a moment of silence. A thought passed through my mind, and I suggested to Staczek that he agree to let me stay in exchange for all the valuables that we had left with the Soviet Doctor in Sokoly.

Apparently the suggestion intrigued Staczek. The expression on his face changed, and he invited us both to come to his house. After we ate a tasty dinner at his table, he brought us to another bunker in the forest where there were a number of radio receivers, automatic weapons, and a pocket flashlight. These things had previously been under Moshe's care. The floor of the bunker was covered with a thick layer of straw.

We went down into the deep bunker, and Staczek sealed the entrance with a heavy cover and disguised it. Without saying another word, he went back home. I felt that we were buried alive, and it was very difficult for me to breathe the suffocating air. There was no possibility of opening the cover alone from inside. I was surprised that Moshe [Maik] did not pay attention to the lack of air to breathe… apparently, from experience and lack of choice, he had become accustomed to the situation.

Staczek brought us food twice a day. He brought a morning meal and ten o'clock and an evening meal between seven and eight o'clock at night. At those times, the cover over the bunker was opened for half an hour, a time to eat and go outside to relieve ourselves. We then immediately returned to our underworld and the cover was put down over our heads. Twice a day would perhaps be enough ventilation for one person, but for two of us it was too suffocating to bear.

The first night in the bunker passed somehow for me, after I had not slept for several nights. Around four in the afternoon, I felt sick from the terrible suffocation. I was afraid I would not hold out until Staczek would come and open the cover between seven and eight o'clock. I spasmodically swallowed air, and it was a good thing that Staczek was not late in coming. Otherwise, I doubt I would have succeeded in bearing the suffocation.

Staczek revealed that Moshe's friends had arrived and wanted to see him. We went out of the bunker accompanied by Staczek and down into a potato cellar to see the guests.

Before us stood six of the nine Plut brothers, the sons of Naftali (the son-in-law of Aharon Eliyahu, the blacksmith); Mordechai Moshe Blustein; Yaakov ['Yankel'] Seines and the two Goldberg brothers (the sons of 'Yisraelke' the blacksmith), my cousins. The oldest of the Goldberg brothers, 'Avrahamel', aged 30, was a carpenter by profession, and had experience in blacksmith work. He was a skilled worker and quick of movement. The day before the expulsion, he went with Moshe Lev (Rashke's son) and his family, among them Moshe Lev's wife's sister Beila, her father, Chaim Baruch Goldwasser, and their children, to the village of Kruczewo.

Moshe Lev was well established and had merchandise and plenty of dollars. He had known many of the farmers since the Soviet occupation, when he was the manager of the Sokoly area dairies. In his position, he would travel in the surrounding villages to receive the milk and butter quota from the farmers for the regime.

As the possessor of many resources and money, Moshe Lev was full of hope that he would find shelter with his farmer friends and rescue his family from death. His hope was dashed when not even one of the residents would give a helping hand to many people in trouble. Possibly they would have hidden him alone, but in spite of the large sums he was prepared to pay them to rescue his large family, his efforts did not succeed.

The family wandered for a few days in the forests and villages. It became clear that all of them fell into the hands of the German murderers during the first week after the expulsion. Moshe Lev himself succeeded in fleeing back to the forest and afterwards, he reached a Christian acquaintance who sheltered him. Moshe knew how to persevere under the most difficult situations, and not to be at a loss. He always knew how to find a way out of distress. As long as he was with his large family, his hands were tied, but when he remained alone, he certainly would not be lost.

My cousin 'Avrahamel' [Goldberg] had been employed by the *Amstkommissar* before the expulsion. He and his brother Chaim 'Yudel' had managed that evening to hide many of their possessions in pits, before they escaped to the Idzki Forest. They wandered in the forests with groups of fugitives, from place to place and village to village. They came across gangs of Polish and Soviet robbers, who took their money and possessions. The robbers even stole the women's clothing and left them almost naked and barefoot. Among the victims who were robbed in this manner were: Chane Kashevitz, the son of Kaladshe's 'Yisraelke', and Malka Ravches, Mendel Fleer's wife. During the Soviet occupation, Mendel had been sent to Siberia, and it was rumored in Sokoly that he was no longer alive. The poor ones who were robbed felt so degraded and depressed that they turned themselves over to the Germans, preferring death to living like pursued dogs.

The Goldberg brothers were miraculously rescued from the gangs. They assumed that Moshe Maik was with the Kalinowski family in Bruszewo, and they therefore walked in that direction. We must not forget that the Goldberg brothers were members of the organization that had sent Moshe to purchase weapons and that he had returned from his errand. The same thing with the six Plut brothers: all of them were young men, as strong as pine trees and all were members of the same organization. The two families of brothers, Goldberg and Plut, weren't together at the beginning, but they met each other on the way to Bruszewo in the area around Dworkie-Noski.

Moshe Maik had previously hinted to Staczek that his friends from the youth defense organization, who had given him 150 marks for the purpose of buying weapons, were likely to arrive. Apparently these friends would come for the purpose of consultations. To others, Staczek would certainly deny that Moshe Maik was there, but being informed by Moshe of their possible arrival, Staczek was willing to grant his request.

On Saturday night, November 7, 1942 -- the sixth day since the expulsion of the Jews from Sokoly -- the members of the *A.K.* organization gathered with Moshe Maik for a talk. They told Moshe what had happened during those six days. They also gave him details about what had happened to 'Shmuelke' Maik and repeated the already-known story about how Shmuel had walked

133

past his house and the scandal with the neighbors. Shmuel had thought nothing bad would happen to him because he was a railroad worker in Lapy. He had confidence, bordering on indifference, that the Polish police, and even the local Germans who were accustomed to frequently visit, would assist him. It is unnecessary to add that Shmuel's father, as a watchmaker and goldsmith, did a lot of craftwork for these *goyim*. It therefore was no surprise that he had confidence in all of them and in his Polish neighbors, with whom he had a good relationship. He thought that they would not harm him, but there was a "good neighbor" who did not hesitate to hand him over to the *gendarmes*. Thus it was that 'Shmuelke' fell into their murderous hands.

One of the Plut brothers told us that the Polish policeman, Kanofka the shoemaker, was the one who shot Baruch Shadlinsky who had tried to flee to the forest. Baruch was the pampered only son of the wealthy carpenter Hershel Shadlinsky and the grandson of the carpenter Elia Burak. Kanofka shot him when there were no Germans around merely to satisfy his animal appetite to murder a Jew.

During that meeting it became clear that in the existing situation there was no possibility of organized underground activities. The Christians would not sell any weapons to Jews at this time and, in any case, the entire amount of money in our possession totaled only 250 marks. As long as the Jews remained in Sokoly it was easier to equip us with weapons, but now the Poles wouldn't sell us any since they were concerned that the bullets were likely to harm themselves. In summary, it was decided to find a temporary bunker where it would be possible to live during daylight hours and go out during the night to the villages in order to supply ourselves with food. We asked Staczek if he would agree to allow us to build a bunker in his forest for a reasonable sum. His answer was a suggestion that we hide among the haystacks in the field at the edge of the forest, but this did not appear possible to us because of the cold and rain.

In consideration of the young men's position and under the autumnal weather conditions, Staczek promised that the next day he would search for an appropriate location in the forest for a bunker. Meanwhile, all of us remained to sleep at Staczek's farm. The Goldberg brothers entered the straw barn and disappeared among the haystacks, the Plut brothers and I remained all night in the potato cellar, and Staczek took Moshe Maik back to his own bunker.

The Pluts bought several kilograms of bread from Kalinowski and returned, meanwhile, to their old place where the members of their family remained. Before they left, they advised that we should strengthen our connection with the Goldbergs and build a large, joint bunker for both families, but they still hesitated and wanted to consider the basics of the matter before they decided. Meanwhile, they remained for one day in the Bruszewo Forest nearby .

In another conversation with Staczek, 'Avrahamele' Goldberg suggested that he agree that they build themselves a bunker for four people, in other words, for the two Maiks and the two Goldbergs. According to the 'Avrahamele' plan, the entrance to the bunker would be from one of the farm buildings, such as the sheep pen, the cowshed or the stable, so that footprints would not be left in the snow. They would do all the handwork connected with the bunker themselves and without bothering Staczek.

In return for his consent, the brothers promised to give Staczek two expensive coats, two suits of clothing made of expensive fabric from the famous *Beiletz* [textile] factory, two excellent watches, and a wagon for two horses. Staczek wrinkled his forehead and closed his eyes, deep in thought. The suggestion perhaps was attractive to him, but he decided to consult his brother Palek and answer the next day.

The next day, the Plut brothers came back to buy bread. In the potato cellar, they also suggested to Staczek that he give them permission to build a bunker for their family. Staczek immediately refused their suggestion because of the great danger involved. The noise of the presence of a lot of people would definitely arouse the neighbors' suspicion, and then a situation would arise that was laden with tragedy. Not having a choice, they remained there that night to sleep in the cellar. Staczek prevented my son Moshe from going out [of his bunker] to meet the men in the cellar.

The next day, Monday, at four o'clock in the morning, the Pluts got up to leave and begged Avrahamele to go with them and to plan a large family bunker somewhere else. Goldberg refused to speak, knowing that the danger was too great for a large number of people.

When the Plut brothers went away, Staczek took me to my son's bunker. On the way, I tried to convince him to accept the Goldberg brothers, because the danger from two men, or four, was the same. It is true that the supply of food would be double, but the payment he would receive would be several times greater. From what he said it was obvious that he was sorry that he had refused to give a positive answer until now, and he was worried that if they would go somewhere else, he would lose all the expensive things that they had promised to give him as payment.

He took off the cover and I went down into the bunker. Towards evening, I again suffered from a lack of air. I breathed with difficulty and waited impatiently for Staczek to come and take off the cover. He came only at nine o'clock in the evening, and then I felt a lot better. Today the first snow had fallen and there was concern that footprints leading to the bunker would accumulate when he brought us food. In light of the coming events that would certainly involve danger, we came out of the bunker and entered the potato cellar, where we would sleep that night. During the night, Staczek would plan a new shelter for us, which would have an entrance from the sheep pen. In the first stage, the area would be enough for two people, and when the Goldberg brothers would join us, it could be widened for four.

We ate the evening meal in the cellar. I remained there, and Staczek took Moshe with him to help him with the work preparing our new place. The digging of a bunker with an area of four square meters and a height of one meter was finished at three o'clock in the morning. The digging work was very difficult because the ground was hard and the soil was rocky, but it was already possible for two to lie down inside the bunker.

We brought in straw and spread it all over the bottom. On Tuesday, the ninth day after the expulsion, we were in our new bunker. As a cover, Staczek used a few boards, upon which he put some earth and sheep droppings from the pen. Our new "home" was a lot smaller than the previous one, but even so I did not suffer as much from suffocation and a lack of air to breathe, like I did in the bunker in the woods, possibly because of the thinner cover and the thinner layer of earth.

Now, Staczek was closer to us for supplying food and he would no longer have to sneak out, away from everyone's eyes, for a distance of several hundred meters. Inside the yard, no suspicion would be raised, and carrying the food was similar to the activity of feeding the cattle and sheep.

That same evening, the cover to the hole above us was opened and Staczek informed us that the Goldbergs had arrived and we should dig that night for the purpose of widening the bunker for four people. After the meal, we crawled outside and the work of digging began. As mentioned above, the ground was as hard as a rock. The soil taken out had to be moved about 50 meters away and poured into pits in a manner that would leave no traces. By four o'clock in the morning, they succeeded in removing one cubic meter of earth. It was necessary to stop working, because the farmers were awaking from their sleep and it was forbidden for Jews to be seen on their horizons. The next night we continued to dig harder, but we still hadn't completed the plan for the minimal amount of space: 1.2 x 4 x 4 m.

It snowed again on Thursday and we were warned not to create any footprints when taking out dirt. Meanwhile, we had to stop digging and busied ourselves with interior arrangements. We fitted boards to the ceiling area and stood supports under them.

More work remained around the bunker. We had to move the opening to another location, because in the event of a search, the opening into the sheep pen was likely to lead to our exposure. It was decided to locate a toilet above the upper hole so that nobody would imagine that there was a bunker here.

On Thursday, the eleventh day after the expulsion, we began to make a new entrance to our bunker. A square pit, 80 cm. wide and of sufficient length, was dug. The digging was done from the inside outward. Actually, almost all the work was done from the inside. From above, the painstaking work of hands working underground in a struggle for their lives could not be detected. At three o'clock in the morning, the entrance was ready. Now it remained to bring a dilapidated old toilet structure, which had previously stood in another place in the same yard, and erect it over the pit we had dug.

Avraham Goldberg, the carpenter, installed the toilet seat over the bunker hole exactly as it had been before. Staczek was not satisfied with this. Being very careful, he thought that somebody undesirable was likely to use the toilet, the board beneath it would move from its place, and the secret would be revealed. Therefore, he commanded us to install a floor made of a single, rectangular piece that would be sized to the measurements of the structure and which would have no possibility of moving, and to attach two rings at the sides of the floor so it would be easy to remove and replace. And that wasn't enough, because the floor had to be covered with dirt so as to give it the appearance of the dirt outside.

'Avrahamele' did everything as requested. 'Shmeig' (that is how Staczek pronounced the word "*shneig*," which means "snow," and sometimes he was called by that name) took care that everything artificial would appear to be natural, and even the Devil himself would not reveal the bunker and its entrance. Our excellent carpenter 'Avrahamel' later installed a table and shelves on the wall of the sheep shed where the former entrance had been, where personal things and tools could be placed. All the work was done during the night, when it was possible to move and saw boards, move dirt, bring water, and relieve ourselves. From five o'clock in the morning until nine o'clock at night, we lay in the dark. The entire day seemed like a long night. We could only see the sunlight for a few minutes in the morning, during the moments when 'Shmeig' took off the cover of the opening so as to bring us food. We had to be careful not to cough, not to snore, and to keep silent; not to let any sound escape to the outside to arouse suspicion that here there are buried live creatures, Jews who are sentenced to death.

Slowly, slowly, the days became colder and frozen. 'Shmeig' no longer allowed us to dig in the ground. 'Avrahamel' of the golden hands was not accustomed to, nor could, sit and do nothing. He always found himself something to do inside the bunker – something to install or something to improve – for the comfort of all of us.

Hidden Treasures Recovered

During these empty nights without any work, the Goldberg brothers decided to try to reach Sokoly and retrieve a few of the treasured possessions they had hidden in their house and left with their Christian acquaintances. They wanted to be able to start paying Staczek as they had agreed and as he deserved and also to buy food.

On November 16th, after midnight, the Goldbergs left the bunker and set out on foot towards Sokoly. They tried to convince my son Moshe to go with them, but I opposed this. I did not agree at all that my only son would endanger his life by possibly meeting up with a German patrol or a Polish guard.

Their trip in both directions took three and a half hours. They brought back with them a feather pillow and cover, a blanket, a few clothes, shoes, and underwear. They swore that they did not even see a dog in the town.

The next night, Moshe also went out with them. I could not hold him back any more. All of them came back at three o'clock in the morning, thank G-d. This time they brought the most necessary household utensils.

The third night I also accompanied them in order to bring away the furs and expensive items that I had hidden under the floor in my house. It was a dark night and a strong wind was blowing. We looked in all directions and listened whether anyone's footsteps could be heard. We went in zigzags through fields and woods, and we avoided going past places where there were dogs.

Finally, we arrived at my house. Chaim 'Yudel' stood guard and looked in all directions to make sure no one was coming. 'Avrahamel' and Moshe opened the floor and took out the furs and the rest of the things.

I stood on a table and took out spoons, forks, knives, and wine cups – all of them silver – from a hidden hole in the chimney of the stove. These were lying in a cloth bag.

All over the house there were signs of a robbery that had been precisely carried out. The clothes closets, the sideboard, and the kitchen shelves were empty. Hundreds of books, certificates of all kinds, family pictures, and artwork that the robbers did not want, were all over the floor. I took only the things I needed the most. I was afraid to light a candle. The windows were broken and the shutters were removed from their frames. I was worried that someone would see that Jews were inside the house. Moshe carried a sack full of clothes that he took out from under the floor. 'Avrahamel' took a second, similar sack and we quickly left the house.

From the priest's pasture behind my house, the new *beit midrash* and synagogue were visible. I saw a light in the windows. Later I learned that that was where the Jews were gathered who had fled, but were caught in the area around Sokoly after having wandered around in suffering and hunger for two weeks. Gangs of Poles and Russians robbed a few of them. Naked, barefoot and hungry, in their despair they handed themselves over into the hands of the Germans. Christian witnesses related that the crying and wailing voices of the Jews who were sentenced to death broke the hearts of everyone passing by. Woe to the ears that hear such things!

The Goldberg brothers also entered their house, which was behind the bathhouse, for the purpose of taking some of their hidden possessions. My son Moshe went with them and I stayed in a hidden corner behind a wall with the sacks.

Suddenly, I saw the shadows of five men. The fear of death seized me and my body started to tremble. My heart started to beat faster. My companions in the Goldberg house also saw the five forms, and hid themselves.

Luckily, the images went farther away and disappeared from sight. Apparently, these were Polish thieves who were seizing abandoned Jewish possessions. I breathed easier. We grabbed our bundles and escaped with our lives. On the way, there was a storm that blew us in every direction, but the fear that had attacked us earlier pushed us to run as fast as we could. At three o'clock in the morning, we arrived safely at our bunker.

After a pause of one night, our young men decided without my knowledge to go to Sokoly again. Their estimation was that as long as the gangs of robbers had not managed to empty all the abandoned and deserted Jewish homes, it was worthwhile to take out of there as much as possible. We opened our hearts to Staczek for the purpose of getting him to join our nighttime adventures.

Since we knew many places where there were Jewish homes in which many things were hidden that were worth taking, it was reasonable not to abandon the matter, and to gradually bring the possessions into our joint ownership.

Staczek agreed to the suggestion and added that it was logical to bring in two more friends so as to be able to carry out the plan in all its details. His friends brought with them two rifles, two pistols, and a few hand grenades. If we meet up with Germans or the Polish police, they would be able to fight them successfully.

On Thursday, November 20th, at 11:30 p.m., Staczek called our boys from the bunker to go with him to Sokoly. Three young men, armed with weapons, were with him.

All of them reached Sokoly without any problems or obstacles. First, they entered the apartment of Shlomo Kravchevitz, the tailor. Two of the armed Poles stood guard in front of the house, and the rest of them went up to the attic. There, they found bundles packed in sacks and suitcases. The group carefully and quickly began to take the bundles downstairs. Staczek whispered to the Jews, that on the way back to the bunker we should keep a distance from him and his two companions, and that we should leave part of the booty in a place he would point out, so that he would be able to gather it later without having to give a portion to his two friends.

Our boys were faithful to Staczek in heart and soul, and they tried to fulfill all his wishes. While they were still up in the attic, they gave Staczek a bundle of expensive fabrics, products of the *Vidzabeska Manufactura* factory, out of sight of his two friends. He stuffed the fabrics into his sack. In another place, they gave him a package of tablecloths and other items, without his Christian friends' finding out. Outside, it was pitch dark. Staczek walked near the Jews so as to hide his expensive booty from the eyes of his Christian partners. When he reached the village, he left many things in hiding. In Staczek's house, they started to divide the booty. Staczek took for himself a reasonable portion as the main instigator of the operation and as the representative of "his Jews". His Christian friends also received good, nice portions, in comparison to the three partners who were satisfied with relatively less.

The following night, Staczek no longer had his Christian friends join the project of going to the town. He told them that he wouldn't continue to endanger his life by going at night to Sokoly. However, he brought his brother Palek, and together with the three Jews, they went again to Sokoly. The project succeeded this time as well, and our heroes brought back five additional sacks of clothing and various items. 'Shmeig' [Staczek] and his brother took half of the booty, and the three Jews together took the other half.

The next night, the five of them went out to Sokoly for the third time and again they brought back bundles of things that they divided between them the same way as the night before. In Maik's house there still remained dishes, bowls, cups, mugs, pots and other kitchen utensils, but at this stage Staczek refused to continue the activity.

Among the possessions of the three nights, there was a box of jewelry, gold and precious stones, a long gold chain, a necklace, pearl beads, gold hand watches, bracelets, earrings and gold rings set with diamonds. Staczek wanted to know how to divide the jewelry between all of them. The Jews told him: "For the present, all of it will remain in your hands...in the future; we will make an accounting and even it out among us..."

From the three night operations in Sokoly, Staczek accumulated for himself expensive winter coats, magnificent furs, suits of clothing, shoes, boots, shirts, bedding, and much more, all valued at tens of thousands of marks. Within a week he became a wealthy man.

The Goldberg brothers and Moshe Maik divided the items they brought from Sokoly among themselves and put the items into the bunker.

First, they wanted to pay their debt to Staczek for the bunker as they had promised him. It is true that at the outset he wanted to support Moshe Maik without payment since his friends in the *A.K.* organization asked him to shelter Moshe and provide for all his needs at their expense. Moshe was regarded in the entire area as being an excellent electronic technician and as such he was essential to the very existence of the organization. Nevertheless, Moshe promised to pay Staczek for sheltering himself and his father by means of the clothing, underwear, and various other items that had been deposited with Dr. Volosvitza. As mentioned previously, at one point Staczek had refused to accept Moshe's father.

When the Goldberg brothers joined the bunker and promised fair payment, Moshe also obligated himself to pay for support. Now, the time had come to fulfill these promises almost completely. At

143

this time, Staczek was given four suits of clothing and four valuable hand watches, along with other items. The wagon was deposited with a Christian in Sokoly, and the minute that they get it back from him, it will be given to Staczek without delay. So that he would not doubt their word, the Goldberg brothers paid him, meanwhile, with other possessions.

'Shmeig' was very satisfied, and announced, with celebration and pathos, that even if the War will continue for years, he will take care of all of us at his own expense, without any further charges. Nevertheless, our boys decided to budget a fixed monthly payment to Staczek. They turned to him and asked him to determine for himself how much the monthly payment for food should be. At the beginning, Staczek gave the impression as if he wasn't asking, Heaven forbid, for any more than he had already received, and here, he had promised them support "until the end" of the War. Our youths pleaded with him, explaining that they had paid him only for the bunker and he deserves a separate payment for the food. He refused to accept their suggestion for a few days, but finally he agreed and said that they themselves should determine how much to pay him.

The amount then, which they determined to pay him, was 400 marks per month. The boys asked the man if this would be enough. To their surprise, he answered that he would be prepared to accept no less than 600 marks in products, not in cash, and according to the prices that were in force before the War. What happened here was like the incident between our father Avraham and Efron the Hittite: when Avraham wanted to purchase land from Efron the Hittite to bury his dead, Efron did not at first want to take any money from him, and in the end, he asked Avraham for "400 silver shekels in legal tender."

Behold the daily menu that was served us by our benefactor Staczek, during the first two months: one kilo of black bread for the four of us, and – twice a day – hot cooked food, generally comprising potatoes mixed with beets or cabbage, thin soups, barley and peas. Meat was served us twice a week in an amount of about one-half kilo for the four of us.

I warned my youngsters more than once that by trying to provide 'Shmeig' with everything good for each piece of bread or sip of liquid, they weren't doing us any favor; rather, the opposite was the case, more and more they were arousing an appetite of greed in Staczek. He sees milk cows before him and in the end he will get everything out of them; the rope around their necks is made… To my sorrow, they did not consider my opinion and in their eyes I looked like a stingy miser.

"He thinks we're at home and free men. He doesn't understand that we are buried and our lives are hanging in front of us."

During those days, our youngsters begged 'Shmeig' to try to buy pistols for them, and they promised to pay ten times the accepted price for them. Apparently, the Christian thought in his heart, "Who knows how much gold they still have in their possession if they can spend such fantastic amounts?"

Some time passed until the farmer Staczek decided on the price that should be set for his Jews because no matter how much he would tell them, perhaps he would be cheating himself? Therefore, at the beginning, he tried to get them to turn to his brother Palek. For himself, it wasn't nice to "strip their skins" from them. And if he will be stingy with the food he gives them and they complain, it would be possible to blame his brother. Palek did not want to set a price either, also being concerned that he would cheat himself, and he answered that he trusted our honesty. Our youngsters gave him possessions worth 800 marks and accounted them as only 400 marks. Then the hesitator gained courage and determined the amount of 600 marks per month for support. He tried to make excuses for this amount by saying that these days it is easy to get all kinds of things from the houses of the Jews, which are then sold cheaply. In this situation, the possessions meanwhile remained in our hands for further valuation.

'Shmeig' understood, with his farmer's sense, that the Jews were not paying him such a high price for the food, but rather for keeping them in the bunker, because the food was scanty and was not worth any more than 50 marks per month. He was sorry that until now he had not put pressure on them to give him more and did not know how to exploit them properly. He knew that other farmers knew how to exploit their Jews better than he did. It was said that Yankel Krushevsky had paid his farmer an entire kilogram of gold for keeping him for two weeks. Moshe Lev paid a farmer a gold watch in exchange for a loaf of bread.

Rosenovitz ('Lazerke' Simoner) paid 100 marks for one day's maintenance in a cellar. From that day onward, Staczek came to visit us periodically, telling us about Jews who had enriched many farmers and he could also bring himself Jews like those, who would cover him with gold and foreign currency.

From day to day, our menu grew worse. Sometimes the bread was missing altogether; it was used up because the work of grinding flour had stopped. The cooked food was watery, without any oil or meat. Sometimes the cooked food wasn't brought to us on the excuse that there were guests in the house and it wasn't possible to cook.

The youngsters explained to Staczek that 'Old Maik' was suffering from hunger. They did not have the nerve to tell him that they also were hungry. Staczek heard what they said and ironically answered that there were a lot of Jews running around in the forests who were suffering from hunger and cold, and they would give praise to G-d if they could receive a slice of bread once a day and a roof over their heads. These stories had the purpose of silencing us and making us understand how much we were obligated to be happy and grateful to him – to Staczek.

Upon hearing these things, our young men decided to try to sell some possessions in exchange for food. It was necessary to go to villages that we hadn't passed through and where they did not recognize us.

The Farmer Lapinski

Avrahamel Goldberg had once worked for a farmer named Lapinski in the village of Jezhbin (a distance of two kilometers from the bunker). The Christian was a good acquaintance of his father's and used to give him blacksmithing jobs to do. 'Avrahamel' estimated that the man would want to buy a number of things that he had, such as a horse blanket, a washing sink, a few dozen hand files, and a beautiful winter dress. At eleven o'clock in the evening, Moshe and 'Avrahamel' went out to Jezhbin. The night was very dark. Even on moonlit nights, the way was difficult, because it went through fields and pastures. In the dark, it was impossible for them to signal one to the other. This caused the boys to make more than a few mistakes, and several times they found themselves in the same place they had left a while ago. Finally, they had to knock on the window of a house and ask for directions.

In my hiding place, I cried in worry over the safety of my only son. To go the comparatively short distance of two kilometers should have taken one or two hours both ways, and here, long hours had passed and the boys hadn't come back yet. G-d knows what happened… I preferred to be hungry for days and not to suffer pangs of discouraged expectation to hear the steps of my son coming back to me. Every minute in my eyes was like an eternity.

To my great happiness, the two boys came back after five hours. They were tired and exhausted and their feet were soaking wet. They hadn't worn boots because they were worried that they would be robbed on the way, and instead they wore worn-out shoes that squeezed their toes. According to their estimates, they had gone more than ten kilometers. With them, they brought back one-half kilogram of bread and two kilograms of butter.

They told Lapinski they would come back to him again in three days. From him, they ordered bread for a number of weeks, a significant amount of butter, and a liter of whiskey. In exchange, they were to bring galoshes and a pair of trousers. They begged Lapinski to get them a pistol, since he had connections with smugglers between Warsaw and Lublin. Of course, they promised that the farmer would be paid a good price. Lapinski also agreed that the boys would supply him occasionally with new merchandise to sell, at a low price so that he would be able to make a profit from the business, and in exchange the boys would receive food.

Within a two-week period, Moshe and 'Avrahamel' visited Lapinski several times. He always greeted them nicely. His wife wanted to bake them a cake and honor them with a cup of tea, but they thanked her and said they did not want to bother her in the middle of the night.

One day Lapinski told the boys that apparently, every time they heard the dogs barking at night, his neighbors had sensed that Jews were visiting his home. They specifically told him that they would wait in ambush for the Jews to come and would grab them and hand them over to the Germans. In light of these threats, Lapinski advised the boys not to visit his house any more; he was prepared to return a lot of the things that he had taken from them up to now; he did not want to endanger his life.

However, he was prepared to meet them at a certain place in the forest after one week's time. The meeting was set for the following Monday, at two o'clock in the morning. At the appointed time, the boys arrived at the place, but Lapinski was not to be seen. They waited two hours and he did not come … because he had warned them before that their lives would be ambushed, they did not try to go to his house. Most of the possessions remained in Lapinski's hands, and they did not receive anything at all in exchange for them.

The food that had been brought until now from Lapinski, along with the portions from 'Shmeig', would somehow be enough for a few weeks. Therefore, the boys decided to rest and meanwhile not to go out at night. But 'Avrahamel' did not know how to rest; he always needed to get rid of his abundant energy. From birth, he was accustomed to working hard, and he was unable to sit and do nothing. From the moment that he tasted going around at night, he was drawn to go again, when the night would be moonless. 'Shmeig' did not let him go to Sokoly in any event; in order to go there, weapons were necessary, and the weapons were only in the hands of 'Shmeig'.

Staczek explained to the friends that the snow had completely covered the earth and every step would leave footprints. Besides, he said, it was not worthwhile to go to Sokoly, because the houses of the Jews were emptied of everything; even the furniture had disappeared from each house. It was not worthwhile, if so, to just go and look around in the dark for places where something might be found. It is true that 'Shmeig' himself had prepared to go to Sokoly to bring the enameled kitchen utensils that might still be hidden in the attic of Maik's house, but he delayed this until after the snow would melt.

The Farmer Wladek from Idzki

Because of this delay, 'Avrahamel' [Goldberg] suggested going a distance of six kilometers from the bunker to the village of Idzki. Some time ago, the Goldberg brothers had deposited some possessions with a farmer there named Wladek. I vigorously opposed the idea that my son Moshe [Maik] would participate in the adventure of this dangerous trip. The two brothers went alone and brought back some of their possessions. Wladek's family had begun to use the clothing that they had deposited with them, assuming that their owners were no longer alive. They got one liter of oil and a loaf of bread from the farmer. 'Avrahame' asked Wladek to prepare for him a larger amount of bread, butter, kerosene, three flashlight batteries, and a table mirror for shaving. As advance payment for his order, 'Avrahamel' gave him 100 marks.

After three days, I no longer had the strength to prevent my son Moshe from going with them. This time they took the two rifles and two hand grenades that belonged to the *A.K.* organization, which had been used by 'Shmeig' and his two friends when they accompanied the Jews to Sokoly and afterwards had been left in the bunker.

I remained alone in the bunker. During these difficult hours, full of restlessness and fear, stuttering, I recited chapters of Psalms, those I remembered, such as: *"Song of Ascents"*; *"I Lift My Eyes to the Mountains, from Where Will My Help Come?"*; and the verses, *"My*

149

G-d, My G-d, Why Have You Forsaken Me?"; "*Why, G-d, Do You Stand at a Distance?*"; "*How Long, G-d, Will You Put Us in the Dark Forever?*"; "*David's Instruction When He Was in the Cave*"; and other prayers that I prayed to G-d, that He would watch over the lives of the boys, that they would succeed in their mission that was so full of obstacles, and that they would return in peace. Amen!

After four and a half hours, I was again privileged to see them return. They brought with them a sack full of bread, weighing 35 kilograms. Wladek promised to supply the rest of the things they had ordered, next time.

With regard to the fate of the Jews from Sokoly, Wladek informed us that on the first day of the expulsion, the Germans had gathered 500 Jews and transported them in the farmers' wagons. During eight additional days, through searches and by means of lowly informers, about 500 more Jews were captured. Many of them handed themselves over to the Germans because of hunger, cold and robberies. Those who were arrested were held for two weeks in the new *beit midrash*. The Germans even baked bread for them and distributed regular portions of food.

During this period, the Germans allowed the baking of bread for the Jews. The baking was done by two of the bakers from Sokoly: Alter Radzilowsky and Yechielke Somovitz. The bakers were allowed to walk around freely.

After two weeks, all these Jews were sent to the Tenth Division Fort near Bialystok, where there was a gathering point for all the Jews of the surrounding area, including the Jews from Sokoly who had previously been expelled. From Bialystok, groups of Jews were sent to Treblinka, to the gas chambers.

Wladek was not a simple boor. He had a measurement of intelligence, read the newspapers, and also knew how to speak German. He was familiar with many spheres, and his opinion could be trusted. He told about the heroes' deaths of several Jews from Sokoly, about whom it was hard to believe that they were able to do such heroic deeds.

Benyamin Rachelsky

One of these heroes was Benyamin Rachelsky, the lame son of Avraham Moshe Rachelsky. Only a few of the residents of Sokoly knew Benyamin. They saw him sometimes, toddling on his crooked legs without using crutches or a cane. When he walked, he breathed heavily. One thing everyone knew: Benyamin was a bookworm and a diligent student. He finished public school with distinction and went on to teach himself accounting from a Polish textbook. He was expert at writing requests to government and private offices, to courts and the tax department, and he wrote these for anyone who would place an order or request with him.

During the Soviet regime, Rachelsky worked in the government dairy as an assistant to the bookkeeper. Those who were close to him knew that he had energy and initiative, in spite of his disability. They also knew that he was a devotee of Communist ideas. Recently, he had been accustomed to spend entire days in the house of his grandfather, Berish the *Shochet*.

On November 2, 1942, the first day of the [Sokoly] expulsion, about 500 souls were at the gathering point next to the old *bet midrash*. This is exactly what Wladek, who was an eyewitness, told us. One of the Germans participating in the expulsion screamed an order at 'Benyaminke' to get up on a wagon.

Benyamin lifted his head and, in an emotional voice, addressed the crowd first in German and then in Polish:

> I know that they are transporting all of us to be killed, but I
> am comforted, with complete confidence, by the idea that
> our murderers will soon suffer a crushing defeat. They will
> be forced to surrender! They will turn into a nation of slaves
> to other nations! In the past, the German nation was famous
> as the bearer of the flag of culture and education. Among
> them were musicians and philosophers of whom humanity
> was proud. But now, all the generations of the nations of the
> world will condemn them as a nation of murderers,

barbarians, wild animals, who exceeded the hangmen and inquisitors of the Middle Ages in their cruelty!

Turning to the Christian crowd, he said, "Don't be happy and celebrate the disappearance and destruction of the Jews! The same murderers who are taking us away today will not hesitate to destroy you also when the time comes."

Benyamin was not able to continue speaking. The sound of a shot split through the air. 'Benyaminke' collapsed and fell, returning his proud, pure soul to his Creator.

Velvel Kapitovsky

Additional, supreme heroism was shown by Velvel Kapitovsky, a young man aged twenty, an orphan who lived on Gonosowki Street. Up to the time of the Soviet occupation, the general public in Sokoly did not know him. His neighbors, who knew him from close by, said that he had a witty tongue. During the period of the Soviet regime, he worked as an errand boy for the clinic that was in Janina Palkowska's house. Velvel was among the first 500 Jews who were taken in the farmers' wagons to Bialystok.

The moment that the line of wagons arrived at the bridge over the Narew River, Velvel burst out with a powerful call to the crowd:

> Brother Jews! We should not deceive ourselves, what awaits us at the end of this journey is known. But before the strange death in the ovens, we are destined for more torture and suffering, hunger, thirst, cold, dirt and fleas. Therefore, brothers, it is not for us to be brought like sheep to the slaughter! If we do not have the strength to rise up against our murderers, it is preferable to immediately put an end to our lives. Whoever still has a bit of courage in his heart and wants to shorten his suffering should take an example from me and do the same, and the G-d of Israel will avenge our blood!

When he finished speaking, Velvel jumped from the wagon into the river and disappeared in its depths.

Wladek continued to tell us about dozens of Jews from Sokoly, who were in a certain bunker with their families. In the end they were found by a Polish informer, who pointed them out to the German *gendarmes*, who immediately appeared, accompanied by the Polish police. All the Jews in the bunker were shot on the spot.

Among these victims were Hershel Yismach, the son-in-law of 'Yankel' [Yaakov] Petroshka, Hershel's wife 'Freidel' [Freida], and their two daughters, the oldest of whom, 'Chaicha' [Chaya], was wounded and fainted at the time of the shooting. The murderers thought she was dead and left her among those who were killed. Farmers were drafted to dig a deep pit and bury the dozens of victims.

After their horrible deeds, the murderers went away. Meanwhile, 'Chaicha' woke up from her faint, got up on her weak legs and fled from the valley of death. With the last of her strength, she went to a Christian friend, with whom she had a very close friendship since they were in school. 'Chaicha' was a good student; she had helped, and even prepared homework, for her friend. Everyone in the school loved her. Her fate is unknown. Apparently, she came to an end sooner or later. In any case, she did not find protection with her Christian friend.

Among the rest of the victims of that bunker was the wife of Chaim 'Itza' Fleer and two of their daughters. Chaim 'Itza' himself, and the rest of his children, hid themselves in another location. In the same bunker were Beilah Rachel's son, Alter with his wife, the butcher Hanoch Fleer's daughter, and their two children. The wife and children were killed in the shooting, but Alter succeeded in fleeing with his life.

Mordechai Lepkovsky, who worked the last few years before the War as a professional carpenter in Warsaw, was also shot nearby. Mordechai, with his mother and sister, were hidden at a farmer's house near the village of Idzki when the Jews were expelled from

Sokoly. It was his sad fate that, once, when he went out to buy bread, he met up with a search-team on its rounds and was shot on the spot.

His father 'Avramelke' who passed away before World War II, was a landowner who worked his lands himself. Alone, he plowed, sowed, harvested, and threshed. He managed a complete farm in every sense of the word, and was called 'Esov' by the Jews. This nickname also gained validity because 'Avramelke' had red hair.

Another victim was a beautiful little girl, aged four, and named 'Henele', the daughter of Betzalel Malach and his third wife. She was in the bunker with her older sister, Sarah Esther. The sister succeeded in fleeing from the inferno. Wladek added, in his shocking description, that when the victims were buried in the pit, blood from 'Henele' flowed up like a fountain. The farmers who did the tragic work told this to Wladek.

Another of Wladek's stories was about the carpenter 'Itza' Baran who succeeded in hiding for two weeks in a hiding-place next to his house. His children were staying with a farmer, and every night they snuck into Sokoly to bring some valuables in sacks for the farmer. They were able to do this because, as we remembered from our adventure with 'Shmeig', for the first two weeks after the expulsion the Jews' possessions were not guarded and everything stood ownerless.

From the continuation of Wladek's story, we found out that Germans have recently been seen who were ready to do business with Jews. At a price of 500 marks per person, they are willing to transport Jews to the Bialystok Ghetto from among those who had fled to the forests and were hiding in bunkers. According to rumors, the Jews in the Bialystok Ghetto live freely and work in the factories. The *Judenrat* there conducts a "kingdom," and it has a Jewish police force at its disposal.

Yisrael Maik and Family

The Germans who transported the Jews to the Bialystok Ghetto used private taxis in order to camouflage their deeds. Among the first to reach the ghetto in this manner was Yisrael Maik, his wife Dina, their daughter 'Teibele', and their cousin Hinda [Czernetsky]. Yisrael bore troubles and suffering in the forests during the weeks until they arrived in the Bialystok Ghetto. All his wealth and money, all his faithful Christian friends who flattered him all the years, all his faith in humanity, did not help him find shelter even for one day. Not a single friend was found, at any price, who was prepared to give him a helping hand in his distress. For weeks Maik wandered around with his family in the forest, from dugout to dugout. At times, he got involved with gangs of robbers who stole from him without mercy. They always followed him and found him wherever he went, in order to get money and valuables from him. In recent days, his distress grew inestimably large, because of his daughter, 'Teibele'.

Armed gangs of Soviets and Poles, called 'Sergei', and the Janek Gangs, robbed and raped young women after having kidnapped them. These creatures also attacked 'Teibele', and her father paid a fortune in order to redeem her from their impure hands.

After all these hardships that are difficult to describe, it is easy to understand that Yisrael Maik grabbed onto the decision to move to the Bialystok Ghetto when he had the opportunity to do so. He paid several thousand marks to the Germans who transported him with his family to the ghetto, in spite of the estimation that the Ghetto also would not exist for a long time, but life at the moment is better...

Yisrael's tragedy continued even in Bialystok, according to Wladek. A Polish citizen of German origins (*Volksdeutsch*) used to come to Yisrael's house in the Ghetto for watch repairs. The man did not remain indifferent to Yisrael's daughter; he actually fell in love with her. The *Volksdeutschers* had special privileges. Since these visits continued every day, a kind of friendship grew between him and the entire family. In estimating the situation, the thought occurred to Dina to exploit the lover in order to free from the hands of Janina Palkowska, the suitcase of gold that she had given to her for safekeeping.

The German agreed, without hesitation, to carry out the objective, and he traveled to Sokoly, accompanied by 'Teibele' Maik. Janina Palkowska received them nicely and asked them to come back the next day, because the suitcase was hidden in one of the villages.

The next day, they came again to her house. Janina asked them to wait a bit, saying that she would immediately bring the suitcase from the shed in the yard. She ran to inform the *gendarmes* of her guests' arrival.

Both of them were arrested immediately. The German was accused of having relations with Jews. To this very day, the fate of 'Teibele' is unknown. We assume that she was shot or sent to Treblinka.

Thus, the Maiks lost their daughter 'Teibele', carrying on their consciences the sin that they themselves had caused her death. The pain was unbearable since it was right after they had just completed the days of mourning for their son, 'Shmuelke'.

After 'Itza' the carpenter also arrived in the Bialystok Ghetto via the Germans, he paid the Germans a second time in order to bring his sons in a taxi from the village. The farmer did not want the children to leave him because they brought him possessions from their nightly trips to Sokoly and until then, they had continued to enrich him. But the boys were drawn to their parents with all their hearts, and they reached them safely.

'Aharke' Zholti

Another link in the chain of Wladek's description was about two respected Jews from Sokoly: 'Aharke' Zholti who was found murdered near the village of Jablonka, and 'Shlomke' Olsha who was shot in the Budziska Forest during a search. Both of them were among the wealthy people of the town and each of them conducted a wide-ranging business.

Until the War broke out, 'Aharke' Zholti was the owner of two warehouses of wood and building materials. He built a large, two-story house for himself in the center of town. His wife, 'Freidel', managed a wealthy, luxurious home. She always spoke nicely and no one ever heard that she quarreled or argued with anyone. She was generous to the poor and needy, and was sympathetic to everyone. Her husband 'Aharki' was a wise Jew, who kept his word and was trustworthy. He was a mediator with Judge Jeruzelsky, when the matter involved justice. Whoever had legal problems turned to 'Aharke'.

In his youth, he was educated in the village of Ros, where his parents lived, and he was a frequent visitor of the Squire [*paritz*] of Ros. He was a friend of the Squire's children and grew up with them. They reached high social levels in the community. One was a judge, the second a legal investigator, and the third an army officer. 'Aharke' was a friend to them all. When the Squire's daughter was married, the ceremony took place in the Sokoly church and 'Aharke' made sure that the Jews of Sokoly erected a royal gate of honor, decorated with greenery and colored paper lanterns in honor of the *shlub* (wedding), and they set up barrels with torches the entire length of the road from the marketplace to Prayer Street that were lit at the appropriate moment.

People came to 'Aharke' with regard to divorces, arbitration suits, and mediation in disputes between two parties. At the time of the Polish regime, 'Aharke' served as an administrator of the Jewish community. During the German occupation, he was a member of the *Judenrat*. 'Aharke' was active in community matters in general. During recent times, his status in the community grew even greater, because of his son [David], who had completed his engineering studies and became famous in the surrounding area.

'Shlomke' Olsha

'Shlomke' [*aka* Shlomo] Olsha was a *Chasid* of the Alexander *Rebbe*. His house was wealthy and conducted with aristocratic customs. He was the last official head of the Sokoly Jewish Congregation. 'Shlomke' Olsha's wife, Sarah Miriam, was from the family of *Rav*

Rabinowitz, the grandson of Rabbi Yaakov, of blessed memory, from Sokoly, one of a chain of rabbis beginning with Rabbi Dr. Eliezer Michael Rabinowitz, who translated the *Gemara* into French. The Rabbi of Lapy, Rav Yisrael Rabinowitz, also wrote important and interesting books.

Shlomo Olsha was the father of five sons and three daughters. His oldest son learned in the *Rav* Reines Yeshiva in *Lita* [Lithuania] and married a woman from the illustrious Grossman family of Ostrow-Mazowiecka, where he managed a store selling paper and writing instruments. Shlomo's sons, Michael and Velvel, opened a wholesale store in Bialystok selling paints and chemical products, and they were known as the "Olsha Brothers." The fourth son, Moshe, was Yaakov Ginzberg's son-in-law and was a partner in a wood-sawing factory in Bialystok. He also manufactured baking powder and spices for drinks under the name *"Ofion,"* which was written in Hebrew letters.

The youngest son, Chaim Yehoshua, married the daughter of the studious, learned Pesach Brill, of blessed memory. His wife, Shifra; his daughter, Sara; and his little son, Pesach were murdered in the forest by the Nazis. Chaim Yehoshua was a member of the regional committee for pioneer training and he was active in local town organizations, such as the Merchants' Union and the Cooperative Charity Committee. He was a member of the town local council, and during the Nazi occupation, a member of the *Judenrat.*

The oldest daughter, Tzipora ('Feigel') was married to Yaakov Starinsky of Bialystok. He founded the first textile factory in the Land of Israel, under the name "Manor." The daughter Chana [Olsha]], who was pretty and intelligent, was married to the son of the illustrious Zolberg family from Warsaw. They had a famous firm for platinum products at 14 Genasha Street. Shlomo's youngest daughter, 'Mushka', completed studies at the Teachers' Seminary in Vilna.

Re-visit to Wladek the Farmer from Idzki

After some time, our youngsters went again to Idzki, to Wladek, to get the ordered supplies. Moshe [Maik] wore a rubber boot on his calloused foot which 'Shmeig' found for him. They took two rifles and a number of hand grenades with them. Near Idzki, they heard loud barking of dogs. They stood still until the barking stopped, and proceeded on their way to Wladek's house. Chaim 'Yudel' [Goldberg] and Moshe stood under a large tree with the rifles in their hands and 'Avrahamel' [Goldberg] carefully checked to see whether there was a guard in the area. He carefully jumped into Wladek's yard and knocked on his window. Wladek was alarmed, thinking that someone had come to rob him, and he started to yell for help at the top of his voice.

'Avrahamel' called out to Wladek, trying to calm him: "Mr. Wladek, don't be afraid, I am Avraham the carpenter!"

But the barking of the dogs and Wladek's cries muted Avrahamel's voice. He was afraid to raise his voice because of the guards who were likely to arrive from a distance. Long moments passed until Avrahamel's voice reached Wladek's ears on the other side of the window. Then Wladek lit a kerosene lantern and went to open the door.

He told 'Avrahamel' that only last night there had been robbers in the village. A pig was stolen from one of his neighbors and dozens of chickens from another. The robberies, committed by gangs of Christians and Jews, were continuing in all the villages in the area. When he heard footsteps outside the window, he was convinced that there were robbers in his yard. In Idzki and other nearby villages, they had established a night guard of ten men. Dogs accompanied the night guard on the paths. Wladek advised 'Avrahamel' to be careful of going to the villages at night because of the danger involved in meeting up with the guards who would not hesitate to call the *gendarmes*.

Wladek gave the ordered provisions to 'Avrahamel', including two liters of kerosene in two bottles, but in return, he requested to be given back two empty bottles. Avrahamel only had one empty bottle. Wladek was stubborn and refused to give him the second liter of kerosene. 'Avrahamel' felt degraded, considering the fact that he had deposited many expensive items with the Christian: clothing, shoes, and underwear worth hundreds of marks, and here he was talking about an empty bottle the likes of which could be found in garbage dumps. What did Wladek see in insisting and forcing 'Avrahamel' to put his life in danger and come a second time?

Moments of great anxiety passed for Chaim 'Yudel' [Goldberg] and Moshe [Maik] who were standing guard outside. Four guards, whistling, had passed by right next to them. Our boys thought that the guards had seen them and were whistling to call others, perhaps even the police. The guards had a pocket flashlight, and in spite of the fact that our youngsters had weapons, self-defense could not succeed against an encirclement of many Christians.

To their joy, the guards went away and, at almost the same moment, 'Avrahamel' slid from Wladek's yard. The three returned safely to the bunker.

Again, I shed tears like water and cried bitterly until I was privileged to see the boys come back to me. They told me of the dangerous trip and described the events of the night. They unanimously came to the conclusion that it was better to pay 'Shmeig' hundreds of marks for a dry crust with water than to endanger their lives chasing after better food.

The boys determined that going to Sokoly was less dangerous than going to the villages. In Sokoly, they did not meet up with a single living soul or with barking dogs.

I tried to convince them that now it was no longer necessary to go to the villages, because we had a stock of food, and in combination with the servings of 'Shmeig', we would be able to exist for a long time. It was not to be even thought of that a special trip should be made for the single liter of kerosene that was left with Wladek. We will manage with what we will receive from Staczek, even kerosene, though at a higher price, but...so be it.

In spite of everything, the youngsters went out a number of times to Jezhbin, saying that on the way there there were no dogs. There indeed was another defect – the road was not straight and it led round and round, and on a dark night it was possible to make a mistake and get lost, but since they had already visited Lapinski a number of times, they had grown accustomed to the way and hoped to succeed.

To our disappointment, these trips bore no fruit. Lapinski did receive them generously, and they left merchandise worth 1600 marks with him in exchange for an order for food items. At the beginning, Lapinski jumped onto the proposal, seeing a significant profit in the transaction, and he told them to come back to get the food. But when they appeared at his house the fifth time, he postponed the matter to another time. The "other time," Lapinski was not at home. They did not give up, and one day they did meet him in his house, but then he told them that he was not able to do any more business with them. He was prepared to return everything he had received from them because, simply, he did not want to put his life and the lives of his family in danger. It is enough for him that the neighbors have seen, and they know very well that Lapinski has connections with the Jews. The whole game is playing with fire.

Finally, Lapinski told them that they should no longer dare to cross his threshold. The boys promised him that they wouldn't come to him any more and requested that he not allow them to leave empty-handed this time, but the Christian did not listen to their pleas and they returned the same way they had gone.

The boys knew that they could no longer go to the villages. One small hope remained to them, to turn to Moshe Maik's friend, the Soviet Doctor.

The Soviet Doctor

Dr. Claudia Nikolievna Volosvitza was 35 years old. Before the expulsion, when there were only two Jewish doctors in Sokoly, Dr. Guttenplan and Dr. Makowsky, the Russian Doctor was loaded with work. She was an expert in women's and internal diseases. She was friendly in her relations with, and the care of, her patients, and it was told that, more than once, she waived payment for a house call from those who were unable to pay. Her husband was a high-ranking officer in the Soviet army, and was at the warfront.

During the first few days after the Nazi invasion, Dr. Volosvitza tried to cross over to the Soviet side and reach the city where she was born, Tembov. Since all means of communication were already disconnected, the Soviet Doctor was forced to remain in Sokoly.

She received good recommendations from Manikowski, the Polish mayor at that time, and from other important people. The German *Kommandant* issued her a permit to treat the sick in Sokoly and the surrounding area.

Dr. Volosvitza was the mother of two children: Igor, a 16-year-old lad and a girl aged six.

My son Moshe became acquainted with the Soviet Doctor in 1940. As a technician, Moshe occasionally received radio repair work from her, and he refused to take payment for his efforts. In such cases, the woman sent him 40 marks for each repair with her housemaid.

After Dr. Volosvitza failed to cross to the Soviet side, she invited Moshe to come to her and asked him to visit her home occasionally, telling him that she regarded him as a son. It is no surprise that Moshe quickly became friendly with her son, Igor.

Now that we were in the bunker, Moshe] and 'Avrahamel' Goldberg decided to exploit this friendship with the Soviet Doctor and get food with her assistance, so that it would not be necessary to endanger their lives by going to the villages.

The two sent some dresses and children's clothing to Dr. Claudia Volosvitza with Staczek. These articles appealed to her, and when she remembered her relationship with Moshe, she sent him a letter with Staczek, asking him details about his situation, including a request to set a price for the things that had been sent to her. Moshe answered that with regard to the price, he trusted her, but instead of money he requested occasional packages of food, because of his unique situation.

The Soviet Doctor answered immediately that she was prepared with all her heart to send packages, even daily, if she will only have the possibility and opportunity to send them with someone. Meanwhile, she sent 100 marks with Staczek, along with a package of food that included a large cake, a fried goose, a jar of oil and one-half kilo of sausage. On a note that she attached to the package she wrote that she wanted to send a lot more, but the messenger was worried that guards would stop him on the way and would be interested in seeing what was in such a large package. For the coming Christmas holiday, she was prepared to send a sufficient amount for all the days of the holiday...to our great disappointment, Staczek refused to accept everything that the Soviet Doctor occasionally prepared.

'Shmeig' visited Dr. Volosvitza once a week. Since she knew that [Moshe] Maik was under his protection, she would run to meet him, leaving the patients who had come to her in the house in the middle of a treatment, as if Staczek were a guest who had arrived from abroad after many years. She brought him into her room, so she could hear details about Moshe Maik. By the way, she showed him enormous affection. Staczek would return home from these visits in high spirits. He was a single man, 36 years old, a wealthy farmer and owner of a variegated farm. He had not had opportunities to meet the fair sex and therefore the doctor's attitude was a special experience for him.

Outside of that, he was interested in meeting the doctor's son Igor, who had learnt from [Moshe] Maik how to charge batteries and had tools for doing so. At Moshe's request, Igor would charge batteries for Staczek without payment. The batteries were necessary for the *A.K.* organization's radio broadcasting and receiving. As is known, Staczek was an active member of the underground.

Staczek came to the doctor's house without crossing through the town of Sokoly, and thus it was less likely that he would be seen.

Moshe Maik made tiny batteries for the organization from chrome and nickel that could be carried in a pocket without being detected. Staczek, in spite of this, became more and more hardened towards us from day to day, and he acted indifferent. He did not give Moshe the letters from Dr. Volosvitza and refused to accept any food from the doctor for him, evading this with all kinds of excuses and pretexts. He accepted only small items, such as medicine for Chaim Yudel, who suffered from asthma.

Once, Staczek brought a message from Dr. Volosvitza that the Chairman of the Sokoly *Judenrat*, Alter Ginzberg, his wife the dentist, her son Monik, Yona Ginzberg and his wife Selina the teacher, had handed themselves in to the German *gendarmes*. They had wandered for a time in the forests, hiding in bunkers, and finally they could no longer bear the suffering and torment. They were still being held prisoner, but there was a chance to send them to the Bialystok Ghetto. All this was written in a note from the Soviet Doctor to Moshe, which this time Staczek was decent enough to give to him.

Seeing that no food would be obtained from the Soviet Doctor by way of Staczek, our young men looked for a strategy as to how to contact her in a different way. Moshe sent a letter to her son Igor in which he asked him to meet him behind the cemetery on a certain day between one and three o'clock in the morning. Igor answered immediately and set a meeting for the next Saturday night, behind the Christian cemetery, on the Warsaw road.

The youngsters put a lot of hope in the meeting, knowing that Igor was a faithful friend and was devoted to Moshe Maik with all his heart. They decided to ask Igor to put a package of food in a certain place under a pile of stones, once a week. To their great disappointment, the plan failed, because Igor received an order to present himself in Lapy for work, and he wasn't able to come to the meeting. However, he sent a message with Staczek that he would get in touch with him next week.

But Staczek avoided the matter for a few weeks, wishing to cancel the exchange of notes between Igor and Moshe. When Igor did meet with Staczek after several weeks and wanted to send a note to Moshe, Staczek emphatically refused to take the note, with the excuse that there were now German guards on all the roads and they inspected everything that was brought from one place to another, even searching people's pockets.

Every night between nine and ten o'clock, Staczek would open the cover over the opening of our bunker and lower food to us. Once every two days, he would come down to us to talk a bit and hear the news on the radio. By the way, he would investigate to see if the youngsters sometimes went outside…they had told him that it wasn't worth endangering their lives for things that were already being supplied to them.

Once, they suggested a few plans to Staczek that encouraged him to participate with them in these missions:

a)   to go to the deputy *Amstkommissar*, who lived in a suburb of the town. It was easy to reach his house, and since he was fattening geese and turkeys for the Christmas holiday, it would be a very good deed to cause him trouble and disturb his holiday by stealing the birds;

b)   to go to the government dairy and take the butter, the tools, the telephone and the typewriter;

c)   to go to the steam plant and cut strips of leather that could be used as soles for shoes; and

165

d)   to go to the *gendarmia* stables (Avrahamel had worked there and he knew all its secrets, how to take the walls apart with no especial difficulty), take out bicycles, expensive furs, and other valuables, and then set the stables on fire with the horses and vehicles inside.

The youngsters awakened Staczek's appetite and he promised to study their plans and choose those he preferred. Meanwhile, he told us that he had heard from Christian acquaintances about some Jews from Sokoly. We were so accustomed to hearing shocking stories about the torture of Jews that our hearts were hardened from hearing them, but even so, the stories still had a depressing effect on us.

Six young girls, who had succeeded in escaping from the German hunt during a search in the forest, remained hidden for a certain length of time. The girls were happy that they had succeeded in miraculously being rescued from the danger of death that had hovered over their heads in the forest. They met a farmer who appeared to be respectable. They asked him to show them the way to a quiet, safe settlement and told him everything that had happened to them during the hunt and what miracles and wonders had been sent to them by a good redeeming and rescuing Angel, who rescued them from death. They followed him.

Suddenly, the girls saw that the road where the farmer was leading them went in the direction of Sokoly, and they could already see the church steeple in Sokoly. They turned to the farmer, "Sir! Doesn't this road lead to Sokoly? Here is the church...".

Just then, the farmer took up a club and started to chase after them. They began to run away, and the farmer ran after them with his club, to force them to run in the direction of Sokoly, the way they bring animals to the slaughter. He handed them over to the *Amstkommissar*. The girls fell into the hands of the German murderers and the farmer received three kg. of sugar for his trouble.

Staczek further told us that in Sokoly, there was a store for manufactured goods owned by Shmuel Tzvi Kravitz, the son-in-law of 'Yudel' Goldin. Before the Jews were expelled from Sokoly, Kravitz hid the majority of his merchandise with his Christian friends. After the Jews were expelled from Sokoly, Kravitz's two daughters, 'Sheindel' and 'Shashki', remained. At the beginning, they lived in the forests. They tried to go to their Christian acquaintances to search for shelter in their homes, but their acquaintances did not even allow them to cross their thresholds.

Once, 'Sheindel' Kravitz met Chane Segal, the son of 'Yudel' from the village of Czeika, who was the head of a group of Jewish partisans. The girl told Chane Segal that their father had hidden merchandise with a farmer in the area and now the farmer wouldn't even allow them to cross the threshold of his house. The girl asked Chane to help her get their merchandise from the farmer. Chane was willing, and accepted her request, but he advised her not to claim all the merchandise at once, only bit by bit.

When Chane and the girl approached the farmer, he suggested that they come back in another two days, since he had hidden the merchandise in different hiding places. Therefore, they had to wait two days until he could take the goods out of hiding. After two days, the girl went with Chane Segal and his men to the farmer. Chane and the girl went inside and the rest of them waited outside. The farmer had prepared a few friends in his house, and the minute that Chane and the girl arrived, the farmers attacked Chane and the girl began to scream.

Chane's men, who stood outside, understood that the farmer had set a trap and they ran away in panic. The farmers tied up Chane Segal and handed him over, along with the girl, to the Germans guarding the Jamiolki Bridge who murdered them in cold blood. The village farmers buried the dead next to the Jamiolki Bridge.

Staczek also told us that the Jew, Tzvi Namzinsky, Alter Radzilowsky's son-in-law, was hidden at Staczek's neighbor's house and was paying a lot of money and possessions for shelter.

When the other neighbors found out, he worried that they would inform the Germans about him, and he then murdered Tzvi Namzinsky and his wife. How he did so, Staczek did not know. He knew his neighbor very well, but as a respectable person...

Now, writing my memories, I doubt whether we will be privileged to see the light of the world after the Holocaust and whether my writings will reach the hands of Jews who will be able to publish them. At the moment, the end is not in sight. We lie, day and night, like living dead, buried under the ground in a dark bunker. We light the *"Kopshtakel"* (a small lantern without glass for the smoke and soot to rise through), which blackens our faces and the entry like a bellows, only for two hours. I write my writings during the day, under the weak lines of light that penetrate through a small hole in the bunker's cover. Will my writings be privileged to reach the hands of Jews? I doubt it! I wanted them to study these works well.

So be it, if the Germans have the task of destroying the Jewish nation, it is still possible to understand them, because they were poisoned with anti-Semitism, which blames the Jews for all the tragedies in the world...and to them, it is a great good deed to fulfill the orders of their leader Hitler, may his name be blotted out! But simple Polish farmers have become wild animals thirsty for blood, ready to hand over innocent Jews into the hands of murderers, for a kilogram of sugar...

When Staczek told us these facts, we began to fear for our own fate... Who knows if Staczek won't also embroider some plots to get rid of us and inherit all our possessions? We were attacked by the suspicion that sooner or later, Staczek would want to get rid of us by putting poison in our food. And therefore, 'Avrahamel' suggested that for each pot of food that Staczek serves us, one of us, by turns, would refrain from tasting it. In the case of poisoning, one among us will remain alive to take revenge and set the entire farm on fire. Thus, several weeks passed, during which, every day, one of us, in turn, did not taste the food that Staczek served us.

Geese and Turkeys

A week before the Christmas holiday, Staczek called our youngsters to go with him to the deputy *Amstkommissar*, to bring the fattened geese as they had previously suggested.

At midnight, the boys took two rifles, a few hand grenades, and sacks. After three hours, they returned to the bunker, bringing eight fattened geese and twelve turkeys. They could not put more into the four sacks, and had to leave the rest. 'Avrahamel' was an artist and was able to break in and open locks. 'Avrahamel' could do everything in a few minutes.

Staczek was afraid to keep the stolen geese in his house and he lowered 'Avrahamel' and Moshe into a second bunker that he had in the woods near his yard, to kill the turkeys and geese there and pluck their feathers. They worked for many hours. Finally, only three geese remained that weren't plucked. 'Avrahamel' and Moshe were hungry and tired from their tense job. Then, Staczek advised them to feast as much as they wanted, after a workday of tension and fasting. Chaim Yudel and I went to finish the plucking of the three geese that remained. After that, Staczek brought a pail and salt. We cut all the geese and turkeys into pieces and salted them. Staczek made an accounting of the fowl: to us, he brought the entrails and giblets of twenty fowl (*drioviski*, in Polish). He gave us a little bit of *greibenes* (fried pieces) from the fat.

On Sunday, Staczek told us that the Germans had made a scandal in Sokoly because of the stealing of the geese. The *Amstkommissar* told the priests that a gang of Polish robbers had broken into his storeroom and removed dozens of geese. He therefore requested that they proclaim in the churches that their religious congregation had to supply the Germans with 50 fattened geese. The priest made a strong speech in the church about the contemptible act done to the representatives of the German government, breaking into his storeroom and stealing dozens of geese, thereby putting the safety of the religious community in danger. And therefore, he proclaimed, it was a great good deed to inform the regime of any information about the criminals.

The Butter from the German Dairy

Apparently, Staczek found the fattened geese to be delicious, and seeing that Avrahamel was an expert in opening complicated locks in a few minutes, and that his Jews were quick and daring, he decided to also accept the second plan of 'Avrahamel', and carry out an attack on the German dairy. Since the second plan was a more dangerous operation, he decided to take a partner and carry it out with his faithful friend Tzeshek. Staczek and 'Avrahamel' took two rifles and Moshe and Chaim Yudel took hand grenades, tools for the break-in and a few sacks.

I remained in the bunker and recited verses of Psalms. At the beginning, I tried to stop my son from participating in these dangerous missions, but he did not want to listen to me on any account.

They returned after three hours, bringing 40 kilograms of butter, a few kilograms of paper, two scales, and other items. The youngsters had also wanted to dismantle the machines and the telephones and bring them to the bunker, but Staczek and Tzeshek were standing outside and were in a hurry to return.

Our youngsters did not have time to carry out their plan of destruction. They only damaged the pipes, and poured out all the milk and cream. If they had gone a day later, they would have been able to bring three more crates of butter. Their mission took place on a Sunday, after the weekly dairy transport had been sent.

Thanks to Staczek, this time the division of the spoils was just. Each one had a portion of 8 kilograms of butter. But our youngsters waived 2 kilograms of their portion, as well as their portion of the scales, which were worth 500 marks.

The burglary of the German dairy was skilled work. The lock was very complicated. Simply, it was impossible to open it with a tool. Besides, there was a double door, and Avrahamel had to break the doors; he had to be very skilled in order to carry out a large break-in within only a few minutes without making a sound.

The boys tried with all their strength to satisfy Staczek's wishes, so that he would not embroider any plots to get rid of them. After the two missions of the geese and the butter, the youngsters stopped being afraid of being poisoned by Staczek, and as a result of that, they stopped fasting in turns.

Staczek wanted to prevent suspicion that Poles had carried out the burglary of the dairy. Therefore, he requested that the boys prepare notes in Russian and Yiddish, as if Russians and Jews were behind the operation. The Russian note was written in a humorous tone, and ended with the words, "Don't worry about the burglary damages, Comrade Stalin will pay for everything!" They showed Staczek and Tzeshek the notes, which they liked. But the boys did not actually leave the notes in the dairy because they had decided that it was not worthwhile to transfer suspicion from the Poles, whose hatred of the Jews was no less than that of the Germans, and whose cruelty occasionally surpassed that of the Germans. The notes would cause the Germans to increase their searches in the forests for Jews and there would be more victims.

The local farmers expressed their opinion that the burglary was the work of Jews. The daughter of the Polish police officer Yanchenko even said that once, at a late hour of the night when her father was at work and she remained alone in the house, Feivel Jezevitz (Mordechai's son and Yaakov Goldberg's grandson) entered the house with a pistol in his hand and asked her for some pork. The Polish girl began to scream and Feivel Jezevitz fled. The police chased after him, even shot at him, but Feivel succeeded in fleeing.

Staczek said that the same night the dairy was robbed, the Germans found, through an informer, a bunker in which Naftali Plut, four of his sons, and Dr. Guttenplan were hiding. In that bunker there was a radio receiver belonging to Dr. Makowsky who had recently been living in Naftali Plut's house, and since the Plut sons knew about the radio, they had taken it out of its hiding place and brought it to their bunker. The Germans shot Naftali Plut and two of his sons, Dov and Shlomo. They had previously been injured, but the Germans did not want to take care of injured Jews. Naftali's other two sons, Yaakov and Nachum 'Yudel', and Dr.

171

Guttenplan, were arrested by the Germans and sent to the Bialystok Ghetto.

At that time, there was an order to send Jews caught in the forests to the Ghetto. The Christians said that the Germans suspected Naftali Plut's sons of participating in the burglary of the dairy.

The Germans did not have a unified way of acting towards the Jews. In the beginning, they sent them to the Bialystok Ghetto, but after that, they started to shoot them on the spot. That is what happened to the son of Yosef Blustein, who turned himself in together with his wife and three sons so as to be sent to the Ghetto. Apparently, the *gendarmes* changed their methods that day and the Jews were killed on the spot.

Sokoly Is Burning

After the butter from the dairy was distributed, we had a stock of 16 kilograms of butter. Part of it remained for daily use, and the rest of the butter was fried with onions to preserve it for a length of time. The bread that the youngsters had brought from Idzki the last time they were there was a sufficient addition to Staczek's portions of food.

But our youngsters could not sit and do nothing. It was a shame to lose a night. In the beginning, they thought of burning the *gendarmerie* warehouse, but first they would have had to take out the bicycles and motorcycles. 'Avrahamel' had built the warehouse, and was familiar with every corner of it. He knew how to open the walls without making a sound. Staczek craved the good things in the warehouse, but he delayed the operation from day to day.

When they saw that they couldn't depend on Staczek, the boys decided to burn down the town, without his help and without his knowledge. As long as the War continues, we do not have a chance to remain alive.

From day to day, their ambition grew, especially after the *Amstkommissar*'s decision to destroy the Jewish cemetery. It wasn't enough that they had taken all the Jews out of the town to kill them (men, women and children), robbed their possessions, and burned their homes. Their wish was also to harm dead Jews and not to allow their bones to rest in their graves. The *Amstkommissar* ordered the destruction of the fence around the cemetery, the uprooting of the trees in the cemetery and the removal of all the monuments, so they could be used to build sidewalks and floors. Therefore, it was our holy obligation to nullify the *Amstkommissar*'s program as soon as possible and burn down the entire town.

The youngsters planned to ambush the Germans at a late hour of the night, when they returned in a drunken state, to suddenly fall upon them with clubs and kill them. It was also part of their plan to attack Polish police, kill them, and take their weapons. I, on my part, tried to delay them and prevent them from carrying out their dangerous plans, arguing that it wasn't worthwhile to put four people's lives in danger for a questionable plan. Perhaps they would succeed in killing one German or Polish policeman, or set a few houses on fire.

But the youngsters started to reproach me for interfering with their plans, and regarded me as an idle, selfish transient who worries only about himself. They added that as long as we are still alive, we should do something, and we shouldn't have guilty consciences that we did not take revenge on our oppressors.

I tried to argue with the youngsters and contradict their excuses. I argued, what gain would there be in burning a few houses? It isn't worthwhile now to endanger the lives of four more Jewish souls because of a questionable plan. Every Jew who will survive is important, and from him a new generation will arise. Is it worthwhile now to abandon four souls, four generations of Jews, for a few houses? Nobody would request such a thing from you…not the *Torah*, not the nation of Israel…

But they stood firm in their decision that the voice of the blood of their parents, their brothers and sisters, women and children, is crying out to them from the earth to take revenge upon the enemy. I tried again to argue that they would be able to take revenge on those who hate us when the United States, the Soviet Union, and England would conquer Germany, but now every soul that would be abandoned and endangered is to be regretted. As much as I tried to influence the youngsters and delay them from carrying out their plans, I did not succeed.

The night before they decided to set the town on fire, they went to explore the situation and the night guard, and see from what locations it would be easier to ignite a fire. They did not take any kerosene with them that time. With regard to their plans to attack the *gendarmes* going home after visiting in Janina Palkowska's house, or the Polish police, as mentioned above, the youngsters promised me that for the moment they would waive these plans.

When they went to the town, my calmness left me. Nightmarish sights filled my imagination. Who knows? Who could guess what dangerous deeds they would decide to do? As was my custom, I began to recite the Psalms that I thought to be protection against danger. I prayed the evening prayers and said *Kriat Shma* with special concentration. I had a *"Tefillat Yaakov"* *siddur* with large letters, and almost every evening I would learn a few chapters of Psalms until I knew them by memory. I had to lie in the dark for 18 hours a day, and during the day not even a little bit of air to breathe penetrated into the bunker. The bunker was covered up from four o'clock in the morning until ten o'clock at night, and a lantern could not be lit during the entire day. We lit a small lantern, without any glass (called a *kopatchek*) only during mealtimes and for two hours at night when Staczek brought us our food, because it raised smoke and soot. Thus, we had to lie for complete days, day and night, in the dark.

When thoughts touching on sorrow and laments gnawed at my heart, the only remedy that eased the suffering of my soul and bitterness of my discouraged heart was reciting Psalms, mainly at the time of the long hours almost every evening, when the youngsters went on their dangerous trips to find food.

Before dawn, at four o'clock in the morning of the day when they went to explore the town, all of them safely returned to the bunker, bringing with them a few pieces of thin plywood that they had found in Sokoly. The plywood was needed for the ceiling of the bunker, so that raindrops would not fall on us when the rainy season began. They also found pieces of mirror for shaving. They couldn't ask Staczek to buy a mirror with cash, because they had asked him to do so ten times and every time he "forgot".

The youngsters admitted to me that they had lain in waiting for a German or a Polish policeman under a fence on Bathhouse Street until two o'clock in the morning, so as to kill them and take their weapons. But they did not meet up with either. The plywood they brought was from Pesach Brill's storeroom.

The next night, they took with them one and one-half liters of kerosene, and the brothers 'Avrahamel' and Chaim 'Yudel' Goldberg, and Moshe Maik, went to burn down Sokoly. I again tried to delay them, and the youngsters scorned me. My son Moshe promised me that there was nothing to fear, and that they knew how to watch themselves and be careful. Before the fire would spread, they would already be in the forest.

The plan was to set three sides of the town on fire: a) near Chaim 'Itza' Fleer's house, a quiet corner, hidden in all directions and together with many other houses; b) at the home of 'Motke', the engraver, which bordered the enormous *gendarmerie* warehouse; c) in the center of the marketplace, where all the shops and restaurants were located. Thus, the fire would take hold of the entire town.

After the boys left, I started to recite the Psalms. Tonight, my fear was inestimably larger than the night before. The prayers also could not calm my mood. Every moment I ran to the bunker hole to listen for any sound outside. Perhaps I would hear footsteps, the barking of a dog, or some noise?

At four o'clock in the morning, I finally was privileged to hear footsteps. With feelings of joy and tears in my eyes, I praised G-d, "Praise and thanks to the Holy One, Blessed Be He, that the boys have returned safely!"

The youngsters called me to come out of the bunker to look at the flames, and to say the *Shehechiyanu* [thanksgiving] blessing.

The sky was red. The entire horizon around was filled with flames, and I recited the *Shehechiyanu* blessing, not because of my feelings of revenge, but because my youngsters had succeeded in fulfilling their dream. With them, the matter was a holy operation, a kind of sanctification of G-d's name.

The 'Yellow Satan' was not satisfied with harming living Jews, but coarsely desecrated Jewish graves. He ordered the uprooting of the monuments in the Jewish cemetery and their use to pave sidewalks upon which the impure feet of those who hate and oppress us, into whose hands the homes and possessions of the Jews had fallen, would tread. The anger of 'the Satan' certainly would burn even more, if he were able to imagine that three young Jews had stood in his satanic path and interfered with his barbaric plan to desecrate the holy...

But the boys decided to deny and not to admit, even to Staczek, that they were the arsonists. Staczek came down to us, as was his custom, at five o'clock in the morning to inspect the bunker cover to make sure it was sufficiently camouflaged. The boys pretended that they did not know and innocently asked about the fire. Did it break out in Bialystok, or in Lapy? The sky was so red that it appeared that the fire was very large and spread out.

The next day, Staczek came again to us, this time to give us a detailed account of the fire. According to what he said, all the buildings in the marketplace and the main streets, Tiktin Street, Lomza Street, and Bathhouse Street, which led to the train, were destroyed. Almost the entire town, one hundred houses and farm buildings, went up in flames. Only 'Aharki' Zholti's two-story house, which the Germans had worked especially to rescue because the *gendarmia* was located there, was saved. It is clear that the damage caused to the building was great, and without serious inspection and repair of the building, it was impossible to live there. The fire departments of Bialystok, Lapy, Wysokie-

Mazowiekie, and Zambrow were called to put out the fire, but it did not help.

Warehouses of merchandise in large cellars were also burned. Many skins for leather, stored in barrels that stood in the cellars, were burned. Meanwhile, the men of the *gendarmia* were forced to move into the church to live. It is superfluous to add that all the "possessions" that they had stolen from the Jews were burnt, as well as their horses, their vehicles, and everything they owned.

Our boys enjoyed hearing these things, how they had succeeded a lot more than they had expected, in realizing their desire to avenge the blood of our people that had been spilled like water. Pride and satisfaction in their deed accompanied them for a long time, when the thoughts arose that the officers had lost their lives of plenty and luxury and that they would not ride so fast on princely horses on their daily excursions, as they had been accustomed to do, that there no longer was a stable with a fancy fence around it, and they no longer had dwellings with every comfort.

But more than everything else, the boys were happy that they had interfered with the desecration of the monuments of the holy ones. Now, the 'Yellow Satan', in his great embarrassment, was forced to leave aside the idea of the monuments because the streets of Sokoly no longer needed sidewalks.

Thank Almighty G-d, that we also have been privileged to take revenge against Troskolski, the restaurant owner, and a number of Christian shop owners who enriched themselves from the destruction of the Jews, settled themselves in the homes of Jews and stole their shops. These despicable Poles got what they deserved and came out of the fire with their bodies, but without firm ground beneath their feet, without even a shoelace.

Our heroes, excited for activity and vengeance, were not satisfied until now with what they had done. They already began to talk about completing the arson operation, down to the last house in Sokoly. It was clear that they had to wait "until the anger would pass" and the mood after the first arson would quiet down.

Even though the plan was to be carried out in a number of weeks, my peace of mind was already gone, especially because, according to Staczek, the night guard had been enlarged and strengthened and the fire department and police were in a state of readiness.

With the increased danger in the entire area, the bravery of our boys grew; any sense of fear that they had before, disappeared. They distanced themselves from thinking, what will happen if…?

A zealous fire to take revenge burned within them. Revenge against the Germans is a national and moral obligation, for history and for themselves.

That same week, something happened to Staczek that partially took revenge upon us. The incident occurred on Sunday. All day we were in a bad mood, without any peace of mind. At nine o'clock in the morning, Staczek did not come as usual to take off the cover of the bunker and lower our breakfast down to us. We knew that Staczek had guests from Warsaw at that time: the wife of a high Polish officer who had been taken prisoner by the Germans, and her two grown sons. Staczek was very careful in their presence so that they would not detect that there were Jews under his protection, hidden in a bunker. To the question of the sons why he had to cook in two pots, Staczek answered that he was fattening hogs, and, out of their sight, he took the pots to the sheepfold and at a later stage – to us. That same day, as mentioned, Staczek did not show up and the bunker cover remained sealed.

We knew that Staczek was accustomed to visit Dr. Volosvitza on Sundays, but the food had always reached us as usual, at the regular times. We were seized by gloomy thoughts, assuming that Staczek had been arrested on his way back from the Soviet Doctor's house when they found him with a hidden battery. Maybe they arrested him in order to send him to work in Germany? Thus we lay all day, upset and expecting the worst. During the late hours of the evening, we heard footsteps. It was Staczek, who took off the cover and came down into the bunker with a pot of food in his hands. He gave Moshe a note from the Soviet Doctor, and after that he told us what happened:

Because of the presence of the visiting lads in the yard this morning, Staczek decided to go earlier to the Soviet Doctor and bring us the food later. Everything proceeded properly, but on the way back home he met a farmer with a wagon, who invited him to climb up and he would give him a ride part of the way. In Staczek's pants pocket, there was a small battery that Igor, the Soviet Doctor's son, had given to him when he was at the Doctor's house. Because of the rattling of the wagon over the rutted road, the acid spilled out of the battery and he was badly burnt between the thighs. When he got home, he took off his clothes and saw that the burns had turned into wide, black wounds that were painful and caused him a lot of suffering.

He is not yet ready to tell his brother Palek what happened to him, because he is worried that he will tease and mock him about his dealings with the Jews and about the radio receivers for the underground, because of which he is endangering himself and his entire family.

Even so, he showed us the wounded places on his body. We advised him to request immediate help from the Dr. Volosvitza. Staczek had no other choice, but to nevertheless tell Palek of his trouble and send him immediately to the Soviet Doctor, tell her what had happened and ask her for medicine for this type of burn, until he would be able to go to her himself.

From that day onward, the cover of the bunker was opened only once a day, at ten o'clock at night, instead of twice a day, until now. The food that was served to us also became worse from day to day, and we had no choice but to be silent.

The Soviet Doctor informed us in a letter, among other things, that Alter Ginzberg, his wife the dentist and their son Monik, who had been transported some time ago to the Bialystok Ghetto, had been expelled with the first transport of Jews – to Treblinka. On the way, Monik had succeeded in jumping out of the train and, according to rumor, he was hiding in one of the villages.

The Soviet Doctor also told us that Shlomo Jaskolka also jumped from the train. In doing so, he received a hard blow on his head that caused a brain concussion, and he became insane. Instead of hiding, he ran to the police in Lapy and prattled about all kinds of things. He told them that until the War, he had been occupied in selling crops, that his wife traveled to visit her relatives in the United States and returned from there close to the time the War broke out. He said he was the father of sons and the grandfather of a grandson, and lived a good, happy life until the Germans came and destroyed the lives of all the Jews. He was forced to flee with his entire family to the forests, from fear of the mass murders that the Germans were committing. From the forests, he later reached the Bialystok Ghetto from which he was taken to be killed in Treblinka. He succeeded in jumping out of the train, and turned to the *gendarmerie* in Lapy, so that they would protect his life from the Gestapo murderers.

They did not let Jaskolka go on. They took him outside to the yard of the police station and shot him in the back.

Another story is about 'Itzele' Roseman. The Germans employed him for a long time to polish their shoes, and regarded him as "an efficient Jew." They promised him that nothing bad would happen to him. On the day of the expulsion, they even suggested that he hide in the forest with his entire family. This week, Roseman was caught, together with Benyamin Okune, the sexton of the synagogue and gravedigger. Both families were shot in the forest.

Among those who were murdered in the forest under similar circumstances were Shabtil Zlotko, the son of Bracha, the seamstress; the butcher 'Betzalelke' Fleer; Hanoch the butcher, the son of 'Bezalelke'; and Hanoch's wife, Nechama who gave birth to a son in the forest; Avraham Fleer; and Hanoch Fleer's son-in-law (Alter, son of Beilah Rachel). Avraham ran around searching for milk for the newborn, since Nechama was unable to nurse him. The farmers knew Avraham and had always been friendly to him, but when he was in trouble, they sent him away empty-handed and avoided him. All these fell victim to the Germans and were shot.

'Shmeig' told us about daily transports of Jews to Treblinka in closed cattle cars. Many people succeeded in jumping out of the trains, but the sentries shot them and the tracks were seeded with those who had been killed. Gangs of Poles roamed the length of the tracks and robbed those who succeeded in fleeing of everything, down to their shoelaces. There were incidents where those who jumped off the train were killed by injuries from objects in their way, such as telephone poles or rocks, or were injured and broken by the jump itself.

This week, continued Staczek, there was an incident involving four Jews, two men and two women, who had succeeded in jumping from a boxcar. They were happy that they had been saved from death and that they did not meet up with Polish gangs. They wandered in the forest, slept in pits and suffered from hunger, until finally they came to Giemzino, a village at the edge of the forest, about four kilometers from where we were located. The four survivors calmed down a bit when they found out that they were far from the train line and from a traveled road and, as they had thought previously, there were no Germans in the nearby surroundings, nor were there any robbers.

The people sat down under a tree to rest, and suddenly they saw a farmer coming toward them. The man appeared innocent and, for some reason, they trusted him, and told him who they were and what their situation was. He listened carefully to every word they said and gave them the impression that he was shocked and took pity upon them. The farmer asked them to follow him to the village and promised to get them some bread. They did not think of suspecting him, and walked after him, feeble and broken, in the hope of quieting their hunger and finding a corner where there was no danger to their lives.

Suddenly, the farmer turned on his heel, pulled out a pistol, and shot a round of bullets. The two men and one of the women collapsed and fell in their places. The second woman, who was young, succeeded in fleeing and found a safe place to hide. She told the whole story, and it also reached Staczek's ears.

The Apostate Meizner

An apostate named Meizner lived in Sokoly with his wife and two children. When the War broke out, their son was 20 years old and their daughter was 17. Meizner was circumcised; even the lines of his face bore witness to his obvious Jewishness. At first sight, his wife also looked like a typical Jewess; her manner of speaking also could not hide her origins. Since he was an apostate, people stayed away from him, both Jews and Christians.

Meizner's apostasy was a matter of livelihood and maintenance, and nothing else. He did not go to church, and he never went to the priest to confession. During the Soviet occupation, his daughter married the *Kommissar* and moved with him to Russia.

With the German invasion of Sokoly, the apostate, like the rest of the Jews, did not enjoy any preferences and he was not granted any privileges. Even so, at the time of the expulsion, Meizner found shelter in the villages, in spite of the fact that the farmers knew of his Jewish origins and the recognition that they would be given the most severe punishment for hiding a Jew. The Polish police also knew who Meizner was and were silent. The apostate went around freely, as if the entire matter of the persecutions did not relate to him. He was carefree and certain that no one would inform on him and that he was regarded among the Poles as "a man of our own." During this time, his son became ill and passed away.

Trouble with the Bunker

In February 1943, three months after the expulsion from Sokoly, the warm winds of spring began to blow, contrary to the usual weather at this season. Suddenly, the snow melted and the walls of our bunker became waterfalls. The water streamed down from the ceiling and burst forth from the bottom like a gushing fountain. 'Shmeig' had predicted to us that in the spring, we could expect flooding in the cave, but at that time we did not relate seriously to

182

what he said because we thought he was interested in getting rid of us and wanted us to go find somewhere else to stay.

We began to look for ways of protecting ourselves against the forces of nature. We found it correct to dig a pit at the bottom of the cave, as deep and wide as possible, so that the water would gather there and gradually subside.

We moved our possessions and bedding to a higher location in a corner where the water had not yet started to flow. The four of us had no choice but to sit on our possessions, being terribly crowded. We could not stretch our legs, and the water came up to our knees. We were worried that the flood would be complete and that the water would fill the entire space within the bunker. Towards evening, our fear grew greater, when the pit in the bottom of the cave filled up and the water overflowed its sides and covered the part of the bunker that was still dry.

On Sunday, we waited impatiently for 'Shmeig' to come. He came at ten o'clock in the morning with portions of food, served to us as usual. We took advantage of the entire time the cover was open and, using the vessels we had at our disposal, fervently drew water and carefully poured it out at a distance away from the bunker without leaving any footprints.

On Monday we could not wait any more for Staczek to come because the water had risen too high. We lifted the cover ourselves and with pails drew out the rising water. One pail was always with us; we took a second pail from the farm well, and in this manner we poured more than 70 pails of water outside. Two of us stood outside and took the pails of water into our hands, while the other two, inside the bunker, passed the filled pails up to us. The pails were hooked onto the ends of gnarled wooden poles to aid in passing them up where we could grab them.

On Tuesday, frost covered the surface of the bunker and the water stopped dripping from the ceiling and flowed only from the bottom.

When the flood ended, the walls of earth and sand were saturated with dampness. When the walls dried, they split and clumps fell off them. This time, there was a danger that the entire cave would collapse.

It was urgently necessary to find boards to support the walls of the bunker. It was clear that we couldn't obtain them for any amount of money. We remembered that on the Idzki road, a board fence had been put up to protect the train tracks from the snow, and the youngsters decided to pilfer boards from there. They went out on their mission at eleven o'clock at night and returned at three in the morning, each of them carrying on his back a section of fence comprised of 15 boards – all together, 45 boards. I tried without success to lift one of these sections and found that it was beyond my physical ability to do so. I wondered at the strength of the boys who had traveled a distance of eight kilometers through fields and woods with such a heavy load without meeting a living soul.

After the boys returned, they did not allow themselves to rest until Staczek came at four o'clock to camouflage the opening. A great deal of work still remained. The boards had to be taken apart, nails had to be removed from them and they had to be lowered into our "house." Then, the area around the place had to be camouflaged so that no footprints would remain. All these jobs were strictly carried out within 45 minutes.

The next night was devoted to supporting the walls with boards that were sawed to size and made appropriate to the shape of the walls and the ceiling.

The third night, the boys went out again to the train track, to bring more boards from the fence to cover the floor of the bunker in a raised manner, so that in case of heavy rain, the bedding would be higher and the water collecting below would be deeper.

The next night, our heroes went out to the forest to cut birch trees to support the floor. 'Avrahamel' had carpentry tools and a sharp saw in good condition. During the next stage, hooks were made to hold personal possessions and clothing.

After completing the bunker house repairs, the boys raised the idea of a repeat mission to the regional dairy to bring another load of butter, since the previous load was used up. In addition, they planned burglaries of farms in more distant villages in order to get food and anything else that was useful.

My heart again filled with unrest, depression, and discouragement, and I was in constant fear that we would be:
    1) killed by the Germans;
    2) murdered by gangs of Poles;
    3) annihilated, following flooding or collapse of the
     bunker, from strangulation as a result of the lack of air,
     or from illness; and
    4) threatened by danger as a result of the boys'
     missions.

I tried, with all the means at my disposal, to restrain the hot-headed youngsters from their dangerous plans and persuade them, with logical arguments, to desist from additional heroic acts after the burglary of the government dairy, the robbery of the geese and turkeys from the *Amstkommissar*'s house, and last, but not least – the burning of the majority of the town. There is no doubt that the guards have been strengthened in all corners of the town and in the villages, and any attempt at burglary or arson is doomed to complete failure and puts the lives of four people in danger. In my heart, I added myself as the fifth and last victim of our community.

I advised them to contact Dr. Claudia Nikolievna Volosvitza in whatever way they could, and ask her to send– as far as could be done – a regular delivery of food packages in exchange for the items that we deposited with her which were worth 1,000 marks. The boys thought my suggestion was a good one, and it was decided to act in that direction.

Since the acid had burned him, 'Shmeig' had stopped visiting the Soviet Doctor. This week, he was due to go out to Sokoly and we convinced him to jump over to Dr. Claudia Nikolievna's house at this opportunity and give her a letter.

On Monday of that week, Staczek came down to us, and together with the food, he gave Moshe a letter from the Soviet Doctor containing 100 marks enclosed in the envelope. In the letter, Nikolievna justified herself and apologized for not immediately sending a package of food, since she was not able to estimate that somebody would be prepared to accept it and bring it to us. However, she informed us of her readiness to send us food, as long as someone would be found who would bring it to its destination.

'Shmeig', in his conversation with Nikolievna, got the impression that she was upset by the rumor that the Germans had killed a Soviet doctor in Wysokie-Mazowieckie. A number of men, dressed in Soviet uniforms and speaking Russian, came to the doctor's house and shot him on the spot. There were those who said, she added, that the partisans in the forests took revenge on the murdered doctor because he did not cooperate with them. As for herself, she did not think that the partisans related to her negatively, because she did as much as she could for them, and thereby she showed support for the Poles.

In comparison, her son Igor had been in a state of depression and discouragement since the doctor in Wysokie was murdered, and he worried that the days of his family were numbered and the voices of death were being raised high.

On Friday of that week, Staczek informed us that he wanted to go into the town. We again gave him a letter to Claudia Nikolievna. Towards evening, 'Shmeig' returned, with Job's message: last night, two men dressed in Soviet uniforms had murdered Dr. Claudia Volosvitza. The housemaid had also been murdered along with her. The son Igor had succeeded in escaping through the window, along with his six-year-old sister.

We were dumbfounded by the news, and the shock did not leave us for many long hours. I was worried that the youngsters would again awaken to rash actions, since their support – the Soviet Doctor – had collapsed and was gone. My heart also was grieved by the tragedy of Claudia Nikolievna who, in our eyes, was one of the world's righteous gentiles.

A few days after the Soviet Doctor was murdered, the men of the *A.K.* underground broke into the apartment of the Polish police officer Yanchenko in the middle of the night and opened fire. At that time, Officer Kanofka's daughter was in the apartment and she was injured. She was taken, in serious condition, to the hospital in Bialystok. Fearing additional attacks, the police headquarters moved to the house of 'Little Alterke'.

The men of the *A.K.* were not afraid, and one day they shot and killed Kanofka, who faithfully carried out the orders of the Germans. Kanofka was sitting in Kraweicz's restaurant, sipping beer from a cup that stood on the table. At that moment, a young Pole entered the restaurant and raised panic by telling everyone that out in the street, they were kidnapping Poles to be transported to Prussia for forced labor. The people who were in the place fled in panic, which the young Pole exploited. He shot Kanofka and ran away from the place without being seen.

This was Sunday, and the church was completely filled with worshippers. The *A.K.* men took advantage of the large gathering and caused panic in the crowd by shouting that outside, Poles were being kidnapped for forced labor in Germany. Their plan was to awaken panic in the congregation and hatred towards those cooperating with the German enemy. In panicked flight, the men of the underground escaped. One innocent farmer hid in a dark corner of the church, from fear of the Germans and being kidnapped. The Germans found him immediately, arrested him, and accused him of murdering the policeman Kanofka.

The death of the cruel policeman Kanofka awakened feelings of revenge within us. During the expulsion of the Jews from Sokoly, Kanofka had excelled in his murderous and cruel acts. He shot many Jews with his own hands, both during the "action" and also when they were searching for Jews in the forests.

Immediately after the German invasion of Sokoly, Kanofka threw 'Yechielke' Blustein (Mondritzke's son) out of his beautiful apartment and stole the furniture and all the possessions in the house from him.

The men of the underground killed Kanofka, not specifically because of his murderous attitude towards the Jews, but also because of his satanic attitude towards his Polish brothers. Not too long ago, the policeman Kanofka shot and killed the daughter of the musician Washilewski, a young Polish girl who had dared to criticize him and his criminal behavior. She announced, publicly and in Kanofka's presence, sarcastic instructions that wounded the policeman to the depths of his satanic heart.

'Shmeig' further told us that this time, the Germans decided to destroy the men of the *A.K.* underground around Sokoly. For this purpose, they had drafted 50 soldiers of the Gestapo, who were combing the roads, pathways, and villages.

During the last days of March, our economic situation worsened and our supply of fat and butter was used up. Only a bit of dried bread remained to us, which we ate with water. Having no choice, the boys decided to plan some kind of "little break-in" at one of the village farms, in order to fill our basket with fresh food.

A Guest in the Bunker

On April 6, 1943, Staczek informed us that tonight Monik, the son of the dentist from Sokoly, had come to his house. Monik had succeeded in jumping out of the train at the time his entire family, along with thousands of Jews from the Bialystok Ghetto, were being transported to the gas chambers in Treblinka. 'Shmeig' told us that Monik had proposed a high price in dollars if he would give him shelter, but he and his brother Palek were afraid to take on their shoulders the burden and responsibility of keeping five Jews, which would involve an additional, multiplied danger. As of now, no answer had been given to Monik, nor had Staczek told him any information about our existence and our bunker. He only gave Monik permission to sleep that night in his threshing house, promising that he would give him a final answer tomorrow morning.

We were happy upon hearing this news and we all spoke together as one, trying to convince Staczek to agree to let Monik join us because it was no more trouble and the same danger was involved in taking care of five people as in taking care of four. For doing so, Staczek would receive a significant payment from Monik in dollars and it was a shame to delay such a wonderful opportunity. We kept trying to arouse Staczek's appetite for money until he decided to agree to let Monik enter our bunker.

'Avrahamel' asked Staczek to supply him with three boards so that he could enlarge the area of the bunker a bit to make it ready for a fifth occupant. We did not ask Staczek for any help doing the work or for any effort on his part.

We were very happy that a new neighbor was being added and we hoped to hear news from him about our relatives.

The next day, Monik, the son of the dentist, went to his Christian acquaintances to get from them the money and possessions that he had deposited with them.

On April 8th, Monik came back and Staczek lowered him into the bunker to us.

At that time, Monik was 25 years old. His father [Roseman] was the son of the owner of real estate property in Warsaw and died at a young age. His mother was a dentist in Sokoly and her second husband was Alter Ginzberg, the Rabbi's grandson. Alter owned a leather goods store and a number of houses in Sokoly. The mother continued her professional work also after her second marriage. Occasionally, she would receive sums of money from the houses she had inherited from her first husband, which were intended for Monik.

Monik completed his high school studies in Bialystok and went on to learn medicine in Italy, where he learned for one year. Close to the start of World War II, when the Nazi propaganda and its influence became stronger in Italy, the Jews were expelled from the institutions of higher learning and at that time Monik returned to Sokoly.

During the German regime, Alter Ginzberg was the head of the *Judenrat*. When the Jews were expelled from Sokoly, he and his family escaped to the forests with the rest of the fleeing Jews. They searched in vain for shelter with their good acquaintances and friends "from the good times." None of them allowed the family to cross the threshold of his house, and certainly not even to sleep in the threshing house. They wandered around in the forests for days, in constant fear of German searches, the Polish police and the gangs of Polish robbers, who swarmed like locusts and attacked their victims, stripping them of everything. Finally, the Ginzberg and Yisrael Maik families found a dugout; later, they found a number of merciful farmers who supplied them with food in exchange for a suitable and high payment.

These good days did not last for long. Polish hooligans found the dugout and bothered its residents, blackmailing them into paying them a ransom, under threats of handing them over to the Germans. The heads of the gangs were famous: 'Sergei' the Russian and Yanek. They appeared to be armed partisans, but their deeds were robbery and rape.

Suddenly, it became known that the Germans had stopped shooting the Jews that they caught, and were sending them to the Bialystok Ghetto at a ransom of 500 marks each. The two families decided to proceed in that way, and handed themselves over to the kindness of the Germans. They were held under arrest for two days and on the third day, they were sent to the Bialystok Ghetto.

In the Bialystok Ghetto

In the Bialystok Ghetto, the Ginzberg family gradually organized themselves. Compared to their life in the forest, in the ghetto they felt they were in Paradise. There, they could at least walk around freely without constant feelings of fear. For coin, it was possible to obtain all the food they needed. Alter was promised a position in the local *Judenrat*, as the secretary of our uncle, Rafael Gutman, Hertzel's son. Alter's wife, the dentist, worked in her profession, and their son Monik was offered a position as a policeman in the ghetto militia. Monik was rescued from that despised job when he coincidentally met up with two policemen who were forced to hang two lads who had been caught for the sin of filling their pockets with seeds on their way out of the factory where they worked.

On February 5, 1943, the first mass transports from the Bialystok Ghetto, known as the 'first action', began. Among the rows of these Jews, the Ginzberg family marched to meet their deaths. The Gestapo soldiers took them out of a camouflaged hiding place that they found with the aid of large search dogs. With great sorrow, it must be added that they were also aided by despicable Jews who handed over their brothers into the hands of the murderers.

A few of the Jewish informers were eliminated by organized youths, whose existence was known only in the Ghetto. Every day, there were thousands of victims of the "first action." Men, women, and children were cruelly taken from their hiding places and brought like a herd of sheep to be slaughtered by dozens of armed Germans accompanied by wolf dogs. The murderers lashed the heads of the poor unfortunates with whips and the dogs bit their flesh. Thus, they were pursued until they came to the Bialystok Train Station, where they were loaded like cattle into closed boxcars and transported to Treblinka.

Inside each of the boxcars stood an upright soldier, who was ready to shoot with his automatic weapon at anyone who would dare to jump out of the car and flee from the death awaiting him when he reached Treblinka. Even so, there were those who tried their luck at this most dangerous jumping. Many of them were killed immediately when they crashed into telegraph poles. One Jew instructed Monik as to how one should jump out the window of the boxcar at a lower location, so as to prevent the upright soldier from having a direct line of fire. The Jew had prior experience, having once succeeded in escaping from a train, but he had been injured and required continuous medical treatment. After he recovered from his injuries, his fate again pushed him into the boxcars of death.

Monik dared to do it, and jumped out successfully, but his knee was lightly injured. He was able to get up immediately and proceed forward in the direction of the nearby forest. On his way, he saw many dead Jews near the train tracks who had tried, like himself, to flee from death. He directed his footsteps toward a village he knew in the hope of finding shelter.

On his way, he met up with a Polish lad and started to talk to him. He was familiar with the Polish language and his accent was such that it was impossible to identify him as a Jew. The boy brought Monik, who had difficulty in finding the path to the village, to the correct road. One of his mother's regular clients, a good-hearted, merciful farmer, took Monik in and kept him in his house for a number of months without any concern that somebody was likely to reveal that he was a Jew because his appearance, speech, and customs were the same as those of the people of the village. Monik even went around among the people, thereby removing any suspicion as to his identity.

Monik's situation was good. The village was far away from Sokoly and far from any busy road, and it was very unusual for Polish police to visit there. But one day a gang of 'Sergei' men appeared in the good farmer's house. They stripped Monik of his clothes and took away his boots and everything they found on him. To his joy, he had hidden his money earlier in a safe place in a crack in the wall. He begged the robbers to at least leave him a pair of torn pants, some worn-out shoes, and a hat. The Poles in the gang did not even want to listen to him, saying that it wasn't worth it and it was forbidden to have pity on a Jew, but one Russian among them did take pity upon him and gave him some patched trousers and an old pair of shoes.

Towards evening, Monik carefully went out in the direction of Sokoly and reached the home of a friend of his mother where some of their possessions had been deposited. The woman, a midwife by profession, gave him a suit, some shoes, and underwear. Monik was afraid to go back to the good farmer's village and decided to find a new, safe place. He thought that the farmer's son had traitorously told the gang members about him. Previously, they had robbed a number of Jews in this same farmer's house, who had paid the farmer 100 marks for sheltering them for three days.

Monik found out where Moshe Maik was staying while he was still in the Bialystok Ghetto, and that is how he came to us on April 8, 1943.

Monik Tells About the Jews from Sokoly

Monik told us about the fate of many of the Jews from Sokoly who escaped to the forests, as well as the way of life in the Bialystok Ghetto. Of a population of 2,000 Jews, that Sunday 500 souls were expelled and the rest fled to the forests and hiding places. During a number of weeks, hundreds of those who fled fell into the hands of the Germans, some by means of searches and some being handed over by Poles. As is known, there also were some who turned themselves into the hands of the murderers in despair, after they had been robbed by Polish, and even Russian, gangs. Many Jews were shot in the forests. Some of them were sent to the Tenth Division Fort near Bialystok, where they were oppressed for weeks with hunger and the most severe conditions. The daily portion of food included 70 grams of bread and one-half potato per person. For that, they managed complete lists and records.

The chief record-keeper there was the respected teacher and talented speaker from Sokoly, Goldberg, the husband of the teacher Friedman. She worked together with Yente as supervisors of the distribution of the scarce food. Those poor souls who became weak and lost their strength from hunger were sent, under strict guard, to the gas chambers in Treblinka.

Monik remembered that, at the time the Jews who had turned themselves over to the Germans and those who had been found by them were transported, 'Avrahamel' Lapchinsky and Rachel Morashkevitz, the daughter of the owner of the ironworks shop, were shot to death in the Kruzewo Train Station. Rachel proudly lifted her voice in the presence of the Germans, the way 'Benyaminke' Rachelsky had done, rebuked them, and predicted their end and that the wrath of G-d would fall upon them. They grabbed her father Yechezkel when he was trying to get into his house in order to take out some of his possessions. He was shot to death on the spot.

The members of the Bialystok *Judenrat* succeeded in getting Rabbi Rosenblum out of Tenth Division Fort together with his wife and eldest daughter Sarah. His two youngest children, the seven-year-old girl 'Nechamale' and the little boy 'Yankele', aged five, who had an open mind and already knew the morning, afternoon, and evening prayers from memory, were also with him in the military camp. When the Germans came to take the Rabbi to the Bialystok Ghetto, the children were playing somewhere in the courtyard. The Rabbi and his wife were not allowed to look for the children and have them join the family. Thus, the poor children were left to their cruel fate in the Tenth Division Fort without their parents. The Rabbi's two middle daughters died in the forest.

After that, the Rabbi remained in the Ghetto for three months. He managed precise lists of Jews from Sokoly and what he knew about their fate. He made lists of those who were murdered, and under what circumstances they were killed. He listed those whose fate was still unknown, those who were wandering in the forests, and of course he did not pass over any Jew from Sokoly who was in Bialystok and what had happened to him until that very day, including those who had been sent to Treblinka to the gas chambers.

Rabbi Rosenblum and the remaining members of his family were sent to Treblinka in February 1943, with a group of Jews from the "first action."

In this first transport, there was a young man from Bialystok named Melamed. At the moment when the men of the Gestapo reached his hiding place and began to drive him and his family out, he took from his pocket a bottle of sodium acid and poured its entire contents into the eyes of the soldier standing closest to him. The German was surprised and it appeared that his face was burnt and his eyesight was lost. Wanting to shoot Melamed, he wounded and killed his German companion. After his heroic act, the young man disappeared. The Germans took revenge on the Jews and killed one hundred Jews right there. After that, they requested that the *Judenrat* hand over the young man to them, promising to stop the mass transportss in exchange for him. Otherwise, they wouldn't leave a single Jew in the Bialystok Ghetto. Melamed appeared of his own free will at the office of the Gestapo, in order to rescue the congregation of Israel by his death. They tortured him cruelly and hung him in public. It is clear that the transports continued more vigorously and the Jews were brought in multitudes to the slaughter.

Yet at the beginning of autumn 1942, the head of the [Bialystok] *Judenrat*, Barash, gave a speech to the Jews. He said that, at his unceasing initiative and with every effort, he had succeeded in delaying the decree of expulsion of the Jews of Bialystok until the spring. "…and who knows, with G-d's help, it would be a real springtime for all of us…".

Things calmed down and everyone made the calculation that it was good to live for the hour. Perhaps, during a period of half a year, a miracle would occur and things would change for the better?

But the first transports began immediately, at the beginning of the month of February 1943, and within two weeks, 15,000 Jews were sent from the [Bialystok] Ghetto to the gas chambers.

In telling about the searches in the forests of Sokoly, Monik described the tragedy of Rachel Leah from Wienda. As I have mentioned previously, Rachel Leah was friendly with the Christians in her village. During the first few weeks after the expulsion from Sokoly, a group of neighbors and acquaintances followed her to the forest and she took care of their needs. At night, they would sleep in the farms. Later, they prepared a bunker for themselves, where they lived for a length of time.

One day, during a search of the forest, Rachel Leah's small son, who was bringing their cow to the cave, saw Germans coming toward him. The boy panicked and started to run in the direction of the bunker. The murderers followed him and killed everyone who was there.

Reuven Gonshak, Shmuel Bronstein's son-in-law, was injured during that same search. When they were digging a pit to bury those killed in the forest, they threw Reuven, alive and groaning in pain, into the pit.

Monik continued to describe the lives of the Jews from Sokoly that he met in the forest. Some of them had arranged permanent places for themselves, and some wandered from place to place.

Shabtai Esterovitz, the son of Shlomo, the owner of the Sokoly flourmill, found shelter for himself and his wife in a threshing house on a farm, among piles of grain. Shabtai was good with his hands and he knew how to do smithy and carpentry work, and knew how to repair things on a farm when needed. The farmer gained a great deal of profit from him. He repaired a machine for cutting straw and other agricultural tools. Shabtai gave his Christian master a significant sum of money and various household items. He was a faithful Jew and observed the commandments, and was especially careful about [not] eating non-kosher food. He ate potatoes with no fat, which were cooked in a pot he had brought with him from his home.

Since the village was isolated and quiet, every once in a while wandering Jews who had heard about the farmer's positive treatment of Jews would come to buy something to eat. Shlomo Kravchevitz the tailor and his six-year-old son, 'Avrahamele' were among these. The Germans had killed Shlomo's wife and his son Fishel. Shlomo would receive tailoring jobs from the farmers and he sometimes stayed with them for a length of time.

In the same group was Sarah Esther Malach, the granddaughter of Yaakov Leib Perlowitz, who had previously been in the forest with her little sister 'Henele'. Following a denouncement, their dugout was revealed and ten people who were found inside were shot and killed. Among those killed were Mordechai Jezevitz and 'Avrahamke' Lepkovsky's wife, his son, and his daughter. By chance, Sarah Esther Malach was absent from the place at that time and thus she was saved from certain death. From that time onward, she stayed in the company of Shlomo Kravchevitz. His other son, Moshe, spoke Polish with the farmers' dialect and disguised himself as a Pole. After parting from his father, he joined a Christian group of partisans. According to rumor, they carried out daring acts of sabotage against the Germans and their possessions.

'Itza' Elinovitz and his son, and one of the sons of Rachel Leah from Wienda, came to the farm where Monik had stayed previously. Schultz also would come to the farmer's house. We heard details about him from Monik.

Schultz (Chaya Zelda Shklarovitz' Husband)

Schultz was a well-known personality in Sokoly. The Christians knew him well, as did the Jews. He had a wagon and had superior strength and quickness of movement. He was famous for his jolly stories and piquant jokes, which he would tell with a unique intonation until his listeners were splitting with laughter. Other than this, he knew how to do acrobatic tricks, such as climbing walls and the high, slanted roofs of houses.

Schultz was especially famous in the whole area after his last victory: A circus came to Sokoly, in which there appeared, among others, an athlete who lifted heavy weights and bent iron. During the show, the athlete turned to the audience with the question whether a man was present who was prepared to wrestle with him and win, for the prize of 100 zlotys (gold coins). Without any hesitation, Schultz appeared on the scene, struggled for a short time, and laid the athlete out on the carpet, according to the rules.

Schultz's wife was also known for her bubbly temperament and witty tongue. Schultz's wife, Chaya Zelda, was the daughter of Yosef Leib Shklarovitz, the glazier. She bore Schultz three children, who were murdered by the Germans together with their mother. Schultz himself fled to the forests, and his portion was suffering and many afflictions.

Life in Our Bunker after Monik Joined Us

After Monik came to us, our situation became a little worse. In our "apartment" under the earth, there was hardly room for the four of us, and here, a fifth resident had appeared. We had to squeeze together even more, but we took the obligation upon ourselves willingly and with full understanding.

For five weeks, we worked hard to add more width and volume to the bunker so that it would be appropriate for all of us. The ground was hard and rocky, and it was difficult and almost impossible to dig with a spade, because the bunker was too low for the movements of the tool. It remained for us to use a pick, and by breaking through, to remove broken-off pieces from the walls and take clumps of the rocky soil outside. It was most important to disguise our footprints around the bunker.

During this period, the place was cramped and the air was stifling. We could not turn over, or even move our limbs, when we were lying down. The food also became worse and there was not enough for all of us. We received the same four scanty portions we had gotten before, now for all five of us. 'Shmeig' did not even enlarge the portion of bread and, to be accurate, he lessened it. Staczek brought us a new custom: twice a week, he did not prepare cooked food. On those days we were hungry. We suffered from his lack of punctuality, since he was periodically absent from home, busy with meetings of the underground, and came home near midnight. Then he would agree to send down to us a pot of cold food that we couldn't eat, in spite of the feeling of hunger that nagged us.

The youngsters conducted savings of the bread they ate and cut it into very thin slices so that it would last them the entire day or more. When hunger nagged them more and more, they found carrots, cabbage, and turnips outside and chewed on them. They gathered these findings on their nighttime walks when they went outside to get some fresh air. As for me, I wasn't able to enjoy such a meal, because I had lost my false teeth some time ago and the fresh, hard vegetables could not be chewed in my empty mouth. Thus, the hunger bothered me incessantly.

We suffered during the months of February and March from flooding and in April, May, and June from a lack of air. So that no one would detect us, we could not make large holes in the top of the bunker for air, and small holes occasionally became blocked.

Once, we were frightened to death and the youngsters blamed me. The incident occurred at midnight. The youngsters went out for their usual walk and I went out for a few minutes to the nearby forest to relieve myself. When I came back to the bunker, I did not have time to cover the entrance with the temporary wooden cover.

Suddenly, somebody opened the door of the toilet and asked in the Polish language, "Is Staczek here?"

I was very frightened. I thought that they had found our hiding place and that by morning the matter would be known all over the village and all of us would be lost.

When the boys came back to the bunker, I told them what happened and immediately panic set in. 'Avrahamel' attacked me in a very loud voice and with insults, yelling, "The 'Old Man', the idle sinner, has buried us! Where will we turn to now to find a new shelter?"

My son Moshe was angry with me for not being careful. "Why didn't you look around you to see that no one was there, or if you could hear footsteps?"

I felt a deep stirring of conscience and pangs of repentance that I had caused a tragedy and endangered five lives.

My son Moshe and 'Avrahamel' immediately ran to Staczek, to find out from him and his brother Palek who the man was who had asked the old man about Staczek. Moshe knocked softly on the window of the brothers' room. They were still awake and immediately came to the window and asked why he was coming to them in the middle of the night. Moshe told them that his father had caused them sudden fear and about the strange man who had asked for Staczek. Palek burst out laughing, saying that he himself was the "strange man," and that he had come home late and found the door of his room locked, so he came to the bunker to see if maybe Staczek was there so he could take the key from him. Palek was surprised; how could the 'Old Man' not recognize him?

All of us calmed down, and I gave thanks to G-d for the kindness he did for me in taking me out of my spiritual distress. After these events, the boys spoke to me and told me not to go out alone from the bunker, but always accompanied by one of them.

A short time later, again something happened to us that caused us a sudden fear of death. The event was as follows:

At that season, every day at six o'clock in the morning, 'Shmeig' was accustomed to closing and camouflaging the bunker opening with a cover having dirt on top of it. A short time ago, he would do this at four o'clock, when it was still dark outside. This time, Staczek appeared exactly at six o'clock. As usual, he took off the wood cover that covered us at night and put it in its accustomed place, so as to replace it with the camouflaged cover.

Suddenly, we heard the barking of the three 'Shmeig' dogs. Moshe put his ear near the bunker hole and said, "Germans in the yard!"

And the bunker was still opened! All they had to do was to open the door of the toilet, and we were lost! They will find us! Trembling seized my body and my teeth began to chatter. I started to mumble the *Viduy* [Confession of Sins].

'Avrahamel' ordered us: "Boys, grab the weapons! First we have to kill a few Germans!" He grabbed a rifle loaded with bullets and handed a second one to Moshe. Monik and Chaim 'Yudel' grabbed hand grenades. 'Avrahamel', who had experience in the Polish army, stood each one in his place and instructed them how to shoot, when to throw the grenades, and in what direction to flee. In case it will be impossible to flee, the last bullets should be used for ourselves, we shouldn't just fall alive into the enemy's hands.

Meanwhile, the dogs hadn't stopped barking, and the entire terrible campaign had continued for a quarter of an hour.

Suddenly, the barking stopped. 'Shmeig' approached us with the heavy cover in his hands, and told us that he had just had some nightmarish moments. Germans really were in the yard, but they did not come to conduct a search; rather, they came to ask for butter and eggs. It was a miracle that they did not see him carrying the cover, which would certainly have brought horrible results. These Germans were guards on the Jamiolki Bridge. Staczek immediately brought them ten eggs and refused to accept payment from them. He told them that today he did not have any lard or butter, and they went away, the same way that they came.

Thank G-d, it all finished only with fear. From that day onward, 'Shmeig' covered the opening at an earlier hour, when it was still dark outside.

At that time, the boys planned a daring, dangerous mission. They decided to burn down all the houses in Sokoly that remained after the previous fire.

Sokoly Burns a Second Time

The boys decided that not a single Jewish house in Sokoly would remain in the hands of those who hate us, neither Germans nor Poles. So that the mission would succeed, it was necessary to carry it out in three stages, and each stage in itself would be satisfying. There were three separate parts of the city that had to be burnt: Mountain Street, where there were a number of two-story buildings; part of the houses in the market that had been saved in the first fire; and some houses that stood alone on a number of different streets.

Since the first fire, a large fire department had been established in Sokoly along with a continuous night guard. Therefore, the mission was difficult and extremely dangerous. Besides the Jewish houses, the youngsters swore that they would burn down the house of the notorious, antisemitic, hard-hearted, and corrupt Janina Palkowska.

A special plan was necessary in order to set a large house on fire that was very far from the others; it stood near the Wysokie-Mazowieckie road and belonged to a Jewish crop merchant, Mordechai Surasky.

It was necessary to begin to act immediately, while the nights were still misty; it would be a shame to miss the opportunity.

The hour to act has arrived! The boys went out to Sokoly on a quiet night, and when they arrived, they immediately set fire to the cowsheds that belonged to Shlomo Leibel Itzkovsky. From there, the fire would naturally spread to the row of houses.

To our disappointment, the next day we learned that only a few of the houses caught fire. However, the flames ate up the cowsheds and shacks all along Mountain Street, up to the house belonging to the Christian blacksmith, Garabowski. This time, the fire department controlled the situation and arrived quickly at the site, located the fire, and prevented it from spreading.

This angered the boys very much and they decided to repeat the deed, and this time "not to come back with empty hands." The second attempt, and after that a third one, also did not succeed, and because of new events in our lives, there was no further opportunity to complete our revenge.

We Leave the Bunker

During those days, some things occurred that brought about changes in our life underground. Staczek's *A.K* organization decided, in its last, secret meeting, and according to the instructions of its leadership, to carry out a series of elimination activities against the Polish police, who faithfully served the Germans. In the continued activities of the organization, attacks will be made against the German *gendarmerie* for the purpose of robbing them of weapons and equipment, but not to kill them. The members of the organization did not want the Germans to take reprisals by burning down an entire village and killing dozens of Poles in revenge for one [dead] German.

One of the most daring operations carried out by the Sokoly *A.K.* organization, during the entire German occupation, was without a doubt the attack on the *Amstkommissar*'s establishment in Kulesze. Thirty well-armed Poles, with masks over their faces, participated in the sudden attack, which took place in the middle of the night. They tied the hands and feet of the Germans that they found in the place, took away their weapons, and stole a great deal of booty, including additional weapons, ammunition, telephone instruments, radio receivers and a stock of various merchandise from the storerooms. All this they loaded onto wagons and brought it to safe locations. The actions were done with great precision and exceptional dexterity. During the entire time that the operation continued, there was a strict guard over the tied-up Germans. Before the *A.K* men left the place, they blotted out all the footprints that could lead to the attackers.

A large portion of the weapons and rich booty was brought to our bunker. There were machine guns, pistols, and a great number of bullets.

After the successful attack by the *A.K.*, the Germans sent a reinforcement of Ukrainian and Latvian police to patrol all the roads, streets, alleys, and paths.

As an act of punishment, the Germans burnt down a few villages and destroyed some farms, suspecting that participants in the Kulesze robbery were hiding there.

Now we had periodic visits in the bunker from Staczek, who came accompanied by his cousin Czeczek from Warsaw, who was his confidant. Czeczek had known about us, and everything that happened to us, for a long time. As an active member of the underground, Czeczek had a significant part in the Kulesze operation. Once, Czeczek remained in our company while Staczek was absent, and our youngsters took this good opportunity and started a conversation with him. Monik gathered his courage and went straight to the point, asking the guest to sell us a pistol for a reasonable price – in dollars.

By chance, Czeczek kept a pistol from the Kulesze booty in his house. He also did not hide the fact that he needed money, and he agreed to sell the pistol to Monik with seven bullets. He mentioned the sum of 30 dollars. Monik did not hesitate for a moment, and handed the seller 50 dollars, on the condition that he would add another 50 bullets.

When this transaction was completed, Monik pulled out another fifty-dollar bill from his pocket and turned to Czeczek with the request that he neither forget us nor our difficult situation, and that he would supply us from time to time with a few kilograms of *slonina* (pork meat) at a doubled price. Czeczek took the bill and promised to take care of us as much as he could. The two of them agreed to meet in the forest every Monday night, at an exact time and at an exact place.

To our boys' satisfaction, these meetings took place a number of times. Czeczek gave Monik a pistol and bullets, and even fulfilled his promise with regard to the *slonina*.

Meanwhile, a sad thing happened. Following a denouncement, a number of Polish youths who had participated in the Kulesze action were arrested. Czeczek was worried that the Germans would torture them to loosen their tongues, so as to get out of them the names of all those who had participated in the robbery, among whom, as mentioned above, was Czeczek himself. He immediately decided to disappear from the horizon and moved to another, unknown place. With the disappearance of this man, our rosy hopes began to wither like a flower.

A short time later, Monik suggested to Moshe that they go to a Christian woman who was one of his family's acquaintances, and who lived in the neighborhood of their house in Sokoly. She was the wife of the principal of the school in Bruszewo. Her husband had escaped some time ago with the Polish army, and had reached England. Through that woman, Monik hoped to buy some food in exchange for his dollars and some possessions from each of us.

From that day forward, Monik and Moshe visited the Christian woman to bring essential food items from there. Our life in the bunker returned again to a state of normalization. We listened to radio broadcasts for long hours and received signals from Moscow and London. Among the booty brought from Kulesze were many different radio parts, batteries for pocket flashlights, and other parts. Moshe, like any expert, knew how to use every part in order to improve the receiver belonging to 'Shmeig', as well as ours, in order to receive broadcasts on all the wavelengths. Moshe and Monik, especially, listened to the broadcasts. They sat next to the receiver for hours upon hours, with earphones on their ears. Monik precisely wrote down important news, the speeches of important people, newspaper surveys and opinions of political commentators from all over the world. Monik later gave these records to Staczek and made sure that he would memorize all of them so that he would be able to pass them on to the *A.K.* organization.

'Shmeig' was accustomed to reading the news and commentaries to his friends, and in their eyes he was a wonder, because of the lovely style and the wise editing. He gave them the impression that he himself had done the work of preparation and they respected him for his knowledge and intelligence. It is clear that not a single one of them was able to imagine that Monik was hiding behind the wings, infusing his writings with his literary style.

At that time something happened that was engraved in my memory for a long time. One evening, at about eleven o'clock, the youngsters went out to the nearby forest for their usual walk before going to sleep. Suddenly, the three farm dogs began a very loud, ear-ringing barking. Staczek immediately stood at the entrance to the bunker, lifted the cover, and asked whether all the boys were present. I answered him that the boys went out to draw in some fresh air.

'Shmeig' sighed and mumbled, "Too bad, too bad!"

"And what happened?"

He did not answer, but took off the light cover of the opening that we used during the nights, and in its place he covered the opening with the cover that was camouflaged with dirt. I understood that Staczek was expecting a search of the farm by the Germans, following the burglary of the government offices in Kulesze. In my imagination, I estimated that my lads would not have time to escape and that they were likely to fall into the hands of the destructive 'Satan' who would go wild here. I trembled at the sight of the visions passing through my imagination, of brutality, cruelty, and the killing of the boys, Heaven forbid! I was sure that after the boys would be seized, Staczek would not help me as he had, and would kill me. As for me, I regarded this as the only rescue I would have and I prayed that Staczek would not delay and would finish me off. Every minute that passed seemed, in my eyes, to be a year.

Thus I lay for an entire day, and tortured myself with the pain of horrible thoughts and nightmares.

The second evening, I comforted myself that it all was a nightmarish dream and any moment 'Shmeig' would appear and tell me that a miracle from Heaven had occurred and the boys had been rescued. Don't I always see false visions? I will beg 'Shmeig' to shoot me right now!

It is incredible. At ten o'clock that night, I suddenly heard footsteps. These were my boys, who were more precious to me than anything else. My happiness was immeasurable, and I wept from an excess of joy. Staczek removed the cover and my boys came down to me.

As became clear, matters had developed in a totally different direction. The Germans in the picture weren't in the yard at all, but I had imagined them in an excess of fear. Actually, the members of his underground organization had come to Staczek to have an urgent meeting at his place regarding the new situation created after the burglary at Kulesze. We must not forget that a number of *A.K.* members had fallen into the hands of the enemy, who was seeking revenge at any price, and the moment was serious for the rest of the members, lest they also be revealed to the Germans.

When 'Shmeig' heard his dogs barking, he thought that Germans had indeed appeared in his yard. First, he ran to ensure the safety of the open bunker, in which there were weapons and hidden Jews. On the other hand, the barking alarmed our boys and they also thought that Germans were searching the farm. They withdrew from the farm like arrows from a bow and hid in a deep pit in the forest, with which they were very familiar, for that entire day.

After the secret *A.K.* meeting, Staczek came to empty all the weapons out of the bunker. Our boys exploited a wonderful opportunity and hid one rifle. 'Shmeig' hid all the weapons and ammunition in a safer place that was unknown to us. Many days went by, and 'Shmeig' did not react to the missing rifle. We came to the conclusion that he forgot all about it, or that he simply did not know how many rifles had been put into the bunker after the Kulesze operation. That is how we came to possess a rifle.

'Avrahamel' shortened the butt and barrel of the rifle as much as he could, so that it looked like a lengthened pistol. Thank G-d, we did not lack any bullets, and we still had a number of hand grenades from before. In this way we obtained for ourselves a significant store of weapons. Their happiness and smiles proved that the comrades were all satisfied.

It is the beginning of February 1944. One Saturday, 'Shmeig' traveled to work in Lapy at the *Dapu* railroad workshops. After the destruction of the Jews, young villagers up to the age of 40 were roped in for labor, and they took turns going to work, once every two weeks.

At the time of Staczek's duty by rotation, his brother Palek brought us our food. That Saturday, we waited all day. By midnight, no one had opened the cover over the entrance and, of course, also no food had arrived. We were afraid to open the cover. In the yard there was utter silence like in a cemetery, and no barking of the dogs could be heard. We estimated that something unusual had happened. We were even more surprised when we did not even hear the footsteps of 'Old Kalinowski', with which we were very familiar, who was accustomed to pass between the stable and the cowshed every day. Did the Germans arrest the entire family?! We worried about pushing the dirt cover upward, lest the Germans had left a guard on the farm after they took the Kalinowski family away.

Even so, we decided to open the entrance after midnight, because if the family really was no longer at the place, then what were we doing staying here as if we were locked up, without any food? We no longer knew the exact time, because we did not have any watch in our possession. Thus we sat in tension until after midnight.

Suddenly, we heard Staczek's footsteps coming closer to us. We were very happy that we had been afraid for nothing. But our happiness immediately vanished when we heard the bad news that we had to leave the bunker completely, otherwise, the next day the Germans would find us. Staczek added that one of the boys had informed on him, telling the Germans that he was hiding weapons from the robbery of the *gendarmerie* in Kulesze, and this morning the *gendarmes* had come to his house to arrest him.

Since 'Shmeig' was in Lapy, the *gendarmes* meanwhile arrested his brother Palek, who was in the house. The *Soltis* (head of the village) and the neighbors all testified to the Nazis that Palek was innocent and that he had no part in political activities, but this did not influence them and they would certainly torture him in order to get information out of him about his brother Staczek's affairs.

Staczek's friends, who met him at the Kruczewo Train Station, immediately warned him that the Germans were looking for him. He hid himself until midnight and he had just arrived in order to investigate his situation and what was happening on the farm. First, he directed a warning to us to leave the farm immediately and get away without leaving any footprints. 'Shmeig' gave us half a loaf of bread, saying that at the moment, he had nothing else in the house.

Fleeing for Shelter into the Mazury Forest

We quickly packed up all the movables that we could take with us. We arranged the rest of the things in such a way that no suspicion could arise that people had lived here. We went out of the bunker carefully and quietly, and set our footsteps in the direction of the Mazury Forest.

We walked though plowed fields and pastures, and were careful not to go on the roads and paths. This was the season when the snow was melting and swamps were formed in the fields, sometimes very deep ones that we sank into.

Towards dawn, the puddles froze over again and the ice broke under our feet. The distance from the bunker to the edge of the Mazury Forest was eight kilometers. I felt weakness in all my limbs, and tried with all my strength to go forward with the group and not delay them from their objective. My feet stumbled, and I fell down more than once; I got up out of the puddles with great difficulty.

All four of the youngsters were loaded down with heavy packages of possessions that they carried on their chests and backs, as well

209

as in both hands. In this difficult situation, I could not expect help from the youngsters. But my son did not remain indifferent to his father's great suffering and he did not abandon me to the wind. He approached me, took the backpack off my back, put it on his own back with the rest of the packages, making his burden much heavier, and suggested to me that I hold onto him and be dragged after him, step by step. To my sorrow, this also did not help me and he had to actually carry me, because my feet would carry me no longer.

Moshe was prepared to do everything for me and made an effort to lead me by one arm, but it was necessary for somebody else to lead me on the other side to make it possible to drag me along. The consciences of the other three boys did not allow them to remain indifferent to the situation. Two of them partially freed the third one from his burden and he helped to drag me along. This was an unusual effort on the part of the boys. I did not believe that they would succeed in bringing me alive to the forest. The walk took over six hours.

We finally reached the Mazury Forest at seven o'clock in the morning. We found a thick, wide wood, where certainly no one had walked all winter, and laid ourselves down to rest and stretch our weary bones. We fell asleep for a few hours, without deciding to do so. We simply fell into the arms of sleep, from total exhaustion. After that, we sat and planned how to keep ourselves alive.

Without any argument, it was decided to immediately begin digging a temporary dugout that would provide a shelter over our heads and a place to put our movables. Then we had to find a source of food and financial means, because most of our things remained at the Kalinowski farm. More than anything else, we had to find a source of water. The entire length of our journey, we had not come across a single living settlement.

After resting, the boys went to look for an appropriate place to dig. A place was found among thick bushes, and it would be possible to camouflage the place from the eyes of passers-by so they would not suspect that people were here. We brought spades with us from the previous digging.

It was very hard to dig, because the upper layer was sufficiently frozen; by evening only one cubic meter of earth had been removed. It was clear that there still was no room in the excavation to lie down, and the group decided to go back to the former bunker to sleep and carefully check whether Germans were there. Tomorrow, they would have to come back to the woods and continue digging. To remain here outside, wasn't acceptable to the boys because of the nighttime frost. It was also necessary to bring a number of vessels of drinking water.

I, who had been made lame on my feet and weak from walking, lay down the whole time that the boys were busy digging. I was covered with two blankets and wasn't able to chew the bread we had with us. From time to time I wet my lips with snow, and I trembled with the cold.

The youngsters suggested to me that I remain there and sleep in the new pit, which would meanwhile suffice only for me. They gave me to understand that I was too weak to walk eight kilometers at night and come back the same way at dawn. I was very afraid to remain alone in the woods all night. I told the boys that I was much improved and that I would be able to go with them, and that I would not agree to remain here alone all night, under any circumstances.

That same evening, we went back to our bunker in Bruszewa. We put our possessions, meanwhile, in the new pit, and the boys camouflaged it properly.

Again the hard journey made its signs. It was a night of a full moon. At a distance there was a road on which vehicles were moving, and they lit the surroundings with spotlights. If the youngsters had been without me, they would have easily progressed quickly and would have avoided going in dangerous places, but they had difficulties with me.

Every moment my feet stumbled and I tripped, and they had to support me under their arms and pull me along. Because of me, they were exposed to danger the entire length of the trip, and we all were likely to fall into the hands of the Germans. Because of this, we mistook the way and had to add a lot of walking. In the hearts of the youngsters, grievances accumulated against the old man because of whom they were weakened, and they cursed their lives more than once.

The boys spoke among themselves about leaving me under a tree on the way, and when they would return to the woods in a few hours, they would take me with them. But my son Moshe aggressively opposed this and he did not agree to leave his old father to the kindness of fate, in a field.

Thus, we finally arrived at the Bruszewo Forest bunker. It was quiet all around. We took off the cover, went inside, and lay down to sleep. We got up at dawn. The boys equipped themselves with a number of vessels, filled them with water, and took more of our possessions with them. The way back this time was easier, or it just appeared that way to us after we had rested, and we already knew the way that we had gone before.

After resting, they began to widen and enlarge the excavation. By the next evening, the new bunker was ready. All five of us could go inside and lie down somehow with all our possessions. Of course, the new bunker was far from the quality of the first one. One could not comfortably lie down and stretch his legs to their entire length, and he certainly could not lie down the way one should. In any case, it was better to lie down that way than to walk again eight kilometers each way, back and forth, and be subject to danger.

Our Boys – As Partisans

The next night, my youngsters decided to go to the nearby villages disguised as armed partisans, in order to obtain food.

Monik Roseman was armed with a pistol and a supply of bullets. 'Avrahamel' Goldberg was armed with the shortened rifle, which the reader will certainly remember. Besides that, he made himself an artificial pistol out of wood that looked like a real one, for the purpose of frightening the farmers and giving himself the image of a real partisan. Our "partisan platoon" also was not lacking hand grenades, as will be remembered.

At nightfall, the four boys went out. Monik went at the head of the line as the officer in charge, since he unhesitatingly spoke fluent Polish and was an educated man familiar with events. By his appearance, nobody would identify him as a Jew. The features of the faces of Moshe Maik and the Goldberg brothers also were not typically Jewish ones.

The platoon reached some country dwellings after midnight and knocked on the doors of the local residents. First, Monik knocked on the door of one of the houses where the people already were asleep, and they woke up to open the door for those who came at unacceptable hours. Monik informed them, in the tone of an order but politely, that he and his companions were gathering food for 30 men, fighters for the freedom of Poland, who were found nearby.

As soon as the residents saw that those who entered their house were armed, in surrender and with fear they immediately gave them loaves of bread, a generous amount of fat and vessels of milk.

After they passed through a number of farmhouses that night, they returned to the dugout with the booty: a number of sacks full of all kinds of food that would be enough for several weeks.

The friends weighed their enormous achievement according to this first attempt, and their appetite grew. Seeing their success, they decided to continue to appear as Polish partisans, for the purpose of preparing a stock of food that would be enough for a long time.

We expected the warfront to come close to our area in the near future and then Germans would swarm everywhere, in their withdrawal from the Russian offensive that had begun during the days of the battle of Stalingrad and still continued at a changing pace. Every day, the Russians were freeing vast conquered areas and they had already reached White Russia, which borders on Poland.

The wealthy farmers feared the Russian advance and hurried to empty their possessions from their granaries and houses. Our boys exploited the farmers' fear and made it a kind of sport for themselves to frighten them even more; thus, it was easy to get whatever we needed out of them. Some of them, who certainly never allowed a Jew to cross the thresholds of their homes, now gave the "partisans" everything good, when they were barefoot and half naked during the late hours of the night.

In this way, our boys prepared a stock of food for several months during a period of two weeks. They brought water in milk vessels.

Soon after we moved into the woods, I was very weak for four days, and could not eat even a crumb of bread, only fresh milk. Slowly, my condition improved and I recovered.

During their night excursions, the youngsters heard news from outside that about 70 Jews from Wysokie-Mazowieckie had been living for a long time in relative comfort in the Mazury Forest. They even had stoves for cooking and baking. They bought sufficient food and drink as needed and even slaughtered calves.

One day a tragedy occurred, following the stealing of an animal that led to their bunker. The villagers sent *gendarmes* there and after a search that they made, the entire group of 70 Jews fell into the hands of the murderers.

This news depressed all of us. We also could be revealed one day because of our footprints in the snow. The matter caused the boys to start thinking. They had already begun to discuss various plans for our future.

Searching for Shelter

Monik suggested that we go to a certain owner of a farm where he himself had stayed for two weeks before he came to us, figuring that the Christian would agree to give us shelter for payment, especially now, when the situation was in favor of the Russians and the success of the Allies was certain. Even if the War would continue another year until the complete surrender of the Germans, our area would certainly fall into the hands of the Russians in another six months at most. With this reasoning, Monik estimated that he would be able to influence the farmer that it was worth it for him to shelter us. Therefore, Monik went with one of the other boys to conduct conversations with the farmer Wladek.

Wladek answered that he doesn't want to take upon himself responsibility to provide shelter, even for a high payment, because gangs of robbers were running around in his neighborhood, whose task it was to eliminate the remainder of the Jews in the forests and the bunkers. The gangs would reveal the Jews' hiding places. However, he was prepared to give us shelter for one month, for the sum of three thousand marks. A few weeks ago his father died and he had paid a significant amount to the church for his funeral. In order to cover the burial expenses, he would agree to provide us with shelter for a month.

It was difficult for us to agree to these conditions. We would have to give Wladek all our possessions and Monik's dollars for only one month, and after that we would remain without any resources.

Meanwhile, we heard that Staczek's brother Palek, who had been arrested by the Germans instead of his brother, had been sent to Danzig. The youngsters thought that the danger was over that Palek would break down and reveal our bunker by being tortured during questioning. And so they decided that now we could return to our previous bunker, especially since we had a supply of food for several weeks and we no longer required Staczek's help to camouflage the bunker cover. Before we had left the Kalinowski farm bunker, 'Avrahamel' had found a way to open and close the bunker cover from the inside in a way that would not leave any footprints above. Therefore, we did not need any outside help.

Return to Kalinowski Bunker

During the four-week interim of our absence, the underground water in the bunker had collected and risen almost to the cover. The silence of death reigned in the farmyard. The boys began to draw out the water. By three in the morning, they had not yet succeeded in drawing out all the water. That first evening they managed to draw the water level down to the shelves inside the bunker. Meanwhile, they brought dry straw from the threshing house and put it on the shelves as a mattress to lie on.

'Avrahamel' was so tired and worn-out from the work that he collapsed, and it took a few long moments until he revived.

The second night, they finished drawing out all the rest of the water and arranged our cave. We knew that 'Old Kalinowski' remained in the house. Staczek was hiding with his friends, from fear that the Germans would come to look for him. Staczek had divided the cows and pigs among his relatives and friends, so the farm looked like it was abandoned. Only 'Old Kalinowski' went about the farm all day, and at night he went to sleep.

From time to time, Staczek would visit his old father. Once, passing by the bunker, he heard a voice and movement, and he understood that we had returned. He panicked, but soon quieted down. He had estimated that over the past month nothing remained of his Jews. How could they bear the cold of the winter for weeks, without a roof over their heads and without food, at a time when no Christian would allow a Jew to cross his threshold for all the money in the world?

Staczek could not hold back his anger, and called out, "You're here again? And you did not see the necessity to ask my permission? I am warning you to leave immediately, and I don't want you at my place at all! If you don't want to leave here, there are enough ways to send you far from my house and my property. I don't want to endanger my own head and my farm because of you!"

The boys tried to convince him with logical reasons that he now had nothing to fear and that the danger had gone. Over a month had passed and if they hadn't come until now to search for him, they certainly wouldn't come any more. All the time that Palek had been in our area, it was possible to be afraid that they would torture him and he would reveal his brother's secrets. But now, he had nothing to be afraid of. After the great defeats of the Germans on all fronts, they had greater concerns than that of the burglary in Kulesze. The boys promised Staczek that they wouldn't bother him and that they had found a source of food. He was exempt from opening and closing the cover of the bunker and camouflaging it, and they had found a way to arrange everything themselves, without any outside help.

The boys managed to convince Staczek and they succeeded in reconciling with him completely. From that evening onward, Staczek had a good attitude toward us. He was careful. During the day, he was afraid to go around on his farm. He came only in the evening for two hours, and would come down to us into the bunker to hear the radio broadcasts and talk with us.

The boys continued to go out to the distant villages at night, even though we had a supply of food for two or three months. They wanted to obtain a stock of food for half a year. Since the front was coming closer to our area, it will be difficult to go out of our cave. It is not possible to prepare bread for a long time; because of the dampness in the bunker, bread would spoil. But fat and other foods could be prepared.

Among other things, the boys planned a daring, very dangerous mission that, according to all logic, was doomed to complete failure at the outset. They decided to rob the Stokowiski landowner's holdings, which were now in the possession of the Germans, under the management of two German overseers who dressed in civilian clothing.

Before the expulsion of the Jews from Sokoly, 'Avrahamel' Goldberg had worked for a number of weeks in the farm warehouses and the broad courtyards. He knew the Germans who supervised the farm work very well, as well as all its entrances and secrets. Therefore, 'Avrahamel' suggested a daring break-in into the homes of the managers and forcing them to hand over the keys, under the threat of using their weapons, as well as cutting off their telephone communications.

Two of us will guard the arrested managers, while the other two will go to the *Soltis* and order him to draft farmers with wagons, so that the food could be loaded up and taken to the Bruszewo Forest, some distance from our bunker. From there, it will be possible to transfer the booty to a new bunker that they will prepare for that purpose and camouflage as required.

I tried to influence the hotheads, to moderate them and prevent them from carrying out their dangerous plans. I explained to them, with the best and most logical reasons that their plan could be expected to fail completely. They did not even want to hear my reasons. They only delayed the mission for two weeks so that they could make all the preparations for the break-in.

Meanwhile, they went out at night. Every time the youngsters went out on their dangerous excursions and left me alone in the bunker, I was seized by fear and trembling from nightmarish visions and soul-suffering, until more than once I envied those who had died and were freed already from a life of hell. After every trip, the boys told me of miracles and wonders, how they were rescued on their way from the danger of death.

Once, they entered a farmer's house to ask for food, apparently for their partisan comrades. By chance, they met up with a group of men from a Polish gang. They started to question our youngsters, who were they, from what political party, for what purpose were they gathering food. Coincidentally, the officer of this gang was not at the farmer's house and Monik, thanks to his ideas and courage, was not at a loss during those dangerous moments, and he found a way out of the trouble.

In another place, one farmer told them that a dangerous Polish gang of the *N.S.Z.* [*Narodwe Sily Zbrojne*, an antisemitic Polish resistance movement], whose task was to destroy all the remaining Jews, had heard that four Jews were running around in the forests with weapons like Polish partisans. That gang was hunting for them and planning to catch them... .

Another time, when our youngsters were returning from Kalinowa with sacks of food loaded on their shoulders, they met up with an armed Polish gang. They stopped our youngsters and asked who they were. Monik stood there talking with their officer. While they were talking, a group of youths and young girls passed by, who were coming back from a dance on this summer evening in the month of May. They stood still, looking at the gang and the four young men carrying the sacks. The officer of the gang wanted to first get rid of the company of celebrants and send them home, lest they interfere with the actions he was planning to take against the youngsters with the sacks, and he ordered them to stand near the cowsheds... .

To our youngsters' delight, they did not want to go away. During the argument between the officer and the dance celebrants, our boys sneaked away and were saved from certain death.

In spite of everything, they would not forego their trips, even with the dangers. They occasionally did not have time to return to the bunker that same night, because the trip in both directions took hours, and then they had to hide between the rows of crops. This was the time before the harvest. I had to remain alone and deserted in the bunker and bear suffering of the soul and a mood of fear and discouragement.

The battlefront drew closer to our vicinity. The boys were worried that they were likely to fall during the last moments before the end of the War ...and truthfully, every day we saw miracles and wonders.

Wounded Germans were passing by on all the roads. In the Bruszewo Forest and in the surroundings of our bunker, there were German artillery units. A German army headquarters unit was located in Staczek's house, 30 meters from our bunker. The farmyard, the cowsheds, and the storerooms were full of soldiers. We had to lie for complete days, day and night, smothered under the heavy earth cover, afraid to put out our heads to breathe a bit of fresh air. We used a pail to relieve ourselves.

There were dozens of chickens in the yard, and the German cook would catch chickens for his kitchen. The chickens were accustomed to sitting above our bunker on the holes that were made in the cover to let air into the bunker. The chickens felt the hot air under the cover. The Germans would hide in corners near the bunker to hunt and catch the chickens.

We had great difficulty getting water to drink. For days, we lay tired and faint from thirst. 'Avrahamel' [Goldberg] tried to dig in the corner of the bunker to reach the source of water. He did succeed in getting a small amount of water but not enough to slake our thirst.

During the last week, we heard the shooting of artillery. The walls and ceiling of the bunker, supported by flimsy and weak boards, started to move. We were afraid that the bunker was collapsing and we would all be buried alive. The posts that supported the ceiling of the bunker were rotting from their foundations because of the wet ground. The bottom portions of the posts were completely rotted. At any moment, the bunker was likely to collapse. A six-meter high pole fell at the edge of our bunker. It served as a lightening rod, but collapsed from the explosions of the artillery shells. We thought there was no hope of remaining alive that day.

My son Moshe heard on the radio that Bialystok, and many places in the direction of the train track to the Lapy Train Station, had been conquered by the Russians. 'Avrahamel' begged us to go out of the bunker in the middle of the night and crawl from tree to tree until we reach the Russians. My son Moshe was of the opinion that it was worthwhile to wait another day and not do anything dangerous during the last moments of the War. Other than that, he was not prepared to leave his father.

Avrahamel Chaim 'Yudel', and Monik decided not to consider the Maiks, and in the middle of the night they went on their way. They parted from us at midnight. 'Avrahamel' opened the cover of the bunker and went up into the toilet. Chaim 'Yudel' and Monik stood below ready to go out one at a time. Avrahamel stood by the door of the toilet and waited, straining his ears as to whether any footsteps could be heard outside. Slowly, slowly, he opened the door of the toilet. He immediately jumped back inside the bunker and quickly replaced the cover. His teeth were chattering.

When he had put his head outside, he saw a few Germans close by who were lighting up the area with searchlights. For a long time, all of us were afraid that the Germans would see something above the bunker when they lit up the ground above, and would find us. After 15 minutes had passed, we calmed down.

During the night, the artillery shooting stopped, and we lay down to sleep until morning. It was August 11, 1944.

Suddenly, towards morning, Staczek's brother Palek] came running toward us and called out: "Friends, come out of the bunker! The Russians have arrived! The Russians have arrived!"

After the Liberation

We immediately opened the cover of the bunker and ran into the yard. The boys went into the forest where the German dugouts were located, in which a lot of food remained, which they gathered. Meanwhile, Staczek came with bad news: the Germans had shot and killed his father. They asked the father something that he did not understand and they immediately shot him.

'Avrahamel' and Monik went to Sokoly to see what the situation there was and find an apartment where we would be able to stay temporarily. The rest of the group remained in Staczek's yard to wait for the return of the two "spies" and their report; then they would decide what to do next.

After two hours, 'Avrahamel' and Monik came back and told us that Sokoly is unrecognizable; it does not look like it once was a town. The streets have disappeared and an empty area remains. The market, Tiktin Street, Bathhouse Street and a large portion of Ganosowky Street, up to Eliezer Rosenovitz' house, have been wiped off the face of the earth. Isolated houses remained here and there, occupied by strange Poles. On Market Street, only the three-story house belonging to 'Little Alterke' and 'Aharke' Zholti's large house, now occupied by the temporary militia, remain. In the house of 'Little Alterke' there are two or three rooms that are empty, but all the windowpanes are broken.

Yisrael Maik's small wooden house next to the horse market is still there, but four Christian families occupy it. The Polish tenant in Maik's house was an underworld figure before the War and his wife was a prostitute. She was called "the black *goya*". Immediately after the Jews were expelled from Sokoly, this *goy* took over Maik's house, the bathhouse, the garden, and an empty lot. He also grabbed Moshe Tzvi Seines' wool spinning machines. He put these machines in the Jewish public bathhouse, and a long row of farmers' wagons was lining up now near the bathhouse. Farmers from all the villages in the area came to spin wool, and the man from the underworld became the heir and was made wealthy by Jewish possessions and the destruction of the Jews.

A few houses remained on Bathhouse Street, but most of them don't have any windows or doors, and Poles occupy the few that are in good repair. The Russian headquarters occupies Mordechai Surasky's large house. Monik spoke with the Russian commanders, who promised to provide apartments for the Jews who had survived.

We decided to return to Sokoly. Not one of us had a remaining shirt, or other clothing, or even a pair of shoes. Everything had rotted.

On August 12, 1944, we returned to Sokoly, the town of our birth. The youngsters felt free and were in high spirits. But I felt myself partially paralyzed. I couldn't even walk a few steps. The boys carried me and supported me in their arms. After ten steps, I had to lie down on the ground and rest. My son and his friends had to wait for me, so because of me, the four-kilometer trip from the bunker to Sokoly took about five hours.

My son and I reached our house that remained whole, next to the bathhouse. We turned to the Christians who had taken over our house and asked them to free at least one room for us, as the owners of the house. The Poles did not want to listen to our request, remembering the tenant protection law. They had grabbed our house, which at the time was an ownerless Jewish house, and now it is forbidden for the owner of the house to take anyone out of his apartment until he receives another one in its place.

We went to the walled house of 'Little Alterke'. There, we found an empty room. The youngsters brought bundles of straw. They spread them on the floor and prepared a mattress for five people. On our lot in the horse market, they dug up a few potatoes for lunch.

The Surviving Jews from the Forests

That same day, other Jews reached Sokoly from bunkers in the forests: Chaim Tuvia Litvak, the blacksmith, with his three sons Shammai, 'Yankel' and 'Sheikele' and his daughter 'Shaintzie'; Avraham Kalifovitz from Dworkie; Issur Wondolowicz with the little girl Yehudit, his murdered wife's cousin orphaned of her father, 'Itcze' Rachelsky; David Zholti, the son of 'Aharki', with his mother Freidel, who had hidden in a bunker in the village of Ros. All the refugees kissed each other emotionally and felt like members of one family.

During the first few days, all of them lived together. They divided all the food as they would to family members. Every one had mountains of miracles and wonders to tell that had happened to

223

them during the years of the Holocaust: about those who seemingly gave shelter to the Jews, but took their money and possessions, and afterwards invented various ways how to destroy them and be freed of them; they were saved from death only by miracles.

On the second day, Zeev Gritczak, his wife, and their three daughters arrived in Sokoly. A Christian friend had sheltered them. Recently, he had tried to force them to commit suicide, for their own good... .

Also among the first refugees to arrive was Bartzi from the village of Dworkie, who had been in the Treblinka death camp. For a few weeks he had watched how thousands of Jews were brought to the gas chambers. It was his luck that they transported him, together with a group of other Jews, to be killed in the Lublin area; during the last actual moments, he succeeded in jumping out of the boxcar of the train.

Aharon Slomasky from the village of Dworkie and a few women from Warsaw and Metshizev were also among the refugees.

During the first week after the liberation, a total of 25 Jewish souls, men, women and children, gathered in Sokoly. We received the news that two refugees from Sokoly had reached Bialystok.

Chaim Yehoshua Olsha and his sister 'Mushka', who had been under the protection of a devout Christian woman as Aryans, with Christian identity cards, were forced to observe the Christian religious customs. 'Rashke', Moshe's mother, was hidden by a Christian, at a price in dollars, in a storehouse full of bundles of wood.

Avraham Yitzhak Lev, Shmuel Leib's son, hid in a bunker with Chaim Tzvi and Zeidel Rachekovsky. The Gestapo found the bunker. They were arrested and until recently they were employed digging graves and burning the bodies of Russian and Jewish prisoners brought from European countries who had been shot before the gas chambers were prepared. There were mass graves scattered in the Augustow, Grodno, and Bialystok areas, mostly in locations close to the train tracks.

After the defeat of the Germans on the Russian fronts, the Germans wanted to wipe out the footprints of their crimes in killing the Jews. The Germans exploited the Jews that they caught after the liquidation of the Bialystok Ghetto for this purpose and gathered them in prisons in Bialystok. A short time before the liberation, when the job of burning the bodies was completed, the Germans commanded the forty workers to dig a large pit. The grave that the workers prepared was intended for themselves. Then they began to flee. Only ten of them succeeded in escaping from death. Among them was Avraham Yitzhak Lev. Among those who were killed there were the brothers Zeidel and Chaim Tzvi Rachekovsky.

Also among the refugees who arrived in Bialystok were Masha Kaplansky and her daughter Rachel. There was tragedy in their bitter fate. By chance, about two months before the liberation, Masha's only son 'Avrahamel' went out at midnight to the village of Lachy to a certain farmer named Troskoleski, to ask for food for his weak mother and the remaining members of the family. When 'Avrahamel' entered the Troskoleski house that fateful night, the farmer Troskoleski, together with his grown sons, fell upon 'Avrahamel', tied him up with ropes, and turned him over to the German murderers.

Others among the refugees from Sokoly in Bialystok were Benyamin the glazier and his cousin Benyamin Gorkovitz, the son of Chaim Dzashesayahak. They had been among the partisans in the Bialystok area. Also among the refugees was Solka, the adopted daughter of 'Itzel' [Yitzhak] the tailor.

Two weeks after the liberation, my son Moshe and the brothers 'Avrahamel' and Chaim 'Yudel' Goldberg traveled to Bialystok to look for work in order to earn enough to buy clothing and shoes because, as stated above, they left the bunker with their clothing worn out and torn. I, who could walk on my feet only with difficulty, remained in Sokoly.

All the survivors moved to live temporarily in Alter Slodky's house. With the intervention of the head of the Wysokie-Mazowieckie district, I succeeded in receiving one room in my own house next to the Jewish public bathhouse. Very slowly, the rest of the Sokoly refugees succeeded in finding a roof over their heads.

David Zholti succeeded, with the intervention of the head of the Wysokie-Mazowieckie district, in receiving one room and a kitchen in his father's house from the Sokoly militia. With a great deal of difficulty, David Zholti obtained a small part of his furniture from the past Mayor of the town, Grabowski, which his brother Chaim had transferred to his house on the eve of the expulsion. At that time, David Zholti sold a clothes closet that stood in his father's building supplies storeroom, and from the payment for this he supported himself and his mother for several months.

Chaim Tuvia Litvak succeeded in freeing two apartments, one belonging to him, and one to his father-in-law, Dov Shaikes. Chaim Tuvia succeeded in gathering the working tools needed for a family and began to work at his profession and to support himself honorably. He was one of the happiest people in Sokoly, who had remained alive with his entire family.

Zeev Gritczak, whose family was happy to remain alive, arranged an apartment for himself in Mottel Shafran's house. He succeeded in his dealings with farmers among his Christian friends and earned a good living.

Moshe, son of 'Rashke' who was in Bialystok during the first days after the liberation, returned to Sokoly, arranged an apartment on the second floor of Alter Slodky's house, and began to do business with Polish merchants.

Chaim Yehoshua Olsha had a great deal of merchandise in Sokoly: paints and other materials. He occasionally came to Sokoly to do business. He bought apartments in Bialystok for himself and his sister.

A few of us supplied various manufactured goods to the farmers in exchange for food. At that time, the only business was in trading, in other words, one type of merchandise was exchanged for another. Very slowly, the economic and material situation of the refugees became relatively stable. Transportation in the Bialystok metropolitan area was mostly by means of military vehicles, which went back and forth day and night. The Russian drivers took one-fourth liter of whiskey for each trip from the travelers.

My son Moshe was one of the few in Sokoly who did not engage in trade or in smuggling. At the beginning, he worked in a textile factory in Bialystok as an electric technician. Every Sunday, when he was off work, he would travel to Bruszewo to see Staczek, who had sheltered us during the Holocaust. Most of the time, when my son Moshe traveled to Staczek, he went together with our cousin 'Avrahamel' Goldberg.

Once, on a Sunday in December 1944, when Moshe and 'Avrahamel' were visiting Staczek and remained overnight to sleep in his house, a search of Staczek's house was conducted by the Soviet security forces. Someone who hated Staczek informed the Soviets that he was a member of the illegal *A.K.* party. Moshe and 'Avrahamel', who were coincidentally present during the search, were arrested together with Staczek and they all were taken to jail by circuitous paths so that their relatives wouldn't know in what direction they had gone.

I had been told that they were going to visit in Bruszewo and would come home the next morning. When the first day went by and they did not come home, I was restless and nervous. All that night I did not close my eyes. At four o'clock in the morning, I went to Bruszewo to find out what happened to my son. There I was informed that Moshe and 'Avrahamel' had been arrested during the night along with Staczek and sent in an unknown direction. I immediately ran fifteen kilometers, on foot, to the Jews of Wysokie-Masowieckie, who had connections with the Soviet civil leadership. I tried to find out, with their help, where Moshe and 'Avrahamel' were located. I couldn't find out anything for three days.

On the fourth day, 'Avrahamel' was released. He informed me that my son Moshe was in jail in Zambrow, suffering from hunger and cold, and that the Soviets had tortured him for three days. 'Avrahamel' argued that Staczek had hidden him from the Germans with a few other Jews, but he did not know whether Staczek belonged to some party...thus, they released him. Moshe tried too much to protect Staczek and they held him because of that, as a faithful friend of Staczek who knows his secrets. They said that Staczek was a British agent who hated the Soviets. I hurried to Zambrow, a distance of 35 kilometers.

There, I turned to every Jew who could mediate with the government. Finally, I reached an intermediary who knew the *Kommissar* appointed over state arrests. The intermediary advised me to bring an acknowledgement from the factory in Bialystok that Moshe worked there and that his behavior was good. I hurried to Bialystok, and there I received an acknowledgement of Moshe's excellent behavior from the manager of the factory. The acknowledgement also stated that Moshe was an expert professional and the factory needed him to work for the Soviet army. After a week, I succeeded in freeing my son from prison.

Moshe's feet had frozen in the cellar of the prison and he suffered from that for several months. Staczek was sent to Russia, and according to rumors, they killed him there.

The Anti-Semitism Remained

A short time after the liberation, the persecution of Jews began in Poland. Young Poles occasionally attacked Jewish survivors in the cities, in the towns and on all the roads. They robbed Jews who made the rounds of the villages with their merchandise, beat them severely, and threw rocks at them. The Jews who earned their living from trading in the villages were in great danger.

David Zholti called a meeting of the survivors. It was decided to establish a few plants for the small Jewish community in Sokoly, such as a cooperative store, a factory for spinning wool for the village farmers, and an oil press. The first to be employed would be the peddlers, who were suffering from persecution. For this purpose, an official Jewish community had to be organized and acknowledged by the Bialystok Regional Center, and through the Center, the community would try to obtain a license from the government entitling the Sokoly Jewish community to sell the Jewish houses and plots of land that remained without heirs, and to be given back the workshops and machines belonging to Jews that had been stolen.

The required steps were taken quickly, and an official Jewish community was established in Sokoly, with a rubber stamp and all the formalities. Chaim Tuvia [Litvak] the blacksmith was chosen as chairman and Michael Maik as secretary. The Wysokie-Masowieckie District Chairman gave the Jewish Community of Sokoly an acknowledgement of Jewish property without heirs.

The Last Battle of the Destruction of Sokoly

Suddenly, a tragedy occurred that put an end to the last Jewish settlement in Sokoly. It happened under the following circumstances:

On *Shabbat*, February 17, 1945, one-half year after our liberation, the survivors had a celebration in Sokoly at Mordechai Surasky's house near the Mazowieckie Road. During the first period of the liberation, the residence of Colonel Dubroshin, the Soviet *Kommandant*, was in that house. Ten days before the fateful evening, Colonel Dubroshin handed over the Surasky house to three Jewish families numbering twelve souls.

The celebration took place: a) as a housewarming for the three families; b) to celebrate the engagement of one of the survivors from Sokoly, Benyamin Rachlav, to Batya Weinstein from Swieciany, a survivor of the death camps; c) that same week, a boy from Sokoly, David Koschevsky, the son of 'Itza' (Yitzhak) the milliner, had arrived from the death camps.

In the house where the celebration took place, about twenty people were gathered. The torn ones celebrated the evening with happiness and joy. The young people played cards, the elderly talked among themselves, the women took care of the kitchen and fried *latkes* [potato pancakes].

In the kitchen, there was a conversation led by the young engineer David Zholti, who accompanied 'Sheintze' Gritczak home after her visit to the Zholti family.

Suddenly, the back door opened. A Pole with a large mustache, dressed in an Army uniform, came in with an automatic rifle in his hand. Zeev Gritczak saw the Pole first, and cried out, "Robbers have come!" He ran to the other room and locked the door. The Pole opened a round of fire. With the first shots, he killed engineer David Zholti and the bride from Swiccienin. Batya Weinstein, who had been frying *latkes*, fell dead with a knife in her hand. A third victim was the pretty, four-year-old orphan 'Tulkale'.

After that, the murderer entered the room full of guests and started shooting again. Panic arose. For a moment, his rifle jammed. A number of celebrants succeeded in breaking the window and escaping through the front door, and they thereby were rescued from death. But a few ran in panic and hid under the beds. A kerosene lamp that stood on the table fell down on the wood floor. The kerosene spread and a fire broke out. Additional robbers entered the room and shot Shammai Litvak and David Koschevsky. Shammai Litvak's body covered Avraham Kalifovitz. The shots did make holes in his clothing, but he was saved by a miracle. Issur Wondolowicz, who was standing behind the closet, was also saved. Shaine Olshak, 22 years old, who had been recently married, fled outside and was shot on the spot by the robbers' guard. The robbers stole the boots and shoes from their victims, as well as possessions from the beds and closets.

In the middle of the robbery, the 13-year-old boy, 'Sheike' Litvak, came in. The robbers asked him "To whom are you going?"

He answered, "To my brother."

One of the robbers shot the boy in the face. The boy instinctively covered his face with his hands and cried, "Oy!"

"Are you still alive?" asked the murderer, and shot him a second time. The boy fell down, rolling in his own blood.

Seven victims fell in that bestial murder, six of them on the spot. The seventh victim, David Koschevsky, was wounded at first and begged, "Jews, have mercy on me! Save me!!!" They took him in a military vehicle to the hospital in Bialystok. After suffering horribly for a few days, he returned his soul to his Maker. He was fully conscious until his last moments.

'Avrahamel' Goldberg arrived in Sokoly from Bialystok in a military vehicle half an hour before the murder. He went to get his sister's daughter, an orphan who was at a farmer's house in the village of Lendowa-Budy, near Bransk. The farmer's wife had adopted the girl as a daughter. The Poles murdered the girl's parents and their sons. Only their small daughter, 'Feigele' Tabak, aged five, remained, who had hidden when her parents were murdered. When 'Avrahamel' found out after the liberation that his sister's daughter 'Feigele' Tabak was in Lendowa-Budy, he and his relative Moshe Lev tried to prove whether the rumor was true.

Passing through the woods near the village of Lendowa-Budy, 'Avrahamel' and Moshe Lev met 'Feigele' who was herding some cows and sheep, wearing a peasant girl's dress and wooden shoes. 'Avrahamel' immediately recognized his sister's daughter 'Feigele' and called to her, in Yiddish: 'Feigele', don't you recognize me? I am your Uncle 'Avrahamel'. I always used to bring you dolls and chocolate."

'Feigele' was frightened and ran away to the forest, screaming, "Jews are chasing me!" She fled to the farmer woman's house and hid under the bed.

'Avrahamel' and Moshe [Lev] spoke to the farmer woman and found out that she did not intend to return the girl to her Jewish relatives. Since 'Avrahamel' was not yet properly organized, he did not want to act with strength and take 'Feigele' away from the farmer woman. But after a short time, when 'Avrahamel' was organized with an apartment and a job, he rented a Russian car and invited a Jewish soldier with a weapon to come with him. When they passed through Sokoly, 'Avrahamel' went to Mordechai Surasky's house. From the celebration, he picked up Benyamin Rachlav and Benyamin Gorkovitz, both of whom had pistols and had volunteered to go with him on a joint mission. They traveled to the village of Lendowa-Budy to take 'Feigele' back from the farmer woman and then returned with the girl to the party. When they returned with the kidnapped 'Feigele', they found the seven victims.

Sketches of the Images of the Seven Murder Victims

The engineer, David Zholti, was born in 1909. In his youth, he received a religious education in his home. When he was 18 years old, he began his secular education. He learned intensively for two years and succeeded in obtaining a matriculation certificate. He continued his studies at the law school in Vilna for one year, but then he was drawn to technical studies. He learned at first in the Danzig Technical College and from there he transferred to the Polytechnion in Warsaw, where he completed his studies in engineering with excellence.

David was fluent in the Polish and German languages. He was an eloquent speaker and his speeches mesmerized his listeners, both Jews and Christians. He was a warm-hearted Jew and believed that soon there will be a complete Redemption of the Jewish people. David was a follower of Jabotinsky's doctrine that a Jewish state would arise on both banks of the Jordan. In his private life, he was modest and a gentle soul. More than once, he waived his personal matters and gave himself over with all his soul for the good of the community.

During the first few months of the liberation from the Nazi hell, David Zholti became the spiritual leader of the last Jewish community in Sokoly. Jews turned to him with their worries and problems and asked him for advice or a recommendation, and he helped everyone, not only with advice, but also with actions, and he rescued people from their troubles more than once. His unique devotion to his elderly mother was marvelous. When he was in the bunker with his mother for 22 months, he took care not to desecrate the *Shabbat* or eat non-kosher food, even though he was not devout and observant of the commandments. He did this to respect his devout mother, and quietly suffered the lack of food, making do with a little.

After the liberation, David was offered a job as an engineer, but he did not accept it so as not to leave his mother alone, subject to the kindness of strangers.

David spoke bitterly about our Jewish brothers; those who quickly forgot what had happened to the Jewish people and worried only about themselves. In his opinion, and according to common sense, the only, greatest desire of any Jew who remained alive should be to immigrate to the Land of Israel and live there among its people, its builders, because we have no future in the lands of Europe, or even in America, and the bitter, tragic lesson of the last few years is enough for us.

David Zholti himself was not privileged to realize his lofty ideals. His pure blood was spilled and he died before his time. May his memory be blessed!

Chaim Tuvia Litvak, the father of two murdered sons – Shammai and 'Sheikele', had rightly been regarded as being happier than anyone else among the survivors in Sokoly. His entire family remained alive and came back to Sokoly. Among his children, he had three tall sons and one daughter. Two of his sons fell victim to the bestial murder at Mordechai Surasky's house, and after that, his third son Yaakov ('Yankele') was murdered by a Polish soldier in Bialystok.

Shammai Litvak was 19 years old when he was murdered. He had completed the public school and also received a religious education. He was a charming boy, talented in all kinds of work, and he was willing to help others. He had a logical approach to every matter. His father, Chaim Tuvia, did not do anything without consulting his son Shammai.

'Yankele' [Yaakov] Litvak was 15 years old when he was murdered in Bialystok.

'Sheike' [Yeshaiya] Litvak was 13 years old when he fell, a tragic victim.

Shaine Olshak was 22 years old when she fell at the hands of the murderers. She was a seamstress by profession. She knew how to do beautiful embroidery and handwork. She was a "woman of valor" in matters of trade, and she managed her matters with intelligence. Shaine married a boy from Zaromb [Zareby Koscielne], Zeev Olshak (with whom she had hidden in bunkers in the forests). She was an energetic woman and a good housewife. She was not accustomed to sit and do nothing; she was always busy with something. She was especially known for having guests. She invited Jewish soldiers who were staying in the hospital for lunch and she was insulted when they suggested that they pay her for the unusual expense.

A few weeks before the murder in the Surasky house, Shaine succeeded in getting her tiny relative 'Tulkale' [Tulka], who was four years old, out of the hands of the Christians. The little girl was orphaned of both her parents, who had been murdered by the Germans in the forest during a search for Jews. A good-hearted Christian woman found the girl and took her home, and over time she adopted her as a daughter. After the liberation, the Jews of Sokoly found out and tried every possible way to get the orphan back. The Christian woman was not prepared to give up the girl, to whom she had become attached. Finally, the girl returned to her origins and Shaine took care of her with great dedication. Fate intervened, and both of them became victims on the same day.

Tulka, the four-year-old orphan, was a cheerful and sweet little girl. She clung lovingly to any person who took her into his arms to spoil her and play with her. She filled every Jewish heart with pleasure and everyone took comfort in her. The beautiful little girl, innocent of any sin, an actual little angel, lay dead with open eyes. Her eyes expressed deep protest against the bestial murderers.

Batya Weinstein, 20 years old, was born in Swieciany to wealthy parents. By profession, she was a bookkeeper. Batya passed through all seven stages of hell. She was, like the rest of the Jews, in constant danger of death, and bore hunger and suffering until she came to Sokoly after the liberation, where she believed she would find safe shelter among other Jews. Fate was cruel to her and she found her tragic death.

David Koschevsky (the son of Itze the hat-maker) was 28 years old when he was murdered. He was a talented young man and energetic at his work. He fulfilled his obligation as a soldier in the Polish army. Before the War, he married Kabula Bialystotzka, the daughter of Nachum the tailor. He hovered between life and death for 27 months. He was in the death camps of Majdanek and Auschwitz. He was sent three times to the gas chambers and was rescued from death only by miracles.

After all his wanderings, he finally was privileged to safely come home to Sokoly, and here he fell victim to a Polish fascist's bullet.

The Last Refugees Leave Sokoly – Permanently

After the horrible murders, representatives of the Bialystok Community Committee came to Sokoly, and it was decided that the last local Jewish settlement must liquidate itself. Life in the small towns of Poland is always subject to danger, and death lurks in every corner. Apparently, the gangs of Poles were not satisfied with what Hitler had previously done, and they strove to destroy all remainders of Jewish survival, at any price.

Thus, the Jews of Sokoly moved to Bialystok, which became a center for Holocaust survivors. Hundreds of returnees, from the concentration camps, the bunkers and the forests, gathered there. The Jewish partisans also were happy to be again with their brothers, the Children of Israel.

Companies of the Russian and Polish armies camped in Bialystok so that the gangs of Polish murderers and robbers would not dare, meanwhile, to run wild and carry out their wicked deeds. Because of this, our brothers felt safer there than they did in the small towns. But it did not take long for the plague of robbery to spread in this city as well. The purpose of the murderers was to plant fear and panic within the Jewish settlement, in every location. One morning, one of the Jewish women was shot and killed when she went out to shop in the marketplace. Another incident occurred in the Bialystoczienska Alley that led to the Jewish shops. Two soldiers wearing Russian army uniforms entered one of the shops and without saying anything, shot the shop owner, Patak, from the town of Rutka. Patak was very seriously injured. A second bullet was aimed at Patak's wife, who was killed on the spot.

And there was another case of mass murder after the War. A group of Jews was travelling in a vehicle on the road between Bialystok and Jasionowka. Robbers, disguised as traffic policemen, stopped them on the way, supposedly for the purpose of inspecting their papers. They were taken out of the car and stood in a row, and all of them were shot to death. And here, another Jew traveled to his town in order to sell his house, and there he was murdered, not far from where he was born.

Incidents like these, and similar ones, aroused panic and fear among the remaining Jews, even in the big cities. Now there was no one to trust and no one to believe. Those who had sheltered us, and whom we regarded as our friends, were those who were behind the events intended to destroy us. To go out during the evening or at night was dangerous, and every rattle of the shutters caused the Jews to tremble, thinking that murderers had come, disguised as police. There were many Poles who robbed the Jews during the Occupation and became rich by taking their possessions. These Poles were interested in sowing panic, so that the Jews would leave and would never claim back their possessions. Simply, they wanted to eliminate Jewish heirs.

In the month of May 1945, the borders of Poland were finalized according to the Potsdam Agreement. Wide areas of German Silesia were annexed to Poland. Jews immediately began to stream there, so as to perhaps find a safer, new refuge, and they did find an intermediate way station there.

At that time, Chaim Yehoshua Olsha presided as the vice-chairman of the *Kommitat* of the city of Bialystok and the surrounding area. He gathered Jewish orphans from the village farmers and left Bialystok accompanied by 48 orphans, after being threatened by Polish gangs. Olsha established a dormitory for the children in Bielsko, Silesia, under the management of Dr. Paula Kammai from Vilna. The Youth Aliya organization sent the children of the institution and the workers to the Land of Israel.

Multitudes of Jews, repatriated from Russia, began to reach Silesia. At that time, many groups began to organize, whose purpose was to reach the shores of the Land of Israel [to Palestine, 1920-1948) illegally. The members of 'Habreicha' were very active towards that purpose, and they succeeded in bringing many Jews to Israel from Poland and the D.P. [Displaced Persons] camps in Austria, Germany, and Italy.

A large portion of the survivors from Sokoly knew that there is no solution for Jews, even in the democratic countries, other than to immigrate to the Land of Israel and there to build our national home. The rest of the surviving Jews of Sokoly went to other countries and dispersed all over the world.

INDEX

Barbinsky, Moshe (son-in-law to Chaim Boruch Goldwasser, 90

Barish, Shmuel the *Shochet* from 'Tiktin' (Tykocin);
        transported to Bialystok Ghetto, 37

Berish, Shmuel Leib the *shochet* from Sokoly; father of Yerachmiel
    Weinkrantz; gpa to 'Benyaminka' and Rachelsky, 13, 151

Bartzi from Dworkie, 223

Beilah Rachel, Alter's mother; mother-in-law
        to Hanoch Fleer's daughter, 153, 180

Beiletz (textile factory), 135

Beitar (Zionist Youth organization), 15, 22

Benyamin the glazier, father of
        cousin to Benyamin Gorkovitz, 225

'Benyaminka' (Benyamin). *See* Rachelsky.,

Berish the *shochat*. *See* Weinkrantz

Berliner, 99, 106

'Betzalelke' (Betzalel) the butcher. *See* Fleer

Bialystok (city in NE Poland),
        3, 12, 14, 20,22-23, 25, 38, 41-42, , 48, 54, 63, 77,
        81,*88, 93-94, 96, 103, 105, 111 150, 152, 158, 176,
        186,189, 194-195, 220, 224-227, 229, 231, 234, 236-237

Bialystok Forest, 84

Bialystok Ghetto, the (pop. 1942, about 60,000 Jews),
        37, 63, *154-156, 164, 171-172, 176,
        179, 184, *187-195, 220, 225, 231, 241

Bialystok Regional Center, 229, 235

Bialystok Teachers' Seminary, 15

Bialystok Train Station, 191, 205

Bialystotzka(-ky),
    Kabula (daughter of Nachum; wife of David. *See* Koschevsky
    Nachum the tailor, Kabula's father, 235

Bielsko (Silesia, Germany),237

Blustein,
    Josef (*aka* 'Mendritska'), 101, 172, 188
    Josef's son (murdered with wife and 3 sons), 172
    Mordechai Moshe, 91, 92, 132
    Yechiel (*aka* 'Yechielke' , Mendritska's son, 33, 188

Chernievsky,
  Leibel (Sarah's husband), 109
  Neta, Leibel's son; a forest guide for Jewish refugees, 109-110
  Sarahke' (Sarah, Leibel's wife), 109
Colonel Dubroshin, 229,
Czeczek from Warsaw (cousin to Staczek), 203-204,
Czeika (village), 167
Czepkin, a German *gendarme*, 53
Czerbonicz, Yechezkel (*Judenrat* member), 24, 58
Czernetzky, Hinda, (cousin to Michael Maik, 99, 155
Czyzewo (village), 113-117, 120-124
Danzig (German city), 215, 232
Danzig Technical College, 232
Dapu (Lapy) railroad factories, 31, 43, 58,
          *60-66, 75-81, 86, 90, 208
David a paraplegic from Bialystok, 42
Delmayer (slave-labor boss), 78
destruction, mass murder and transports,
  Baranowicz, 82
  Bialystok (Ghetto on Feb. 5, 1943), 23, 150-154,
          *179-181, *188, *190-193, *195, 197, 214, 224
  Bransk (on Nov. 2, 1942), 94
  Jedwabne, 38, 82
  Lapy (on Nov. 2, 1942), 41, 93
  Lomza, 37
  Minsk, 82
  Myszyniec, 82
  Radizlow, 38
  Rutka, 82
  Rutki-Kossaki, 39, 98
  Tykocin ('Tiktin' on 2 *Elul*; Aug. 25, 1941), 37-38, 82
  Slonim, 82
  Sokoly (on Nov. 2, 1942), 93, 151
  Trzeszczyn ('Trestin'), 23
  Vilna,82
  Warsaw, 84-85
  Zambrow, 37
  Zawady (on 2 *Elul*--Aug. 25, 1941), 37

Fleer contd.),

Hanoch's daughter; wife of Alter (son
of Beilah Rachel), 153, 180

Hanoch's son-in-law, Alter;
murdered in forests, 153, 180-181

Hanoch (*aka* 'Henich' the butcher), father of 2 children;
son of Betzalel; murdered in forests), 153, 180

Leibel the butcher (father of Chaim 'Itza'), 46

Malka (*nee* Ravches; Mendel 's wife), 133

Mendel the wholesaler and cattle dealer; husband
of Malka Ravches; sent to Siberia during
Soviet regime in Sokoly, 16, 18, 133

Nechama (Hanoch's wife; murdered
with newborn baby in forests), 180

Frankel, a warehouse worker in Lapy, 40

Friedman the teacher (wife of Goldberg the teacher, 193

Garabowski (a Polish blacksmith), 202

'Gelev', 80

German Silesia, 237

Gidrowicz, 64, 75-78, 82

Giemzino (village on edge of forest;
8 km from Maik bunker), 181

Ginzberg,

Alter, owner of leather goods and shoe shop;
Head of Sokoly *Judenrat*; married to the Sokoly dentist
(given name unknown); step-father to Monik Roseman,
19, *23-25, 31-32, 36, 57-58, 164, 179, 189-190

Alter's wife the dentist; after suffering in the forests, went
with Alter and son Monik to Bialystok Ghetto, 191

Selina the teacher in the Polish public school, Yona's wife
and sister to Lutka, 59, 164

Yaakov the wholesaler (father-in-law to Moshe Olsha), 11, 158

Yona, (member of the *Judenrat*), 24-25, 58-59, 164

Golche, Freida, 32,

Goldberg from Sokoly,
    'Avrahamel-e' (Avraham, 2nd son of Yisrael; carpenter and
        blacksmith; his sister (given name unknown) married
        into Tabak family; 131-140, 143, 146, 149, 158, 162,
        174, 212, 217, 219, 212, 225-226, 230
    Chaim 'Yudel' (Yehuda), 5th son of Yisrael
        the blacksmith, 67, 131-137, 139-140, 143, 149,
        158-159, 174, 212, 225
    Mordechai, eldest son of Yisrael the blacksmith, 67
    'Sarachi' (Sarah), daughter of Yisrael the blacksmith;
        wife of Pesach the blacksmith, 67-68
    Tuvia the blacksmith, 35
    Yaakov, *Rav*, 3rd son of Yisrael the blacksmith;
        gpa to Feivel Jezevitz, 67, 171
    Yisrael the blacksmith; wealthy widower; father
        to 9 children; father-in-law of Pesach
        the blacksmith, 67-69
    Zalman, 4th son of Yisrael the blacksmith; Soviet soldier;
        killed in battle of Rostov, 67
Goldberg from Tykocin,
    Dovka (fled to Sokoly; family murdered), 38
Goldberg couple (given names unknown),
    (husband) a former teacher; son-in-law of 'Yisraelke';
        prisoner and chief record-keeper in 10th Div. Fort, 193
    (wife) a former teacher; *nee* Friedman; prisoner and food
        distribution supervisor in 10th Div. Fort, 193
    'Yisraelke' (Yisrael), father-in-law to
        Goldberg (husband), the teacher, 193
Goldin,
    Alter, owner of Sokoly oil factory, 52
    'Chaimke' (Chaim, 12-yr.-old gson of 'Moshele'), 123-124
    Dina, Leah's mother, 70
    'Leishke' (Leah), Dina's daughter, 70
    'Moshele' (Moshe), gpa of Chaim, 123
    'Yudel' (Yehuda), father-in-law to Shmuel Tzvi Kravitz, 167
Goldstein, 16

Goldwasser,
  Beila, (sister-in-law to Moshe Lev), 132
  Beila's sister (given name unknown),
      married Moshe Lev), 132
  Chaim Baruch, father of Beila and her sister;
      father-in-law to Moshe Lev, 90, 132
Goltz (German slave-labor boss), 79, 82
Gonshak, Reuven, son-in-law to Shmuel Bronstein, 196
Gorkovitz, Benyamin (Chaim Dzashesayahak's son), 225, 231, 239
Gozbonda the barber, 34
Grabow, 7
Grabowski, 226
'Grandfather', the. *See* Ozorowski
Gritczak,
  'Sheintze', 229
  'Velvele' (Velvel), father of 'Yudel', 240
  'Yudel' (Yehuda), 14-year-old murdered son of 'Velvele', 90
  Zeev, father of 3 daughters, 226
Grodno, 241
Grossman, 169
Gutman, Raphael (Michael Maik's uncle), 191
Guttenplan, Dr., 173, 183, 184
'*Habreicha*', clandestine Zionist organization
      for illegal immigration of Jews to Palestine, 237
Halpern, 27
Hershel the fisherman, 40
Hirshman, 13
Idzki (village), 100, 149, 153, 158-159, 172
Idzki Forest, 84, 97-98, 106, 126, 132, 149
informers, 8, 27-29, 152, 160, 163, 205, 150, 191
'Itza' (Yitzhak the carpenter). *See* Baran
'Itzel', (Yitzhak the tailor), 225
Itzkovsky, Shlomo Leibel (cowshed owner), 21, 202
Jablonka, 74, 167
Jamiolki (village), 134
Jamiolki Bridge, 179, 216
Jamiolki Forest, 90
'Janek' (armed and dangerous anti-semitic gangs), 155, 190

Kaloshin (town close to Warsaw), 87

Kammai, Dr.Paula from Vilna, 236

Kanarczika, Josepha 25

Kanofka,
    daughter of Konofka the 'policeman', 186
    Polish shoemaker turned 'policeman' (given-
        name unknown), 33, 134, 186, 188

Kapitovsky,
    Velvel, an orphan (age 20), 152
    Yisrael the shoemaker, 123

Kaplansky,
    Masha, mother of Rachel, 48, 224
    Rachel, Yaakov's daughter, 224
    Yaakov, husband to Masha; wealthy owner
        of large fabrics store, 48

Kaposta (Russian General), 21

Kashevitz,
    Chane, son of 'Yisraelke' (Yisrael'), 133
        'Kaladshe', Yisrael's father, 133
    'Yisraelke' (Yisrael), 133

Knishin (town), 90

Kobylin (town), 75-76, 80-81, 90

Koenigsberg (city), 78

Kolno (city), 7

Koschevsky,
    David, 28-yr. old son of 'Itza' the hatmaker; married Kabula
        Bialystotszka; murdered after war, 229-231, 234-235
    Kabula, David's wife, 230

Kozloszczina (small city near Slonim), 69

Kravchevitz,
    Shlomo the tailor, 142, 196-197

Kravitz,
    'Shashki' (Shoshana), Shmuel's daughter, 167
    'Sheindel' (Shaine), Shmuel' daughter, 167
    Shmuel Tzvi ('Yudel' Goldin's son-in-law), 167

Kraweicz (restaurant), 186, 187

Krinski, the Polish steam mill owner and electrician, 12, 42

'*Kroks*' (German *gendarmes*), 63, 80

Lev (contd.),
    'Rashke' (Rachel), Moshe's mother, 224
    Shmuel Leib the *Sho"b*; father to Avraham and Mendel, 6, 224
'Little Alterke' (uncle to Dr. Makowsky), 26, 186, 221-222
Litvak,
    Chaim Tuvia the blacksmith; son-in-law
        of Dov Shaikes, 223, 226, 229, 233-234
    'Shantzie', Chaim's daughter, 223
    Shammai, Chaim's 19-yr.-old son;
        murdered after liberation of Sokoly, 223, 230, 233-234
    'Sheike' (*aka* 'Sheikele' [Yeshaiya], Chaim's 13-yr.-old son;
        murdered after liberation of Sokoly), 223, 230, 233-234
    'Yankele' [Yaakov], Chaim's 15-yr. old son; murdered in
        Bialystok by Polish soldier, 223, 233-234
Lomza, 37
Lopuchowo Forest, 37
Lublin, 147, 223
Lutka (Selina Ginzberg's German-speaking younger sister), 59
Macziewski, 124
Maczuszko, Anthony, 127-128
Maik,
    Dina, Yisrael's wife; formerly hotelier and
        restaurant mgr.), 51, 99-100, 154
    Michael, 27-28 , 51, 61, 64-66 99-100, 124, 127, 135, 146
    Moshe ('Mushko'), son of Michael (*See also* 'boys', *aka* the/
        'youngsters', the) 18-19, 26-27, 51
          *55, 64, 91-93, 96-98, 109, 112, 119, 123,
          126, 129,-131, 133, 135-136, 139-144, 185,
          192, 199-200, 204-205, 209, 212, 220, 225-228
    'Shmuelke' (Shmuel), Yisrael's son, 91, 99-101, 104, 133-134
    'Teibele' (Yona), Yisrael's daughter, 100, 155-156
    'Tsippa' (Yisrael's wife), 95, 97, 107
    Yisrael, *Judenrat* member; watchmaker and goldsmith,
        24-25, 27-28, 58, *99-100, *154-155, 189, 221
Majdanek, mass murder concentration camp, 235
Makowsky, 'Alterke' (Alter), hostelier and restauranteur, 70
Makowsky, Dr.(nephew of 'Little Alterke';
        member of *Judenrat*), 26, 60, 161

Malach,

    Betzalel (son-in-law of Yaakov Leib Perlowitz), 77

    'Heneleh', daughter of Betzalel, 154

    Sarah Esther (gdaughter of Yaakov Leib Perlowitz), 196

Manijenie-Novogrod, 52

Malkin Bridge, 18

Malon,

    Yosef, father of forest guide (given name unknown), 112

    Yosef's son, forest guide to Jewish refugees,

        112-113, 115-116, 118, 120-122

Manijenie-Novogrod, 56

Manikowski, (anti-semitic former mayor of Sokoly;

      advocate/lawyer), 21, 28, 162

'Marok the Silent' (a quiet, German supervisor, 65, 79

Marshlek. *See 'Zekankan'*, the

Martzibur. *See* Rachelsky, Shmuel

mass graves, 42, 152, 154, 224

Mazury (landowner court village), 21, 30, 41

Mazury Forest (about 8 km. from bunder), 92, 124, 209-210, 214

Meir from Wienda, husband of Rachel Leah, 118-119

Meir Gedalia the builder (Beila Gittel Djajeh's,

      father-in-law), 114, 123

Meizner, *181-182

Melamed from Bialystok, 194

Metshizev, 224

Minsk, 82

Monik. *See* Roseman

Morashkevitz,

    Rachel, daughter of Yitzhak, 193

    Yechezkiel, owner of metalworking shop, 35

    Yitzhak, father of Rachel; owner of ironworks factory, 23, 195

Moshe, son of 'Rashke', 224

Moshe 'Yossel' (Josef), father-in-law to

      Rav Avraham Shapiro, 5

'Motke' (Mordechai) the engraver), 175

'Mushko' (*aka* Moshe). *See* Maik

Myszyniec (village), 7, 82

Olsha (contd.),

    Sarah Miriam (*nee* Rabinowitz), wife of 'Shlomke', 157

    'Shlomke' (*aka* Shlomo), father of 5 sons
        and 3 daughters; murdered in Budziska Forest,
        56-58, 86, 156-158, 169

    Velvel, co-owner of paint supply store in Bialystok
        with brother Michael, 158

    Sara Miriam (nee Rabinovitz, wife of 'Shlomke', 157

    'Shlomke' (Shlomo), shot in Budziska Forest, 86, 156-158

Olshak,

    Shaine the seamstress, age 22; murdered after
        liberation, 230, 233-234

    'Tulkale' (Tulka), 4-yr. old orphan relative to Shaine;
        murdered after liberation, 230, 234

    Zeev from Zaromb (Shaine's husband), 233-234

Ostrow-Mazowiecka, 30, 77-78, 157

Ozorowski, slave-labor boss, 63-65, 79

"Pahtcher", the (German sadist and whipper in Gidrowicz's slave-
    labor office), 64-65

Palkowska,

    husband of Janina (no given name); father
        to son and daughter (given names unknown), 49-50

    Janina (collaborator, schemer, and anti-semite), 47,
        49-52, 67, 99-100, 102, 152, 155, 173, 201

Patak from Rutka, a shop owner murdered with his wife, 235-236

'Pekka', step-sister to 'Trotsky', 29-30

Pelchok the fisherman, 3

Perlowitz,

    Sarah Esther Malach, gdaughter of Yaakov Leib, 77, 196

    Yaakov Leib (father-in-law to Betzalel Malach), 77, 196

Pesach the blacksmith (father of 6; son-in-law
        of Yisrael Goldberg the blacksmith), 67-68, 51, 67

    'Moshele' (Moshe), Pesach's ten-yr.-old son, 67-68

    'Sarachi' (Sarah), wife of Pesach; daughter of
        Yisrael Goldberg, 67-68

Petroshka, 'Yankel' (Yaakov), father-in-law to Hershel
        Yismach, 152

'pikatniks' (aka *'pikatnikim'* Polish ruffians and hoodlums)10-11, *49

Rachelsky (contd.),

Seines,
    Chava, wife of Moshe Tzvi, 108
    Moshe Tzvi Hershel (owner of wool spinning
        factory, 23, 52, 54, 221
    'Shaya' (Yishaya, son of Moshe, 91-92, 108
    'Sirkeh' (Sarah, Moshe's daughter, 23
    'Yankel' (Yaakov), Moshe's son; member of
        secret, youth underground organization, 52, 131
'Sergei' (armed and dangerous Soviet and
            Polish gangs, 155, 190, 192
Shadlinsky,
    Boruch, son of Hershel; murdered by Konofka;
            gson of Elia Burak the carpenter, 134
    Hershel the wealthy carpenter, 134
Shafran, Mottel, 226
Shaikes, Dov, father-in-law to Chaim Tuvia Litvak, 226
Shapiro, *Rav* Avraham 'Yossel' (Josef), 5-6
Shklarovitz,
    Chaya Zelda, daughter of Yosef the glazier;
        Schultz's wife, 197
    Yosef Leib the glazier, 197
'*Shmeig*'. *See* Kalinowski, Staczek
'Six Feet', German enforcer with dog, 89-90
Shulmeister,
    Moshe Lipa (son-in-law of David Borovitz;
        wealthy shop owner; *gabbai* (sexton)
        in the large *beit midrash*), 26, 55
slave-labor, 80-82, 93
Slodky,
    Alter, 2-3, 225-226
    Gedalia, 16
Slomasky, Aharon from Dworkie, 224
Slonim (town), 69, 82
smuggling, 12, 18, 40, 82, 89, 118, 226
Sokolow (city), 87
Solka, the adopted daughter of 'Itzel' (Yitzhak)
        the tailor; a refugee from Sokoly, 225

Somovitz,
    Chaim, son of Yechiel, 19, 51, 105, 107
    'Yechielke' (Yechiel), 13, 19, 51, 54, 101, 105, 150
Soviet Doctor, the. *See* Volosvitza, Dr. Claudia
Soviet retake and liberation of Sokoly (Aug. 11, 1944), 221
Squire (*paritz*) of Ros, the, 156-157
Staczek (*aka* 'Shmeig'). *See* Kalinowski
Starinsky, Yaakov (m. Shlomo Olsha's
        eldest daughter Tzipora),158
Stawiski (village E. of Kolno), 7
Stokowiski landholder robbery, 217
Surasky,
    Mordechai, son of Moshe Yitzhak;
      a grain merchant, 33, 201-202, 231, 233-234
    Moshe Yitzhak the blacksmith, 33
    'Yankel' (Yaakov) the blacksmith;
      member of *Judenrat*, 26
Suzin, 63-64
Swieciany (*Svencionys*, Lithuania), 229, 235
Tabak,
    'Feigele' (Faigel *aka* Tsipora), 230-231
    'Moshele', 10 yr.-old son of Pesach, 51, 56, 67
    Pesach the blacksmith (father of 8;
      son-in-law of Yisrael Goldberg), 51, 56, 67
    'Sarachi' (Sarah, Pesach's wife), 67
Tannenbaum, a rent collector under the Soviets, 40
Tashikelski, slave-labor boss, 63-64
Tembov (Soviet city), 161
Tenth Division Fort, the (near Bialystok), 111, 150, 193-194
'Tiktin'. *See* Tykocin
Todras the shoemaker from Wysokie, 123
    Todras twin boys, 123-124, 126-127
Treblinka, *84-85, 87, 150, 156, 179-180,
        188, 191, 193-194, 224
Troskoleski the Polish restaurant owner, 177
''Trotsky',
    Nachum, 29-30
    'Pekka', Nachum's stepsister, 29-30

Wenagrod (city near Warsaw), 87, 93

'whipper', the, (sadistic German whipmaster,
        slave-labor boss), 32, 58-59, 63

Wiczenowski, 62

Wienda (village), 118-119, 123, 195, 197

Wilk from Idzki (old Polish friend of Yisrael Maik), 100

Wladek [Ruszkowski]the farmer, *149-151,
        153-156, *159-160, 170-172, 215

Wondolowicz, Issur, 223, 230

Wysokie (*aka* Wysokie-Mazowieckie district city;
        7km. to Sokoly), *1, 7, 17, 19-20, *39-40, 45, 56 92-93,
        95, 109, 123-124, 176, 185-186, 214, 226, 228-229

Wysokie Forest, 83, 90

Wysokie Ghetto, 39-40

Wysokie Train Station, 45, 189, 199, 214

Yachnes, Zalman, 86

'Yankel' (Yaakov); a disabled youth and Torah scholar;
        murdered in a mass killing of the disabled, 42

'Yechielke' (Yechiel the baker). *See* Somovitz

'Yellow Satan', the. *See* Wassel

Yente (Jewish prisoner in 10th Div. Fort;
        supervised food distribution with Goldberg
        nee Friedman, wife of Goldberg the teacher), 193

Yismach,
    'Chaicha' (Chaya, Hershel's oldest daughter),153
    'Freidel' (Frieda, Hershel's wife), 153
    Hershel, son-in-law of Yaakov Petroshka, 153
    Hershel's youngest daughter (given name unknown), 153

Yisrael Chaim the beltmaker. *See* Roseman

Yisrael the blacksmith. *See* Goldberg

Yosef Leib the glazier. *See* Shklarovitz

Yachnes, 86, 92

Yanchenko (*aka* 'Yanchko'), the Polish policeman,
        73-74, 102, 171, 186

'Yankel' (Yaakov) the 'walking encyclopedia', 42

'Yellow Satan', the. *See* Wassel

Zambrow (city), 37, 69, 95, 176, 227

Zaromb (*aka* Zareby Koscielne town), 234

www.ingramcontent.com/pod-product-compliance
Lightning Source LLC
Chambersburg PA
CBHW060330100426
42812CB00003B/938